D1282832

# UFOs

**An Insider's View of the Official Quest for Evidence**

# UFOs

An Insider's View of the Official
Quest for Evidence

## Roy Craig

University of North Texas Press
Denton, Texas

Library of Congress Cataloging-in-Publication Data

Craig, Roy, 1924–
UFOs: an insider's view of the official quest for evidence / by Roy
Craig.
p.      cm.
ISBN 0-929398-94-7   (pbk. : alk. paper)
1. Unidentified flying objects.    I. Title.
TL789.C686                          1995
001.9'42—dc20                      95-10882
                                    CIP

This book is dedicated to the surmounting of Earthlings' addiction to violence.

# Table of Contents

# PART II
## The Production, Content, and Impact of the Condon Report

# Preface

The United States Air Force had a problem. Its top brass did not consider it a defense or a national security problem. It was a public relations problem. Since "flying saucers" became a part of American lore after Kenneth Arnold's reported sighting in 1947, the demands on the Air Force to check out and tell about reported UFOs had grown through the years. So had criticism of the Air Force's handling of the reports. By 1966, public indignation at Air Force "explanations"—focused then on the "swamp gas" explanation of a multitude of sightings in Washtenaw County, Michigan—became intense enough to create demands for Congressional investigations. The Air Force's public relations people found it necessary to seek assistance to get critics off the Air Force's back.

On 30 December 1947, the Air Force had begun formal investigation of what were then called "flying discs" after a flurry of sighting reports followed Kenneth Arnold's experience. Its first program was code-named Project Sign. After a year of study, the staff of Project Sign prepared an "Estimate of the Situation" and sent it, supposedly classified "Top Secret" to Air Force Chief of Staff, General Hoyt S. Vandenberg, in July of 1948.

This "estimate" reportedly asserted that the staff of Project Sign was convinced that the UFOs they investigated were really vehicles from another planet. General Vandenberg felt that Project Sign's staff lacked adequate proof for such a conclusion, and refused to accept the report. The "Estimate of the Situation" never became an official Air Force document. Copies of it were destroyed. If clandestine copies of it still exist, they are kept well under cover.

Sign's final report recommended: "Future activity on this project should be carried on at the minimum level necessary to record, summarize and evaluate the data received on future reports and to complete the specialized investigations now in progress. When and if a sufficient number of incidents are solved to indicate that these sightings do not represent a threat to the security of the nation, the assignment of special project status to the activity could be terminated. Future investigations of reports would then be handled on a routine basis like any other intelligence work."

One might assume that General Vandenberg had a role in Sign's change in outlook. Letters appended to Sign's final report, written by scientists who served in positions such as membership on the Air Force Scientific Advisory Board, showed that the Air Force then was giving consideration to the extraterrestrial possibility, in spite of the outlook revealed in the report itself.

Early in 1949, the name of the project was changed from Project Sign to Project Grudge. Project Grudge operated less than a year before the Air Force announced its termination on 27 December 1949. UFO reports would henceforth be handled as an ordinary intelligence activity. Grudge's one report discussed 244 sightings investigated, and displayed prominently the conclusions of Dr. J. Allen Hynek, who had been hired by the Air Force as a consultant on astronomically-related UFO sightings. Thirty-two percent of Grudge's cases were considered to have been sightings of astronomical objects. After considering weather balloons, airplanes and hoaxes, a residue of twenty-three percent of the reports was considered as "unknown."

The Grudge Report concluded, "There is no evidence that

objects reported upon are the result of an advanced scientific foreign development; and, therefore, they constitute no direct threat to the national security." It recognized a psychological threat, however, and continued: "There are indications that the planned release of sufficient unusual aerial objects coupled with the release of related psychological propaganda would cause a form of mass-hysteria. Employment of these methods by or against an enemy would yield similar results." It therefore recommended that the Psychological Warfare Division be informed of the results of the study and that it participate in plans for public release of information relative to unidentified flying objects.

Grudge was allowed to rest in peace less than two years. It was reincarnated on 27 October 1951, when Major General C. P. Cabell, director of Air Force Intelligence, ordered its re-activation as a new and expanded project. The new project, which was re-named Project Blue Book about five months after its reactivation, was under the direction of Captain E. J. Ruppelt. Dr. Hynek continued to serve as consultant on astronomically-related events.

The year 1952 saw a tremendous upsurge in UFO sightings and in public interest in them. Reports received by Air Force Intelligence and Project Blue Book jumped from 169 in 1951 to 1501 in 1952.

An amateur UFO study organization known as the Aerial Phenomena Research Organization (APRO), headquartered in Tucson, Arizona, was formed that same year by Mrs. Coral Lorenzen. APRO was the first such organization to operate on a national scale. Its initial mimeographed bulletin was sent to fifty-two members. By 1968, APRO claimed 8,000 members. It had, however, been surpassed in size by the younger National Investigations Committee on Aerial Phenomena (NICAP), an amateur organization based in Washington, D. C., which by 1968 claimed a membership of 12,000, including over 300 scientific and technical advisers.

Public interest in the numerous UFO reports was greatly enhanced by press attention and sensationalized reporting. Magazine articles on UFOs appeared in 1952 not only in sensational publications but also in *American Mercury, Collier's, Life, New Republic, Newsweek, Popular Science, Reader's Digest, Time,* and even *The New Yorker.*

The Air Force came under intensified public criticism for its handling, or mishandling, of UFO reports after NICAP came on the scene. NICAP's major theme seemed to be that the Air Force was keeping the truth about UFOs from the American people. NICAP was certain that "real" UFOs were extraterrestrial vehicles. So was APRO, but that organization felt it was the CIA which was withholding the truth and deceiving the public—even withholding the truth from the Air Force.

The Central Intelligence Agency (CIA) did take an interest in UFOs, presumably out of concern that the generation of mass-hysteria, as mentioned in the Grudge report, might be utilized by an enemy, and that military communication channels might be jammed with UFO sighting reports at a time of enemy attack. The CIA convened a Special Panel of renowned scientists, chaired by Professor H. P. Robertson of the California Institute of Technology, to assist in assessing the UFO situation. The panel's report, produced in January, 1953, after a week of study of the best documented UFO reports and available UFO photographs, not only concluded that UFOs offered no direct threat to the national security, but further stated the belief that there existed "no residuum of cases which indicates phenomena which are attributable to foreign artifacts capable of hostile acts." The Robertson panel further concluded that there was no evidence that the phenomena indicated a need for revision of current scientific concepts. It did recognize potential psychological hazards associated with UFO reports, and recommended "that the national security agencies take immediate steps to strip the Unidentified Flying Objects of the special status they have been given and the aura of mystery they have unfortunately acquired." The panel also recommended launching an educational program to inform the public about UFOs. Its report was classified "Secret," and thus kept from public knowledge until declassified in the summer of 1966.

While the Robertson panelists were renowned physical scientists, their recommendations showed a naive lack of understanding of the nature of human beliefs and desires. Their recommendations were never implemented, and probably could not have been. However, since the panel's report and numerous UFO reports were kept "secret," their existence fueled additional arguments that agencies of the government were conspiring to conceal the truth about UFOs from the American public. Confidence in the honesty of the Air Force, as well as the CIA, continued to decay.

Meanwhile, public interest in UFOs continued to intensify. A 1953 book, *Flying Saucers from Outer Space* by Donald E. Keyhoe, a retired Marine Corps major (and founder in 1956 of NICAP), quickly made the bestseller lists. Significant numbers of readers were avidly consuming the multitude of books and articles about UFOs that appeared on book shelves and magazine stands, and writers were cashing in on the opportunity to make bucks.

Belief in Air Force concealment of the sensational truth about UFOs continued to spread. Since secrecy was known to exist, no one was sure that he knew the truth. Unnecessary Air Force secrecy from 1947 to 1968 regarding UFO matters played a significant role in the development of distrust by American people in their own defense establishment.

The market quickly showed what the American public

wanted to read. Understandably, it was that which offered mystery, a glimpse of the unknown, sex, and fascination. Two other books appearing in 1953 reveal the public's desire for the sensational. *Flying Saucers* by Professor Donald H. Menzel, then director of Harvard College Observatory, explained many UFO sightings in terms of optical illusion, and found no need to invoke extraterrestrial visitors in explaining observations. Menzel's book did not achieve a large enough market to be issued as a paperback, and quickly went out of print. *Flying Saucers Have Landed*, by D. Leslie and George Adamski, was widely read in hardcover and paperback editions. This book gave a full account of Adamski's alleged interview with a man from Venus on the California desert on 20 November 1952.

In 1967, Miss Lynn E. Catoe of the Library of Congress compiled a bibliography of UFO publications. It contained over 1600 entries, including 71 books, 28 pamphlets, and 73 magazine articles in English. Flying saucers might possibly have been illusory, but flying saucer literature was quite real, and still thriving.

Captain Ruppelt, director of Project Blue Book, left the Air Force in September, 1953. Even he was critical of Air Force handling of UFO reports, implying in his 1956 book that investigation of Grudge's twenty-three percent residue of "unknown" cases was inadequate and incomplete.

By 1965, Project Blue Book had received more than 9,000 reports of UFO sightings. It had "explained" all but about seven percent of them in terms of ordinary phenomena or hoaxes, and felt the other seven percent might be similarly explained if adequate information about them were available. The public, however, often did not accept or believe the Air Force "explanations," which sometimes did not seem compatible with the facts. Demands increased for Air Force revelation of the "truth."

The Air Force public relations problem led to the 28 September 1965 request by Major General E. B. LeBailly, head of the Office of Information of the Secretary of the Air Force, that a working scientific panel composed of both physical and social scientists be organized to review Project Blue Book. Addressed to the Military Director of the Air Force Scientific Advisory Board, General LeBailly's letter asked for the review of Blue Book's resources, methods, and findings, and for reviewers to advise the Air Force concerning improvements that should be made in the program to carry out the Air Force's assigned responsibility.

General LeBailly's request resulted in establishment of the "Ad Hoc Committee to Review Project Blue Book," chaired by physicist Dr. Brian O'Brien, and composed of Drs. Launor F. Carter, psychologist; Jesse Orlansky, psychologist; Richard Porter, electrical engineer; Carl Sagan, space scientist; and Willis H. Ware, electrical engineer. The O'Brien Committee reported its findings in March, 1966.

The committee noted that in thousands of hours of observation and filming of the sky in scientific programs such as the Palomar Observatory Sky Atlas, Harvard Meteor Project, and the Smithsonian Visual Prairie Network, not a single unidentified object had been reported as appearing on film plates or sighted visually. After reviewing Blue Book and previous panel records, the O'Brien Committee came to the now common conclusion that there has been no evidence that unidentified flying objects were or are a threat to our national security. The committee also noted, however, that some of the Blue Book cases that were listed as "identifieds" were sightings where the evidence collected was not adequate to permit positive listing in the identified category. For that reason, the O'Brien Committee recommended that the Blue Book program be "strengthened to provide opportunity for scientific investigation of selected sightings in more detail and depth than has been possible to date." To implement this recommendation, they suggested involving one or more of the nation's universities. It was this report that eventually spawned the University of Colorado Project, which is discussed in the following chapters.

Meanwhile, as the Air Force bogged itself ever deeper in what must have seemed to it a UFO quagmire, its public image sank to a new low. Its "explanation" of the Washtenaw County sightings as "swamp gas" was considered insulting to observers, ridiculous by UFO-club members, and ludicrous by the observers' representatives in Congress. Calls increased for a Congressional investigation of the Air Force's handling of UFO reports.

Demands for Congressional action were strengthened by activities of individuals who were considered especially qualified to speak out about their UFO beliefs. In particular, Dr. James F. McDonald, Senior Physicist at the Institute of Atmospheric Physics, University of Arizona, was taking personal time off work to travel about the United States and speak at meetings and conventions of scientists about UFO sightings. Dr. McDonald was amazingly energetic, organized, and convincing in the logic of his presentations. He repeatedly displayed a list of his "20 best cases," which he felt indicated strongly that Earth was being visited by extraterrestrial beings. Dr. McDonald felt that the UFO question was "the greatest scientific problem of our time." Because of his qualifications and the high regard in which he was held in scientific circles, Dr. McDonald convinced numerous scientists, as well as members of the U.S. Congress, that UFO reports were not receiving the attention and investigation they deserved.

Dr. J. Allen Hynek also began to add to the Air Force's public relations problem. Although it was he who suggested to them that swamp gas could account for the flurry of sightings in Michigan, he found himself embarrassed by public reaction to that "explanation." He felt comfortable with the cases he identified for the Air Force as misinterpretations of astronomical objects, but began to feel that the accumulation of good non-astronomical cases was so impressive that there must be something very significant, such as extraterrestrial visitation, occurring on Earth. Dr. Hynek began to express such a feeling publicly, referring to the UFO phenomenon as "the greatest mystery of our age, perhaps the greatest mystery of all time." Dr. Hynek's position as Chairman of the Department of Astronomy and Director of Dearborn Observatory, Northwestern University, as well as his experience as Air Force Consultant on reported UFO sightings, gave considerable weight to his call for more complete investigation of UFO reports.

The voices of such qualified scientists were amplified by APRO, NICAP, and numerous smaller organizations and clubs of UFO believers.

Just a few weeks after the swamp gas incident, the House Armed Services Committee of the U.S. Congress held a one-day hearing on the UFO problem. It was there that Air Force Secretary Harold Brown publicly revealed the existence and content of the O'Brien Committee report. Regarding the report's recommendation for establishment of a university-associated panel of civilian scientists to investigate selected UFO reports, Secretary Brown told the Armed Services Committee, "I believe I may act favorably on it, but I want to explore further the nature of such a panel, and the ground rules, before I go ahead with it. I don't want to have a group of people come in for just one day and make a shallow investigation. They have to be prepared to look into the situation thoroughly if they are to do any good."

Less than four months later, Dr. J. Thomas Ratchford of the scientific staff of the Air Force Office of Scientific Research (AFOSR) asked Dr. E. U. Condon, then at the University of Colorado, if he would take on the scientific direction of the study of

UFOs as recommended by the O'Brien Committee. Secretary Brown had assigned the responsibility of implementing the O'Brien recommendations to the AFOSR, which was asking the University of Colorado, because of Dr. Condon's possible willingness and his tremendous prestige as a scientist, to accept a contract for the work.

Dr. Condon's background was one of both scientific eminence and controversy. His tenure as administrative assistant to Dr. J. Robert Oppenheimer, directing the scientific work in developing the atomic bomb at Los Alamos, was cut short by conflict with Army General Leslie R. Groves, whose oppressive security restrictions on Los Alamos scientists Condon considered stifling to scientific progress. He was elected President of the American Physical Society while serving from 1945 to 1951 as Director of the National Bureau of Standards. At that time, his loyalty to his country was viciously attacked by the now infamous House un-American Activities Committee. Dr. Condon survived the witch-hunting attacks, and became known internationally as an outstanding scientist with impeccable integrity who was willing to fight in support of his beliefs. He was publicly known to be intolerant of official nonsense, and the AFOSR considered him one of the few scientists who would be suitable to head the UFO project, simply because his conclusions, whatever they should be after the study, would carry unquestioned credibility in scientific circles, and likely also with the public at large.

Although many scientists considered UFO sightings not a proper subject for scientific study, some, including Dr. Walter Orr Roberts, who headed the National Center for Atmospheric Research, urged Dr. Condon to accept this assignment as a significant public service.

The news that an official UFO study would be made at the University of Colorado, under Dr. Condon's direction, hit the papers and wires on 7 October 1966. Dr. Franklin E. Roach and Professor Stuart W. Cook would serve as principal investigators. Dr. Roach, an astrophysicist, was renowned for his work on upper atmosphere radiation. He had participated in briefings and debriefings of our early astronauts. Dr. Cook was Chairman of the Psychology Department at the University of Colorado.

On the evening of the day the contract was announced, I unintentionally and literally bumped into Franklin Roach at a party at the home of Professor Frank Kreith and his wife, Marian. One of the very young Kreith daughters was standing on my feet, to keep from being stepped on by those size thirteens, as we laughingly joined the dancing crowd in the living room. We bumped into more than one of the couples there. When I turned to see the Roachs, however, I stopped to chat a bit, since I had known Franklin socially for some time, and the UFO contract was the conversation topic of the day. I told Franklin I envied his participation in this study. He responded that he was interested that I was interested, and suggested I talk with Bob Low, who was an Assistant Dean in the University of Colorado Graduate School, and who would be serving as coordinator of the UFO project.

Mr. Low was cordial at our meeting. Staff was not yet being hired, however. Work was not scheduled to commence before December, and no one was certain yet just how the study would be organized or carried out. It was assumed that scientists from other universities would be sub-contracted to investigate reports of UFO sightings in their respective geographic areas.

In March, 1967, Bob Low contacted me to see if I might still be interested in working on the UFO project. The thought of cooperative agreements with other universities had long since been abandoned. I had a full teaching load as Associate Professor and Coordinator of Physical Science in the university's Division of Integrated Studies, but could do outside research on a one-fifth time basis. We agreed that I would work this part time, getting acquainted with UFO reports, until the end of the regular academic term, then be with the project on a full-time basis until its investigative phase was completed. My assignment would be to investigate the physical aspects of current UFO reports, working with a staff psychologist, who would study the psychological aspects of the report. I would look for physical evidence that the reported UFO had actually been there, and that it was not some ordinary object misidentified by observers. Hopefully, we might even get to the site soon enough to see the reported object. Actually, I hoped—though I would not say so openly—that I might find real evidence that someone had actually seen an extraterrestrial vehicle. My associate would look into the minds of the persons reporting the sightings. We would plan to get to the location of any significant sighting as soon as possible wherever the site was in the United States—and possibly Canada and Mexico. The assignment promised to be both interesting and fun. I would even receive an official UFO Project identification card.[1]

This book is the story of the Condon Study, particularly my participation in it. It is divided into two parts. Part I describes a variety of topics and situations I encountered during field and laboratory investigations of reported UFO experiences. Its purpose is to give the reader an understanding of our attitudes, methods of investigation, types of reports investigated, situations encountered, and the way we dealt with those situations. Actual names of people and sighting locations are used unless stated otherwise.

Part II describes the problems encountered by the Colorado Project resulting from internal dissension, external attacks, and the fears and desires of people and publishers committed to belief in the reality of flying saucers from other planets. It also

reviews the content of the Condon Report, the impact of the report on Air Force and other official government activities, and its lack of impact upon public beliefs.

Part II is followed by a brief discussion of the current outlook regarding interstellar travel.

[1]Actually, I never showed the ID card during the UFO study, for my identification and business on the scene were never questioned. However, shortly after the study was completed, I was in a bar/restaurant/pool-hall combination in Bogota where I had been told one might purchase emeralds. Colombia produces most of the world's supply of emeralds, and has a government monopoly on their sales. I thought it would be nice to have a good emerald crystal, and didn't really approve of government monopolies, so I was surveying this "black market" supply. I wasn't interested in cut and polished emeralds because, with them, I really didn't know how to distinguish the real thing from colored glass.

When I entered this joint, alone, I was hailed by a burly gentleman sitting with two companions at one of the tables. "Hey, Yankee, Esmeraldas??" I didn't want to appear overly interested, but did accept this man's invitation to join his group for a beer—an invitatiion which was understood fairly quickly in spite of his limited English and my almost non-existent ability to communicate in Spanish.

After a bit of somewhat difficult chatter, my burly host went over to another part of the crowded room and returned with two other men who had emeralds for sale. They wouldn't show me the emeralds there, however. We had to go outside and across the street before one of the men secretively opened a folded paper and displayed a half-dozen beautiful stones. I noticed a uniformed policeman watching us from across the street. I pretended to know emeralds, and examined the stones through a small magnifying glass from my pocket. I was quite sure the stones were genuine, and probably very valuable. Then I told the men, "No, I'm really not looking for polished emeralds. I want uncut emerald crystals. Have you any of them?" The men didn't, and insisted they would sell me one or all of these stones at a tremendous bargain. I said I'd continue to seek a good uncut crystal, but if none could be found, perhaps I'd bargain with them tomorrow. "No, Señor, tonight is the last night of the market!" I figured that was a familiar type of pressure bargaining, but made no issue of it as we returned to the pool hall.

It seems the man spoke truth, however. Somewhat later, as I was standing near one of the pool tables, watching the most skillful pool playing I had ever seen, there was a sudden hush and tenseness in the air. The pool playing stopped. I looked around and saw two uniformed policemen at the entrance and two more at each exit. The place was being raided! This was the end of the "market"!

The officers went around the room, approaching each individual, questioning, sometimes searching, occasionally escorting a person or two out the door to a destination I could only guess at. Then one of the uniformed fellows was addressing me, in Spanish words I did not understand. Obviously he was demanding something. I realized I had left my passport at the hotel, and could be in a difficult situation. I played it cool, however, and with a composure that surprised myself, I got out my billfold and withdrew the Unidentified Flying Objects Project identification card, which I just happened to still be carrying. With extreme dignity, I handed the card to the officer, as if it had some significance. He was puzzled. He looked intently at the card, which carried my photograph. Obviously he couldn't read what it said, and didn't know what it meant. I maintained the act. The officer was impressed. He took two brisk steps back, then bowed deeply. I nodded as he respectfully handed back my UFO project ID card. I returned the card to my pocket. Perhaps he thought I was a CIA agent. At least he was satisfied that I was some important person. He and the other officers finished their raid, the pool-playing resumed, and I held my position, watching the pool game, until the time seemed appropriate for me to drift through the door and return to my hotel. I wondered where I'd be had the UFO project card not been in my pocket.

DEPARTMENT OF PHYSICS AND ASTROPHYSICS

1006 JILA Bldg.                                    27 September 1968

Dr. Roy Craig
202 Woodbury
Campus

Dear Roy:

   There have been a lot of minuses associated with the Scientific
Study of Unidentified Flying Objects, but a very big plus which helped
a great deal toward making the ordeal bearable for me was that through
it we became personally acquainted. I hope that our friendship will
continue. You have been a real mainstay of the project, as investigator,
as policy-maker, as author of three chapters of the final report and as
drafter of case reports. Your scientific and personal integrity have
been a great source of moral support to me in trying times.

   Please accept my thanks for your help and best wishes for continued
success in other scientific and academic projects.

   With best regards,

                                    Sincerely,

                                    E. U. Condon

EUC:kes

# Acknowledgments

I should like to thank the Board of Regents of the University of Colorado for granting me permission to quote the official report of the *Scientific Study of Unidentified Flying Objects,* published in 1968. Mr. Wilbert B. Smith's open permission to quote his writings in *Topside* also is appreciated. Thanks also to Jerry McElroy of Pro-Visions Photography for permission to use several of his photographs, and to photographer Gerald Brimacombe for permitting use of the photograph he took for *Life* magazine while we were searching for a saucer nest in Canada.

I appreciate the typing assistance provided by my sister, Carolyn Craig Shryock, and my niece, Gayle Voss Button, during various phases of preparation of this work. John and Ruth Van Sant were helpful in getting material stored on old computer disks transcribed to readable form. Myrtle Nord and Dr. Robert Minturn read the entire manuscript and made helpful suggestions for its improvement.

Special recognition goes to my editor at the University of North Texas Press, Charlotte M. Wright, for her pleasant cooperation and excellent editing work, and to Mrs. Jake (Terry) Hershey of Houston, Texas, without whose enthusiasm, dedication, and active promotion this work might never had been published.

# PART I

## FIELD AND LABORATORY
## INVESTIGATIONS OF REPORTED
## UFO EXPERIENCES

# Chapter 1

# Beeping Sounds from Nowhere

It was 2:35 A.M., May 14. We were on top of a hill in a dense rain forest near the northern Pacific coast. I wondered what the devil I was doing there, and laughed to myself, almost audibly, as I took a disengaged view of what then seemed an absurdly amusing situation. The amusement brought relaxation, and I was no longer aware of shivering as I mentally reviewed the events that led to this improbable way of spending a Saturday night.

Early in the week I had stopped at the UFO Project offices in Woodbury Hall at the University of Colorado. I was picking out some choice reports of past encounters with unidentified flying objects, expecting to read the reports in my spare time as a means of getting acquainted with the UFO question. (Were they real? Were they from another planet?) Jim Wadsworth was engaged in a lengthy telephone conversation with an official of the Civil Defense organization in Washington state. Other staff members were excited about reports he was receiving of strange beeping sounds coming from near the earth's surface, about tree-top level, where there was no visible object or organism to generate the sound.

Apparently, the beeping had been heard each night for several nights, commencing almost on schedule about 8:00, and continuing while scores of curious people tramped about the area, trying to identify its cause. The beeping continued, unaffected by shouts and even a shot-gun blast beneath the spot where it appeared to originate. Although the point of origin varied at different times, observers agreed that the sound seemed to come from a particular point in space which was not far above their heads as they wandered around beneath it. Yet nothing visible was present in that region of space.

Observers had only their own imaginations to tell them what could cause strange sounds to appear from nowhere. To some, the beeping seemed unearthly. The apparent strangeness of the sounds was enhanced by reports of unusual animal reactions to them. Frogs stopped croaking about twenty seconds before the beeps commenced, and cattle in the field at the bottom of the hill acted apprehensive and strangely disturbed. Amateur ornithologists had stated the sounds certainly were not those of any bird, and officials felt the sounds were somehow electronically generated. How? Where?

The state Civil Defense group apparently felt there was a potential threat associated with the beeping. The Air Force's Project Blue Book had refused to investigate, claiming an unidentified sound was outside the realm of flying objects. Flying saucer enthusiasts scattered about the country were showing strong interest in the phenomenon. Should the Colorado Project investigate?

The project had received similar reports of strange beeping sounds from other regions of the United States. Some of these described the cowering and quivering of usually bold dogs when the sound was heard. The reports were intriguing. Project staff personnel had marked a map to show the locations from which such reports originated and were checking to see if these points were along straight lines or displayed any other significant pattern.

I suggested to Jim that he get the best tape recording of the sound that could be obtained. Perhaps sonographic analysis, revealing the various frequency components and the duration of each frequency, would enable us to identify the sound.

How could the exact position of origin of the sound be determined, so one could verify that no material object was there? We had read of "snooperscopes" which could pick up whispered conversations from a distance when the receiving cone was pointed in the direction of the whispering. Perhaps a snooperscope could be used to determine the direction to the sound source from different positions around it. The crossing point of such direction lines would show the location of the source. Directional ultrasonic detectors of a type sometimes used to locate points of corona discharge on power lines seemed to be more precise than the sonic devices in determining the direction from which vibrations came. If the strange beeping sounds were accompanied by vibrations with higher frequencies than were audible, these ultrasonic detectors might help pinpoint the source. I discussed this possibility with Jim before leaving him with his beeping problem.

On Thursday, as I was preparing a lecture for my physical science class, I was interrupted by a telephone call from Jim at the UFO office across campus. Could I leave Friday with him to investigate the persistent beeping and check on reports of visual sightings of unidentified flying objects in the same region?

I canceled plans for a weekend trip to a ranch in Wyoming, and arranged for an assistant to meet my Monday classes. While

I met my classes on Friday morning, Jim loaded our cameras with high-speed film, put a portable tape recorder with his personal gear, and picked up a directional ultrasonic translator-detector which we had located in Denver and arranged to borrow. Any other equipment we thought we might want would be furnished by the Civil Defense group at our destination.

A few hours later we were in Washington, at the home of the Civil Defense official, getting a detailed evening briefing on the strange sounds, and getting addresses of people who had reported sightings of unidentified flying objects.

A large part of the following Saturday had been devoted to finding and interviewing people who had heard the strange sound or reported seeing flying objects. Oral statements by those who had heard the sound merely confirmed the written report that it was something very strange. Those who had seen flying objects gave disturbingly vague and generally inconsistent descriptions of the experiences. There was no apparent relation in time between the objects sighted and the beeps heard, and there seemed to be no relation between the two phenomena.

Another aspect of the beeper's nature had been suggested at a meeting with the Civil Defense group early Saturday morning, as one of the technicians reported that radio interference had been experienced at the time of the beeping, the interference having the same frequency as the beeps. Sound is one thing, radio interference quite another. If this report were true, we wondered, what must be the nature of the beeper?

The early morning meeting had culminated in the evening's attempt to get good tape recordings of the beeping sound, to locate the source, and to learn whatever we could about it.

So there I was, twisting uncomfortably on a bed of damp hemlock branches in the dense forest at 2:40 in the morning. I pulled my light raincoat tight around my waist and piled more boughs on top of my legs in a vain effort to keep warm on a misty, cold night. I was watching particularly the region around the top of the tallest of the trees which zoomed skyward high above, for it was there the beeping had been heard on previous nights. Peering into the darkness around me, I could make out the outlines of two of my five associates. I couldn't tell if anyone else was awake, for I saw no one moving and the last few words of subdued conversation had been exchanged perhaps an hour earlier. We were intentionally quiet as we listened and waited for the strange beeping sound which had no visible source.

We hadn't expected to be there all night, without warm clothing or other equipment to make our stay reasonably comfortable. The assault group, consisting of Jim and myself, four technicians from the Civil Defense group, and two teenage sons of the owner of the farm which served as a base for this operation, had planned to hike to this point just before dark. We would stay only long enough to get what information we could after the 8:00 beeping commenced. If the beeper didn't show by 11:00, we reasoned, we would hike back down to the farm at the base of the hill, and perhaps try again another time.

The farmhouse was only about a mile away. In getting to our site, however, we had waded through a stream at the foot of the hill, climbed a steep, slick slope, and hiked through dense undergrowth that was difficult to penetrate in daylight. We had been guided by the sons of the owner of the farm. The older boy, having Saturday night attractions in town and knowing this wooded region well, had tired of waiting and started hiking out before midnight, taking one of the Civil Defense technicians with him. For the rest of us to try to find our way out of this forest in the dark seemed to be inviting disaster, so we had decided to maintain the vigil until dawn. Thus, I had trapped myself here. Fickle fate seemed to be one up on me now, and the most satisfactory reaction I could muster was to find humor in that fact. Perhaps a greater contributor to my amusement, however, was

7

the thought of how theatrically impressive our assault on this hill seemed. The Civil Defense official and the farm owner had stayed below to man the non-portable tape recording equipment we had set up in the barn. We had rolled out 2000 feet of cable to separate the stereo microphones in the fields on either side of the barn in expectation of determining the time delay in receipt of a particular beeping sound at the second microphone after it was initially picked up on the first. Thus we hoped not only to get a recording of good fidelity, but also one which would help locate the source by telling us how much farther it was from one mike than from the other. The field party had come equipped with portable tape recorders to record the beeping sounds; two-way radios for communication with the official at the farm; a home-made snooperscope and the borrowed ultrasonic transla-tor-detector for determining the direction of origin of sound or ultrasound; a military type infrared sniperscope to possibly en-able us to see a "beeper" in the dark; Geiger counters for check-ing possible deposition of radioactive material; cameras loaded with high speed film, infrared sensitive film, and ultra-violet sensitive film; flashlights; and battery lanterns. If the beeping would only commence, we were ready to collect information.

Unfortunately, the only beeps we had heard so far were during three or four very brief periods when the sound came faintly from the distance. We heard the first of these at dusk, just before we arrived at our present site. Again about 9:00 P.M., and twice again between 9:00 and 12:00, some of us heard the faint sound. We had heard no such sound since midnight, and at no time did a beeping commence by the tall tree above us, where it was re-ported to have appeared almost every night before.

As I looked up at the sky and the top of the tree, I found it difficult to believe the beeping was something unusual. After we had climbed this hill, one of our young guides told us that one night, while the beeping was coming from the top of this

8

tree, another boy had climbed the tree to see what caused it. When the boy got high in the tree, the beeping source left it and circled around him, still beeping, yet he could see no bird or other object there. Whether or not a bird was seen in the darkness, this information clearly indicated the source of the beeps was aware of the boy's presence in the immediate vicinity. The described behavior seemed very bird-like to me, and I thought it would be a good laugh if all this excitement and concern had been caused by some little bird, such as a pygmy owl, whose call the beeping was said to resemble.

At 2:45 my thoughts were interrupted by another brief beeping in the distance. Jim heard it too, but the sound had ceased before he could start the recorder he kept ready at hand. We listened quietly, hoping it would either come closer or cause the beeping to commence near the tree by us. Our hopes faded as neither happened.

Eventually I settled back to musing. I had just joined the UFO Project, which Jim had worked on for several months, and this expedition was my first introduction to field investigations. Staying awake to listen for strange sounds was not really difficult, for we were far too cold and uncomfortable to go to sleep. Just at daybreak, about 4:55, we heard the distant beeping again. Jim caught a bit of it on tape, but it was too distant and faint to record clearly. No beeper had appeared near our camp through the entire night.

We broke camp as soon as it was fully daylight, and started down the hill. As we approached the farmhouse, a youngster ran to greet us, asking if we'd heard the beeping. Carelessly and unintentionally, I revealed the belief I then held when I replied, "The bird didn't show." This response apparently offended one of my companions from the night watch, who turned to me and said, "You're calling it a BIRD!" The tone of his voice was sufficient to accuse me of jumping to unwarranted conclusions, be-

9

cause I had no proof that it was a bird. Sure enough, I didn't have.

Jim and I left further observations at this site near Hoquiam, in Grays Harbor County, in the hands of local residents, and drove around Seattle and north to the town of Seedro Wooley, another area where beeps from nowhere were being reported. On the way, we stopped to talk with other citizens who had a special interest in unidentified flying objects and sounds.

I mentioned to Jim that a major flaw in our mode of investigation so far had been the tendency to interview only those people who had reported seeing or hearing something strange. It would seem equally important to talk with their neighbors, particularly if those neighbors had been in such situations that logically, they also should have seen or heard the phenomenon of concern. Their not reporting anything strange would not necessarily mean that they did not see or hear the same objects or noises their anxious neighbors reported however, for they might have observed, and recognized as something quite ordinary, that which their neighbors considered strange.

We arrived at the second site after dark. Fortunately, this location was near a country road, so we could listen for the beeps from the car. It was raining, and we wondered if the rain would prevent the beeping. Several other cars were parked or slowly cruising in the vicinity, their occupants also waiting and listening. According to reports, dozens of local residents had been tramping through these woods on previous nights, as they had at other such sites, some carrying guns. Luckily, no one had been injured. No beeper had yet been seen.

The rain continued. We were exhausted from our previous night's vigil, and found it impossible to stay awake as we tried to listen for sounds from the wooded region. At midnight, having heard nothing, we gave up the effort and found comfortable beds at a motel. By this time, I could have fallen asleep if a little green Martian were pulling on each ear.

The next morning we inquired about the beeping at the police station in Seedro Wooley. The police had no knowledge of recent activity, and pointed out that the area where the beeping was heard was outside the jurisdiction of town police. They suggested we contact the Skagit County sheriff, whose office was handling the local investigation of the sounds. Upon phoning that office, we were told that the sheriff had just been given a dead saw-whet owl which was said to have been shot the previous night while "beeping" at the famous site which we had left at midnight. The man who brought it to the sheriff said he lived at the edge of the woods and shot the owl to stop the milling of curious people around his yard.

We drove to the sheriff's office in Mt. Vernon and looked at the dead little owl, killed with a 20-gauge shotgun blast. With its wet feathers clinging to its skin, it was not much bigger than a sparrow. I snapped a photo of the dead owl, and then I spoke with the local biology teacher who had identified the owl as a saw-whet. In his opinion, the owl was indeed the source of the sounds. He said the only people who had gotten concerned about the beeping were those who were not familiar with the woods. Lumbermen and kids who spend time in the woods, he said, had all recognized the sounds as the call of an owl.

So the sheriff had a dead owl. Would the beeping in his region now cease? Was this dead owl adequate proof that the beeping was merely that of an owl? I recalled a story a professor had told in one of my classes years before during a discussion of fallacious reasoning. It seems a man heard of a claim that a chicken had killed a tiger. This man traveled into the back country to talk with the person who made the claim, and returned to his friends convinced that the claim was true, saying, "I know it is true, he showed me the chicken!" I told this story to Jim as we drove to the airport, pointing out that the mere evidence of a

11

Saw-whet owl shot near Seedro Woolley, Washington, because it made "mysterious sounds from nowhere."

dead owl did not prove that the owl had done anything in particular while it was living. We had been unable to contact the man who shot the owl to get his full story. Even if we had, we still would want to compare sonograms of recorded owl calls with the beeping sounds from nowhere which had been tape recorded by others before our arrival on the scene. We now had copies of those tapes. If the beeping sounds matched those of the owl in frequency and character, then we would be justified in concluding they were made by owls. Jim agreed to make the sonograms for identity verification.

Upon returning to Boulder, I found Dr. Condon awaiting my arrival. He asked me to eat lunch with him, so I could let him know what we had learned about the unidentified flying sounds in Washington. He seemed amused at the results of the field investigation. Personally, I felt a major result was the knowledge that an investigator of any unidentified phenomenon is likely to learn much about that phenomenon from people who were in a *position* to experience it, but who saw or heard nothing they considered unusual. Listening only to those who reported a strange experience may keep one from learning the true identity of its cause.

We had left instructions with local residents to inform us if beeping sounds without apparent sources continued to be heard after the killing of the unfortunate owl. We heard of no further reports. Apparently the unearthly beeping ceased with the termination of the owl mating season.

# Chapter 2

# His Chest Was Burned

UFO reports are most frequently descriptions of strange lights in the distance. They are interpreted in various ways by observers, but they seldom leave any markings or evidence to reveal their presence or their nature—no calling cards. As Colorado Project investigators, we were most interested in studying cases which involved "calling cards"—something which was left for us to analyze and evaluate, and present to the world as authentic evidence of whatever was indicated.

In late May, a reporter for the *Winnipeg Free Press* telephoned us to inform us of a UFO sighting which might be of special interest. A fifty-year-old mechanic, doing some weekend prospecting alone in the Canadian woods, had reported seeing two domed saucer-shaped flying craft which traveled at fantastic speed. One of them had landed near him and, after watching it for more than a half hour, the prospector approached near enough to touch the saucer. When he did so, it began rotating and vanished quickly over the horizon. At the beginning of its rotation, a blast of hot gases had struck the prospector, who was standing near a patterned exhaust area of the craft. It left him with a rather severe burn on his chest and a scorched pattern on his shirt and undershirt. It also made him violently ill. He was, at the time of the phone call, sick in bed and unable to go back to the site where he encountered the UFO.

This report contained the most detailed description of a flying saucer I had yet heard. It was a craft about thirty-five feet long and eight feet high with a three foot protrusion on top, displaying the rainbow-colored appearance of hot stainless steel. Before it cooled, it was surrounded by a red glow. A bright violet light beamed out of a door-like opening which closed before the craft departed. No welding, bolts, or joints were apparent on the craft.

The prospector also reported hearing a loud hissing sound, like air rushing in and out of the opening, and human-like voices from within the craft. He had tried to talk with the people he assumed to be inside as he approached the craft, addressing them in English, Russian, Polish, German, and Italian. (A Polish immigrant, he claimed to speak 5 languages.) The only response was closure of the doorway and departure of the craft.

It wasn't the description of the craft that interested us so much as the apparent possibility that a project representative could be with the first party to revisit the site of the claimed encounter. The primary question was, "Is there any evidence to verify that the man actually had such an experience"? Unless one could establish the event as factual, details of the description, fascinating as they may be, were meaningless, for study of individual fantasy does not produce evidence regarding a physical reality. If a saucer landing site did exist, with physical evidence there to identify it, we wished to examine it before other

15

human beings obscured or destroyed the evidence. We also wished to be present the first time the site was revisited to reduce the probability the "evidence", such as landing marks, burned areas, or material deposition, would be created by human beings who intended to deceive others.

In this case there were also the burns on the weekend prospector's chest. They, reportedly, were real. Was the experience described also real? There might be some evidence, remote in the Canadian woods at the site where the flying saucer reportedly landed, which could help us answer that question.

For reasons I could only guess at, the decision was made that if anyone representing the Colorado Project were to go tramping through the Canadian woods looking for a UFO landing site, it was to be me. We were in the middle of final examinations at the University, however, and I simply could not get away to chase UFOs until my students' exam papers were scored and their term grades submitted to the records office. That seemed to be no disadvantage, however, for the burned man had not yet recovered from his illness sufficiently to attempt to guide a search party back to the region of his experience, and there was no chance of locating the site of that experience unless he described exactly where it was or led us to it.

As the days went by, news of this UFO encounter spread across the country. *Life* magazine wanted to send a reporter and photographer along if the Colorado Project sent an investigator to Winnipeg. We didn't know yet whether a trip would seem warranted. The staff kept informed of developments through an occasional phone call.

After several more days, we obtained a tentative commitment that the burned witness, now nearly recovered from his illness, would lead a search party to the region of his encounter. This commitment was obtained through Mr. Thompson, a Winnipeg civilian UFO enthusiast who had gained the burned man's confidence. I could see the end of the exam papers by then, and agreed to catch a Friday afternoon plane for Winnipeg. The search party was expected to leave on Saturday.

Changing planes In Minneapolis, I boarded the flight to cross the Canadian border. Two fellow passengers on the same flight were carrying boxes bearing "photographic equipment" and "*Life* magazine" labels. I assumed their mission was closely related to mine, for I had been told that a *Life* reporter had phoned the project office again after my trip was scheduled, learned of our plans, and indicated he would join our search.

As far as I was concerned, my business was to seek information and evidence about unidentified flying objects. Reporters were welcome to conduct their business however and wherever they saw fit, and I would communicate freely with them as long as their business didn't interfere with mine. At this point, however, I saw no reason to identify myself to *Life* representatives, for I chose to avoid the undesirable implications which could develop if we arrived in Winnipeg together.

As I started for a cab stand at the Winnipeg International Airport, I looked back to see the *Life* photographer arguing with a Canadian customs agent. From the nature of the gestures, I assumed there was some question about importation of his camera. I also assumed I would see this man and his companion again soon.

During the long cab ride to my hotel, which was on the outskirts of the city, I listened to the friendly, talkative driver. He told me of the numerous sightings of unidentified flying objects around Winnipeg. I was particularly interested as he told me, "One guy got burned. He's still in the hospital. The thing left a foul odor on him—his wife can't stand the smell of him even yet. That happened a week ago."

I knew that the event he referred to had happened two weeks previously, not one, and that the burned fellow has been sick at

17

home, not in a hospital. Such inaccuracies were of no particular consequence. However, I was interested in observing the manner in which UFO stories were accepted and developed by the public, so I continued to ask questions and listen to the responses. The cab driver never suspected the nature of my mission. He was a willing source of information when he thought he was relating local news to a passing tourist. I did not disturb his assumptions.

I had hardly finished unpacking my suitcase at the hotel when the *Life* reporter telephoned. I agreed to talk with him at a set time later that evening, for Mr. Thompson was already on the way to my hotel to review the case of interest and arrange plans for the search for the UFO landing site.

Mr. Thompson informed me that the UFO witness, whom I shall call Mr. Zellinski, had developed a rash near the burned area on his chest and had an appointment to see the doctor about it the next morning. He was certain the rash was a result of his exposure to the UFO blast. He was reluctant to lead a search for the landing site in any case, saying he wasn't sure his health would permit it. An item in the newspaper revealed that Mr. Zellinski had already made an unsuccessful search for the site the previous day, mostly by helicopter, in cooperation with the Royal Canadian Air Force (RCAF) and Royal Canadian Mounted Police (RCMP). Mr. Thompson had arranged for Mr. Z to see me on Saturday afternoon, after his appointment with the doctor. He hoped we could convince Z to lead us on another effort to find the landing site. By this time, the *Life* representatives were included in all plans, and it appeared that both Mr. Thompson and Mr. Zellinski anticipated some financial benefit from a *Life* article.

Since I had some free time Saturday morning, I phoned the *Free Press* reporter who had originally notified us of the reported UFO encounter. He came to my hotel to give me his version of the original story and what he knew of subsequent developments. He was delighted to get an exclusive interview with me, although I told him I knew, as yet, nothing more about the UFO case than such people as he had told me. His response, which constituted the beginning of my initiation into the public relations aspect of being an "official" UFO investigator, was, "Your coming to town is news!"

The *Free Press* reporter was an impressive man of about thirty-two, with a neatly trimmed heavy red beard. He was intelligent and independent in his thinking. Although we quickly covered what he then knew of the total UFO situation around Winnipeg, present and past, we talked for a couple of hours. We spoke "off the record", after his agreement not to print anything I said about anything other than UFOs, since that was my sole business here.

As we chatted, this red-bearded citizen of the world revealed his effective method of teaching languages to his children. At home, the family spoke nothing but German, which was his original native tongue. English was spoken at school. The family television set was tuned only to French stations. Thus, his children had naturally become trilingual.

I was admiring this man's system of education as he left my hotel with his story. Apparently he was right when he said my coming to town was news. The Saturday edition of the newspaper was already made up when he left my hotel, and the *Free Press* did not print on Sunday. When the Monday edition hit the street, however, it carried a front-page headline, in bold red letters on the lower half of the page, "U.S. UFO Expert in Winnipeg." This was 5 June 1967. The only headline which was in larger type announced the outbreak of what proved to be the six-day war between Israel and her Arab neighbors.

I learned later that this high degree of public interest in local UFO experiences was not at all unusual. I laughed at the "expert" label, however, and agreed with the definition of an expert as anyone more than fifty miles from home. I had been working one-fifth time on the UFO study for about six weeks, and I was already an "expert."

By the time the news article was published, we had already been searching the Canadian bush for the landing site. The Saturday afternoon interview had found Mr. Zellinski reluctantly cooperative. He started by saying we would get the details of his experience from the recording of an earlier interview he had granted Mr. Thompson, so he would not repeat those details for me. Leading questions, however, got him to review every aspect of his claimed ordeal. I recorded this interview on tape as the *Life* representatives took notes and shot roll after roll of film. The photographer got pictures showing our expressions during the question and answer process, pictures of Mr. Z's sketches of the saucer-shaped craft, and pictures of his scorched undershirt and partly-burned cap.

Mr. Z had said he made one of his sketches at the site while watching the craft and waiting for someone to emerge from it. The undershirt had been "confiscated" by an RCAF officer who returned it, at Mr. Z's request, during my interview. When he brought the undershirt to Mr. Z's house, the fact that Colorado Project and *Life* representatives were there was kept secret from him. I got the officer's name and telephone number for later contact.

Mr. Zellinski agreed to guide us on a search for the landing site on Sunday, warning us not to let RCAF, RCMP, newsmen, or anyone else know of our plans. He explained that if the public knew we were going into the area, there would be so many people there that a search would be impossible.

Saturday evening, after the lengthy interview, I compared notes with reporter John Fried and photographer Jerry Brimacombe from *Life*. We all agreed that, fantastic as this man's

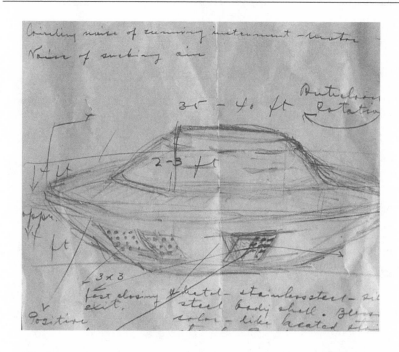

Sketch of UFO at Falcon Lake, Canada. Sketch said by observer to have been made at the site while he was observing the object.

story was, he seemed sincere and told his story convincingly, as if he were describing an authentic experience. Other people considered Mr. Z to be a stable and reliable man. There were some incongruities in the story, such as a compass which spun wildly in the presence of the UFO, and yet told exactly the direction one UFO departed while the other hovered nearby. Nonetheless, the case seemed to all of us to be worth further checking. We were anxious to find the landing site to see if evidence there supported Mr. Z's claims.

Besides a landing spot where the lichen had been burned or blown from the rock by the hovering and landed craft, there should be remnants of Mr. Z's burned shirt, evidence of a small moss fire started by the burning shirt when he threw it to the

21

*Life* photographer's picture of Roy Craig chasing flying saucers in Canada. (*Life* Photo used by permission of Jerry Brimacombe)

ground, and a 6-foot rule he had neglected to put back into his prospecting bag while gathering his equipment after stamping out the fire. Mr. Z didn't know if there might be other physical evidence there, for he said his illness commenced within minutes after the blast of hot gases struck him. He had said earlier that he vomited and passed out briefly several times during his struggle back to the highway. He did recall finding a small saw, evidently left by a lumbering crew, and placing it on a stump he passed before he saw the UFOs. This saw had been found again on the unsuccessful site search with the RCAF and RCMP, so Mr. Zellinski felt he knew just about where his UFO encounter took place.

Sunday morning we drove about eighty-five miles east of Winnipeg and a mile or so off the highway to park by an abandoned gravel pit. We had been warned that this would be a rugged hike in remote bush country, and the site would be about five miles from the highway. We were appropriately equipped for a rugged all-day hike, with individual canteens filled with water and lunches packed for the occasion. I stuck my lunch in a light backpack which already contained cameras, a Geiger counter, sample containers, and other equipment I thought I might need for a reasonably thorough examination of the landing site.

We taped our trouser legs tight around our ankles, wore long-sleeved shirts with tight wrists, and sprayed insect repellent on our hands and faces, following Mr. Zellinski's advice, to keep the black flies from "eating us up." Then, we headed into an area of small trees, brush, and beaver ponds. We noticed a fire look-out tower about half a mile behind us when we started out.

The search party consisted of Mr. Zellinski, his eighteen-year-old son, Mr. Thompson, the two *Life* representatives and myself. Mr. Zellinski took the lead and proceeded fairly slowly as he

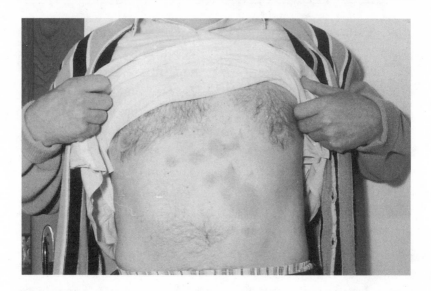

The residue of the claimed burn from the hot exhaust of departing saucer from Canadian woods near Winnipeg.

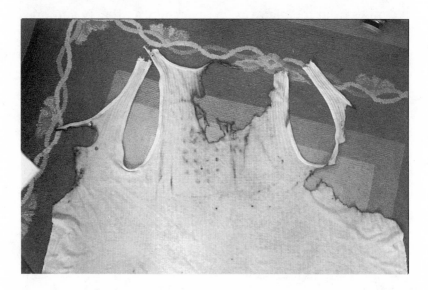

The undershirt said to have been burned by a UFO. Patterned burn shown is apparently the *back* of the shirt.

was, he said, trying to retrace the path he took while searching for veins of ore the morning of his UFO encounter. This, he hoped, would lead him to where he saw the UFOs. He frequently recognized places he had been, and pointed out spots where he had chipped off segments of rock for examination. We were on the right track.

It was hardly past noon when Mr. Zellinski suggested that we could not find the site that day, but, since he was determined to find it, he'd have to come back and search again some other time. The day was still young and we were not likely to be with him "some other time," so we urged that the search be continued. Mr. Z's efforts so far had already impressed me as those of someone who was trying to create the appearance of searching, rather than of one who was actually searching for something. Although he talked as if he were leading us deep into the bush country, we had actually wandered around a small area within two miles of our cars, frequently doubling back and crossing our own path. It seemed like rather aimless wandering. The fact that Mr. Z wanted to give up so easily strengthened my suspicions about the nature of the outing.

Mr. Z agreed to "look some more." After additional wandering in the same general vicinity, I was convinced that what he said was true—we were not to find a UFO landing site that day. Either there was no landing site to be found or, as Mr. Thompson suggested, Mr. Zellinski had found valuable ore where he was prospecting when the UFOs arrived, and didn't want anyone in the area until he staked his claims. In any case, if Mr. Z said he didn't think we would find his landing site, it obviously was futile for us to insist on trying.

I took advantage of the early termination of this search to talk with people who had seen Mr. Zellinski after he reached the highway and before he returned to Winnipeg on the day of his UFO encounter. I also visited with those persons who were in

The group, including media personnel, starting off to search for a flying saucer nest in the Canadian woods.

charge of manning the fire look-out tower we had seen, and with people who reported having observed an unidentified flying object in this region on the day Mr. Z was burned. I returned to Winnipeg with the feeling there was no UFO landing site to be found. The other object observed had the appearance of a box kite, rather than of Mr. Z's UFO, and conservation officers were sure the watchman on the fire tower would have seen both the smoke from the small moss fire and the flying objects themselves had the described event actually taken place.

I spent three more days investigating this report and other UFO reports in the Winnipeg region, with full cooperation of RCAF and RCMP personnel, medical personnel, news reporters, and regional radar operators. Each afternoon when I returned to my hotel, the girl at the telephone switchboard handed me a stack of messages from people who wanted to tell me about their UFO sightings, wanted to tell me where UFOs came from or how they worked, or wanted an interview for their radio or TV station. This switchboard operator was most helpful, putting through on schedule the calls I desired, screening incoming calls and checking with me before connecting the caller with my phone, and letting visitors cool their heels in the lobby until I could get a chance to talk with them. She would be a superb secretary.

I left Winnipeg still puzzled at how this gentleman had gotten burned. He had initially convinced his family, RCAF and RCMP officers, and several of the half-dozen doctors he encountered for various reasons regarding his burn, as well as UFO enthusiasts, that he told a strange tale of an actual experience. Beyond the burn itself, however, I had found no evidence to verify or even support his story. I had encountered so many discrepancies and incongruities that, however the man got burned, I felt the case could not be used as evidence that flying craft like he sketched in such beautiful detail existed outside human minds.

Mr. Zellinski had agreed to phone the Colorado Project office immediately if he were to locate the landing site on a later search. The office received no such call. We heard rumors a week or two later that the site had been found. After a few more weeks, I received from Mr. Zellinski a copy of a booklet he had published which described his experience and what was found at the located landing site. Those findings included the presence of radioactive material in the cracks of the rock upon which the UFO had landed. Upon checking with the Canadian officials who had been involved in investigating Mr. Z's reported encounter, I learned that the radioactive material from the rock cracks was similar in nature to uranium ore from a nearby valley. Since it appeared that the landing site had been prepared by humans for "rediscovery," I could see no reason to expect useful information could be gained by further investigation of this case.

27

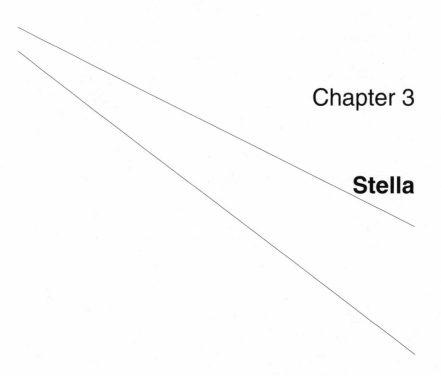

# Chapter 3

# Stella

It was nearly midnight when co-investigator Jim Wadsworth and I drove up to Stella's motel. We had rented a car at the airport which serves Youngstown, Ohio, and driven through the small Pennsylvania town a few miles from which a man and his eleven-year-old son reported seeing and photographing a flying saucer the previous day. We had a 10 A.M. appointment with the dairy farmer who had notified the world of his neighbor's experience, and had just driven past his farm to note its location. As we were about to turn around to find a place to stay, a sign announced that right here was Stella's motel. It was most convenient, and the "vacancy" sign was up.

We entered the motel office to find the late TV news showing the flying saucer photograph we had come to examine, document, and obtain for analysis if we could. The two women in the office were watching the broadcast and talking excitedly. As soon as the news broadcast had finished the UFO item, the younger woman waddled her 300-plus pounds majestically to the counter and handed Jim a pen to register our presence.

This was Stella.[1] And she was in her glory. She told us of the photograph of a UFO which had been taken in her neighborhood, and showed us the front page article about it in the local newspaper. She had known someone would get such a picture one of these days, for there had been numerous sightings of a UFO like this one around the neighborhood for the past four or five years. It was most often seen between June and September, and there were several instances in which young couples had been frightened when it came right down near them in the lover's lane region to the west. The nephew of the dairy farmer down the road had had such an experience a couple years ago, and other young people periodically told Stella of such experiences. Stella commented that there was a tremendous amount of interest in the UFO photographs. This really tickled her, for now she could gloat at the state police. A state policeman she knew had phoned her after the department received a call from Stella's farm neighbor informing them of the photographs which had just been taken about 300 yards from the dairy barn.

"Your pet has just been photographed!" he said. "Run down and see if there are any little green men in the picture!"

She had immediately driven over to check out the report. When she saw a real picture of a genuine saucer, she called the state police, gleefully, and told them the man really had photographed a flying saucer. Officer Bell then went out to the dairy farm to look for himself, and the news hit the press.

"People have been coming here from all over—making appointments from that University of Oregon, and all." Stella talked on and on about UFOs. "Some people think they come from under the water. I've heard that someone saw one emerging from the lake north of here."

We finally managed to get our keys and say good-night to Stella. Since only Jim had signed the register, she had made no connection between us and the Dr. Craig who was known to be coming out from "that University of Oregon."

Neither Jim nor I had been favorably impressed by the newspaper reproduction of the polaroid photographs we had come to see. The outline of the flying saucer obviously had been sketched in by hand. This made the photo appear faked. However, we acknowledged that the sketched outline could have been added by newspaper people for increased clarity on reproduction. We'd have to wait until the morrow to see what the original photographs revealed.

Stella called us the next morning forty-five minutes after the time we had requested. We were already up and showered. Since breakfast was included in the motel price, and there was no cafe within several miles, we went to Stella's kitchen where she fed us a routine Continental breakfast. It was tolerable but plain. The digestion was aided, however, by Stella's interesting stories of past events at her motel, which she was telling to a man and wife at the next table who apparently were friends of hers. She told of these events as exuberantly as she talked about UFOs, and soon we were listening and laughing with the rest.

She spoke of one elderly couple who had spent the night at her motel. They had already raised a nice family, but now, because of some social security requirement, wanted to get married. Stella, as Justice of the Peace, was to perform the ceremony. The time for the wedding had arrived, but the old gent suddenly decided he didn't want to marry that old woman—he wanted a young one. Why should he marry an old woman like that? Stella agreed that a young woman would be nice. She told him if he got a young one, though, he'd have to buy her new dresses and take her out to expensive restaurants. By the time Stella finished, the old man and his mate were happily wed.

30

Stella's good humor spread to everyone around her. Both of her chins and her full body seemed to participate in her friendly laughter, which was immediately contagious. She was still entertaining her guests when we departed, somewhat reluctantly, to get about our UFO business.

The dairy farmer had in his custody the polaroid photographs which had been taken by a divorced machine operator who lived in a small house at the edge of his farm. I shall call this man Mr. Mason. The two photographs, taken at midday, showed different views of an obviously solid flying saucer with two rows of square windows or ports. The photos were interesting, though overexposed and covered with fingerprints from careless handling.

According to the report of the flying saucer incident, Mr. Mason was about to take a picture of his eleven-year-old son, who spent weekends and vacation periods with him, when a high-pitched humming noise attracted their attention to the sky. There they saw a UFO about sixty feet in diameter, probably some 500 feet away, moving about thirty to forty miles per hour. Mr. Mason swung the Polaroid camera around and got the two pictures during the few seconds before the object made a sudden transition to high speed, estimated at 2000 miles per hour, and zoomed out of sight.

There were some trees, bushes, and other objects in the foreground of both pictures. These should serve as good reference points, useful for precise determination of the flying saucer's distance. If the distance to the object were determinable, its dimensions could be computed from the focal length or angular field of the camera. We went to examine the site where the photographs were taken and to talk with Mr. Mason and his son Bobby.

Mr. Mason loaned us his Polaroid camera, with which we duplicated his photographs, without the UFO, using the same type film he said he used previously. As we did so, we stayed beyond the reach of an angry beagle with one red injured eye, tied to a run line in front of the dilapidated house. As we were measuring distances to various objects which showed in the photographs, Stella arrived on the scene, laughing and thrilled. She was accompanied by the wife of the dairy farmer, who had told her that the investigators from Colorado University were staying at her motel!

"If I'd known that's who you were, I'd fixed you bacon and eggs this morning. And to think of all those things I said last night!"

"I heard that," I said. "We'll expect bacon and eggs for breakfast tomorrow morning."

"You'll get them too."

The curious were too ubiquitous to allow private conversation with the withdrawn Mr. Mason and his bright young son, Bobby. We made an appointment to take the pair to dinner that evening. This was to be followed by private conversation at Stella's motel. Meantime, we checked out reports that others had seen Mr. Mason's UFO, and also talked with people who seemingly should have seen it if the event had occurred as reported. If the photographed object were the size Mr. Mason claimed, it would have been directly over a gravel pit when his first photograph was taken. Workmen in the gravel pit, on lunch break at the time, saw no such object. They did not doubt that it had been overhead, however. After all, this man took a picture of it! They regretted that equipment noise had kept the UFO sound from attracting their attention.

We arrived at the motel that evening after dinner to find Stella waiting for us to witness a wedding ceremony she was about to perform. She was decked out in a full black robe with a corsage of plastic lilies of the valley. Fancy ear pendants hung beneath her neat coiffure. It was obvious that she took this business of marrying people quite seriously.

We watched as Stella went through the wedding ritual. She gave the participants the full treatment, and then impressed upon them the seriousness of the obligations they were assuming. Although we knew Stella had performed about 260 marriages the past year alone, and aspired to perform the first such ceremony in a flying saucer, she was as nervous and concerned as if this were her first such experience. She misread a couple of lines and had to try them again, but she did not let this distract from the impressiveness of the ceremony. As in all other matters, Stella had command of the situation.

Stella indicated to us that the couple, both of whom appeared to be in their thirties, had come in quite depressed. They were going to be married, but they had no witnesses, and the occasion was to be nothing special. Now, as all four of us—Mr. Mason, Bobby, Jim, and I—signed the wedding booklet on the "reception" page, Stella told the newlywed couple, "Nobody will ever believe you—your wedding witnessed by the man who took the UFO pictures, his son, Mr. Wadsworth, and Dr. Craig, whom you saw on the TV news this evening."

We tossed rice on a departing couple, who were thrilled by their wedding experience. They would not soon forget the night they were wed by Stella.

Our request for a 7 A.M. call was promptly honored the second morning—on the minute. Stella checked back after a half hour to make sure our breakfast would be hot out of the pan. "When would you like your bacon and eggs, your honor?" Ten minutes later she was serving us all we could eat of orange juice, apple sauce, coffee, toast, stacks of delicious home-cured ham, and eggs "lovingly cooked and served with a smile."

We mentioned to Stella that we needed to have the UFO pictures copied, since Mr. Mason did not want us to take his originals for photographic analysis, and we also wanted a map of the area where Mr. Mason lived, as well as reservations for our return flight to Colorado, which we then thought could be that evening. The fact that this was Saturday could have been a handicap to us, for the town's photographic studio didn't open until 9:30, the most detailed map of the area was said to be obtainable from the Highway Department, which wasn't open on Saturdays, and the town's only travel agency was located in the bank building, which also was not open on Saturdays.

Stella reached for her telephone. Within ten minutes the dairyman's wife was on her way to town with the UFO photographs. The studio owner would open for us at 8:30, would make the copies according to our instructions, and have them out as soon as possible. There also would be someone at the Highway Department office especially to get a map for us, which would be picked up by the same woman. The travel agent, phoned at home, would assist us with reservations. Stella knew everyone in the community, and everyone knew Stella. Her requests seemed unanimously to be their commands.

As we left to check other UFO reports by local residents, Stella was preparing for three weddings and a hearing on her day's schedule. She was in the midst of the hearing on marital problems of a young couple when we returned at noon, and was roughly telling the kids how they could straighten out and just what it appeared to her they were up to. The youngsters listened, and agreed to try to do as Stella suggested. This appeared to be the end of the hearing, so we asked Stella, in her capacity as Notary Public, to compose a binding statement for my signature which would assure Mr. Mason that we would use our copies of the UFO pictures for research only and not to reproduce them or use them for commercial purposes.

Stella selected bathing trunks our size, gave them to us, and insisted that, while she prepared our statement, we see for ourselves how delightful the spring water in her pool was to swim in. We chose between swimming and having lunch, and decided on the swim. Before we dived into the refreshing water, Stella, always laughing and joking when not engaged in serious business, checked the fit of our trunks. Stella and her friend found it most humorous.

We tied together some loose ends of the investigation and picked up the copies of the UFO pictures at the neighboring dairy farm before checking out of the motel with a jolly farewell. Jim returned our keys to the motel office and gave Stella a departing hug. He had quite an armful.

"Tell your friend I didn't get any lovin' from him," were Stella's parting words.

We laughed, sighed, and waved as we drove away.

That was Stella—Justice of the Peace, Notary Public, motel operator, counsel, friend and weightiest power in the county. Full of laughter, smut, fun and devilment. A woman who understood humanity, lived every minute of the day, and enjoyed life as few in this world dare.

Stella said she would lose faith in all humanity if this UFO picture turned out to be a hoax. However, preliminary analysis of the photograph indicated just that. One photograph showed the UFO, as well as a near-by clothesline across the top of the photo, in fairly good focus, while more distant bushes and trees were not in focus. There is no way the clothesline could be in focus, intermediate distance bushes and trees out of focus, and a more distant UFO in focus. The picture appeared to be of a small object about the distance of the clothesline from the photographer. Our photographic consultant concluded, from the photos and our distance measurements, that the object photographed was about ten or twelve inches in diameter—the size of a pie tin, which its lower half resembled, or of the lid of a frying pan, with which the upper half had much in common. It would appear that Mr. Mason and his son had stuck together some kitchen

A spoof photo by Jerry McElroy, which he captioned: "The famous 'Flatirons Flying Saucer' photo taken by Ned Perkins in 1962. It was later determined by scientists that it was swamp gas from nearby Lake Chautauqua."

These spoof photographs demonstrate that photographic evidence alone does not serve as proof of the existence of what is shown in the photo. Not only were the Boulder Flatirons not visited by a flying saucer (*above*)—appearing much like an old Studebaker hubcap, but there also is no Lake Chataqua in the vicinity, nor moose or moose hunters. (Photos by Jerry McElroy, ProVisions, Boulder, Colorado.)

*Annual Moose Hunt*
*Lake Chataqua*

materials, painted "windows" on the bottom portion, hung their "UFO" on the clothesline, probably with a monofilament fishing line attached to the bakelite knob on top of the frying pan lid, and photographed their "UFO." We had noticed fishing equipment on their porch. Monofilament line would not be visible in such a photograph.

We never told Stella what project staff determined about her pet UFO pictures. To do so would have been like killing Santa Claus in the mind of a previously excited child on Christmas Eve.

[1] Not the real name of this marvelous lady.

# Chapter 4

# Venus and Her Charms

The investigative phase of the Colorado Project was still young, and a visiting scientist from the West Coast was telling us, at a June 1967 meeting in Woodbury Hall, what he thought we should be doing. Mary Lou Armstrong, an enthusiastic young woman who carried the title of Administrative Assistant with the project, burst in with the news that the staff members who had driven to a Denver suburb in response to a UFO call had phoned back to report there indeed was an unidentified light in the sky. They were keeping the light under surveillance, watching it move toward the west, and trying to get data on its position and speed. They needed simultaneous observations of the object from two different locations to determine how high it was. The person who originally reported the UFO said it had caused his "magnetic UFO detector" to sound the alarm, and when he went outside to look, sure enough, there was the UFO straight overhead. He had pointed out this distant bright object, high in the sky, when the staff team arrived about an hour later.

A check for large balloons known to be in the vicinity at that time brought a negative response from the National Center for Atmospheric Research. Mary Lou phoned the UFO officer at one of the Air Force bases in the region to learn if he had knowledge of an unidentified object then in the sky. She was most indignant when it was suggested to her that they were "probably chasing Venus," and she commented upon the nerve of anyone who would suggest that Ph.D. scientists would be chasing a planet without recognizing it.

One of the team observing the light in the sky was a Ph.D. scientist. Mary Lou's indignation must have mellowed considerably the next day when he arrived at the office with figures which showed the light had moved westward at fifteen degrees per hour, and expressed the suspicion that the observed light must have been an astronomical object, since this is the apparent motion that rotation of the earth would give an astronomical object.

We checked the positions of the brightest planets. The coordinates of Venus matched those of the observed bright light. We went outside to look at the sky where Venus should then be. Once located, the planet appeared with surprising brightness in broad daylight. If one looked away, however, the planet was difficult to locate again, and its presence was not then obvious.

While this experience may have left some staff members slightly embarrassed, it was a valuable lesson to those who were to conduct field investigations of UFO reports later. Although most casual students of astronomy know that Venus can be bright enough to be seen during the day, few have actually made that impressive observation.

Venus proved to be ever present and ever charming—though one might still wonder how she managed to trip the suburbanite's magnetic UFO detector.

An earlier project experience had given an indication of another aspect of Venusian charms. An individual who lived within an hour's drive of the project headquarters phoned to report that a flying object was making frequent evening landings a few miles from his house. Before landing, it appeared as a green light as large as a two-story building, round or oblong in shape. When he observed the light through binoculars, he saw a dome-shaped object with two rows of windows. The object seemed to have jets firing from its undersurface, and it lit up much of the surrounding area. After landing, the object would cut off its lights, making it no longer visible.

Project investigators had driven to this man's home and found him watching Venus descend in the evening sky. He agreed the flying object then looked like a planet or star, and he would believe it to be such if he hadn't seen it closer and larger at other times, including the occasions when he and his wife observed surface features through binoculars.

Months later, when Venus shone brilliantly as a pre-dawn "morning star," she was even more beguiling, and was commonly reported as an unidentified flying object.

One morning in October, 1967, we received a call from the UFO officer at an air base in Georgia reporting repeated sightings of an unidentified flying object which could not be explained away in terms of something as simple as Venus, even though it was seen in the pre-dawn hours on successive mornings. This object, appearing as large as the moon in the sky, had been pursued by law enforcement officers in a dozen or more neighboring towns, and had, in turn, pursued police officers traveling seventy miles per hour on the highway. At one time, it had come within 500 feet of a group of officers in a police car, lighting up the whole vicinity so brightly that the officers could read their wrist watches by its light. It was a large object, usually red, but sometimes changing color to green or white.

As the information developed, it became ever more interesting. A pilot of a small aircraft had participated in one of the early morning chases. As he neared the region where the officers were keeping the object under surveillance, he saw it rise from the swamp or river area. He immediately gave pursuit, but the object easily outdistanced him, flying up and away into the distance. During the chase both the small aircraft and the unidentified object were seen as images on the nearest Federal Aviation Agency traffic control radarscope. In addition, during the afternoon, a boy had photographed a domed saucer-like solid object hovering over an open area in a near-by wooded region.

At last, we had an ideal case to investigate! The presence of a strange flying object, with capabilities exceeding those of earth-made craft, was indicated by the testimony of multiple witnesses, including a trained pilot and numerous police officers, and their testimony was supported by ground radar observation and at least one photograph. Moreover, the object had been reappearing each morning, so there was a chance that on-site investigators might be able to take appropriate photographs from which the object's distance and dimensions could be determined. If the distance to the object were established, the investigators could then compute its actual speed. Hopefully, they might be able to get additional information about the object.

By noon, John Ahrens, a psychology graduate who had recently joined the project staff, and I had checked the field equipment and were packing our bags to get to this site as quickly as possible. Because of poor plane connections to the distant rural community, the "possible" was not very quick. Spending the entire night on short flights to intervening cities and long waits for the next flights, we arrived at the Macon airport at 7 A.M., somewhat tired and hungry. The UFO officer with whom we had been in communication met our plane and immediately took us to breakfast at the officer's club at Warner Robins Air Force Base. A full briefing at the air base was the next order of business. The base commander placed a car at our disposal and offered any assistance we could use in our investigation.

As usual, public interest in the local UFO sightings was intense. Front pages of town newspapers were covered with the reports. A photograph of the main street of one small town, taken at 2 A.M., showed the street filled with cars at that hour, as the curious citizenry joined the UFO chase.

Before driving to Milledgeville, the town where the closest sightings had been reported, we stopped at the FAA air traffic control room to verify the observation of a radar image of the unidentified object. We transcribed the tape-recorded conversation between the radar operator and the airplane pilot, recorded during the pilot's chase of the UFO. The recording was part of routine temporary records of control room operations, and would be destroyed later if there were no special reason or requests for its preservation. Transmission of the voices had not been clear, but the conversation did indicate that an image from the small aircraft and possibly a second image were visible on the radarscope. The second image was reported as seen intermittently during a period of one minute.

The radar operator who had been on duty during the UFO-airplane encounter was not on duty at the moment of our visit, so I contacted him later by telephone to get his full version of the incident. He informed me that he was not even certain he had seen radar returns from the aircraft, let alone from the unidentified object. His scope showed a steady target which he assumed to be the aircraft. At the time, he thought another object might be indicated; after thinking about the incident later, however, he wasn't at all certain about the second object. The second target had "painted" on only two sweeps of the radar, separated by several sweeps in which no such target showed.

It appeared that the supporting radar evidence had evaporated.

The flying object may or may not have caused a blip or two on the radarscope. Even the radar operator was not convinced it had. Without the radar confirmation, however, there was still adequate information, if it could be verified, to establish the presence of a strange object in the vicinity.

We spent the major portion of that afternoon talking with police officers who had chased the UFO. It was described as a bright red, football-shaped, moon-sized light which officers chased for eight miles into the country, lost sight of, and then found to be pursuing them as they returned to town. On other occasions, it changed shape from oblong to round and even to the shape of a cloverleaf. To one highway patrolman, it had appeared rectangular. Others saw it as a sphere about twenty-five feet in diameter. On one occasion, the object had resembled a piece of floating tin foil, looking flat, with a bend in it. It bobbed and floated about its otherwise relatively constant position.

Color descriptions varied. Sometimes the object was seen to change color from red to green to white. Others observed a red or blue object with red, green and white flashing lights.

As our pointed questions were answered, certain uniformities developed. The object was always seen near the eastern horizon. When it had been said to come to within 500 feet over the police car, it was not meant that it was directly overhead: it was, rather, about 500 feet behind the police car, toward the east, and guessed to be 500 or 600 feet above the ground. When the object was accompanied by a second, smaller object, the two maintained a constant separation. The object not only appeared about the same time each morning, but, at the end of each chase, took a position in the sky where it remained, looking like a star and still visible after the sun came up.

The more we heard, the more it appeared that our old friend

Venus was performing her dance for a new audience, with less-brilliant Jupiter playing a supporting role.

We arranged for police officers to pick us up at our motel at 3 A.M. the next morning, so we could observe the object or objects with them. By midnight, however, a continuing steady downpour of rain had set in, and there was to be no observation of unidentified flying objects in such a sky. While we were disappointed to miss the observation, at the same time we were thankful the rain gave us a chance to sleep. Having not had such a chance the previous night or during the past couple of days, the sleep was indeed welcome.

The pilot's description of what he and his companion had seen, which we listened to the following day, also strongly indicated that they had been chasing Venus. They had not actually seen the object rise from below them in the river area. In fact, as they were searching for the UFO, after taking to the air following the alert that law enforcement officers had again spotted it, they were at first unable to locate the object. They were told by the airport manager, who had radio communication with the pilot and walkie-talkie communication with the officers on land, and thus could relay messages from ground observers to the pilot, that they had flown past the object. They turned back, and looked in the direction the lights of the police car had been pointed to show the direction of the object. They were then told the object was above them. Looking up, they did see the white light, which appeared half to two-thirds the size of the moon. They flew directly toward the light, but it receded from them. By the time the plane had reached an altitude of about 3500 feet, the object was so far away that it appeared as only a fraction of its original size. However, when they turned back toward the airport, the object moved back toward its original position. It was about in its original position when the plane landed.

To officers on the ground, observing the plane chasing the

object, the object continued bobbing and moving upward. It did not appear to get dimmer or smaller, and they couldn't tell it was moving away from the airplane.

Both the ground and air observations were just how one would expect a very distant bright light, such as the planet Venus, to appear if observed through a typical early morning haze over the river region.

The only "evidence" that did not seem to be observations of Venus was the pair of photographs of a solid, sombrero-shaped object, taken in the woods during the late afternoon. We contacted the thirteen-year-old photographer, who willingly took us to the spot where he had taken the pictures. There he reenacted his experience for us.

He was a bright youngster, and he was consistent in his story. His strong interest in UFOs was evident from pictures on the walls of his room. He was president of a UFO club consisting of himself and four or five friends. Yet, when a thirteen-year-old boy, taking his B-B gun and Polaroid camera, heads into the woods alone specifically to hunt UFOs, and indeed succeeds in finding and photographing one, such improbable success taxes credulity. Such success may be more probable when UFOs are known to be in the region, as observed by many other reliable people. However, when the other observations are actually of the planets Venus and Jupiter, the chances of seeing a solid UFO in the woods did not seem logically enhanced thereby.

We arranged to obtain the original photographs for later analysis, although we could see no objective relation between the boy's pictures and the early morning observations.

The position in the sky, which the morning UFO had taken after each chase, corresponded nicely with the listed coordinates of Venus at that time, and Jupiter was properly located to be the dimmer companion. We pointed out Venus in the forenoon sky to the police officers. They agreed that was what their UFO looked

45

Polaroid photograph of UFO taken by a 13-year-old boy near Milledgeville, Georgia. Craig's notes on the back of the photograph read: "18 yds to high weed at 178° bearing; 290 yds to three trees in clearing, 178° bearing; 240 yds to dead tree, 192° bearing; 90 yds to berry bushes (under UFO), 157° bearing."

like when they gave up the morning chases. By this time, it was so obvious that planets had been responsible for the morning excitement that we saw no cause to pursue the case further.

Returning to the air base, we met with the base commander, General Gideon, at his request, to inform him of our observations and conclusions. At the same time, I denied a request from news media for radio and TV interviews. In most circumstances, I granted such interviews, for our study was open, paid for by public funds, and carried considerable public interest. If interview requests were made at the time of my arrival on the scene, I could speak in general terms about our project and state truthfully that, as yet, I knew no more about the case of immediate interest than the news media had already reported. At the end of this particular investigation, however, any comments I could make about our findings would only embarrass individuals who had failed to recognize a familiar planet seen under unusually impressive conditions. Reporters could easily make those individuals appear foolish. I felt that unusual foolishness or stupidity was not indicated at all, however, for I was well aware that ignorance of physical and psychological factors affecting observations of distant bright lights near the earth's horizon is the common condition on the American scene. If anyone should be embarrassed over this incident, it perhaps should be the American educators.

What accounts for the apparent ability of a bright planet to dance about, change colors, change size and shape, and chase automobiles traveling at high speeds?

The apparent pursuit of moving vehicles, or flight from them, is characteristic of any distant object which is imagined to be close to the observer. Because of the object's great distance, it remains in essentially the same direction from the observer as the observer moves. Compared with trees or terrain nearby which change in direction as the observer moves past them, the object, retaining a constant direction, does seem to be moving the same speed and direction as any observer who thinks it no more distant than the reference terrain. This holds true for the moon and stars, as well as planets, and is particularly noticeable when the object is fairly close to the horizon, where the reference objects, such as trees, buildings, or hilltops, are located.

It is characteristic of this "pursuit" that the object stops when the observer stops, resumes its motion as the observer resumes motion, goes the opposite direction when the observer reverses direction, and travels at whatever speed the observer happens to travel. This often gives an observer the impression that the

This full-disc image of Venus was taken on March 3, 1979 at 66,000 kilometers (40,920 miles) from Venus by the Pioneer Venus Orbiter. The Pioneer Venus Multiprobe and Orbiter spacecrafts are managed by NASA's Ames Research Center in Mountain View, California. NASA Photograph object is indeed pursuing his particular automobile. One man reported that such a UFO stopped in the sky while he had breakfast at a cafe, but again "locked on" his car after breakfast and resumed chasing it. His UFO may have been Venus, but could have been any bright planet or star.

The brilliance of Venus is also unbelievable to some observers. When this planet is relatively near the earth and shines with a brightness as great as minus 4.2 magnitude on the astronomer's scale, it is 126 times as bright as the average of the couple dozen brightest stars in the sky (first magnitude stars). Venus had a magnitude of minus 4.2 during the time of the above described early morning chases by police officers.

How does one account for apparent size exaggeration?

Most people have noticed that the moon looks bigger when it is close to the horizon than when it is high in the sky. This is a purely psychological effect. M. Minnaert, in his classic treatise "The Nature of Light and Colour in the Open Air" claimed that, to the average observer, the moon near the horizon appears two and a half times as large in diameter as it does when high in the sky. The same psychological factors would cause Venus to appear bigger near the horizon, and accounts for some exaggerated size estimates.

Viewing a light through haze or mist also causes apparent increase in size of the light source. In the airplane incident mentioned above, Venus would appear to get smaller as the plane gained altitude both because the plane rose above the morning mist hanging over the region and because Venus would appear farther from the horizon as the plane gained altitude. Such apparent reduction in size is logically interpreted as recession of the object.

Venus's apparent "bobbing about" and changing colors and shapes is both psychological and physical. Experimental psychologists have established the fact that, to almost any human being, a stationary light will appear to move when it is observed intently, particularly if the light is not near other lights or visible objects. The motion, known as autokinesis, occurs only in the mind of the observer.

When the distant light is near the horizon, however, its apparent dancing about and changing colors is generally caused by particular atmospheric conditions, such that the light beam travels through pockets of turbulent air of varying density, causing variable refraction of the beam. Such conditions are fairly common. The observation is merely an extreme example of "twinkling" of starlight. The variable refraction causes color separation and "scintillation" of the light, which is observed rapidly fluctuating in brightness, sometimes even flashing as if the light source were throwing off sparks. The light appears to change both color and position rapidly, oscillating about a central point. A flashing red, white, and green appearance is frequently noted, as variable refraction in the atmosphere brings different colors to the eye of the observer at different times. Distortions in shape of a bright object that is larger than a point source also result when such atmospheric conditions prevail.

Scintillation is more likely when the distant light is near the horizon, where it passes through more of the earth's atmosphere in reaching the observer. However, I have observed an impressive display of scintillation of starlight when the star was about forty degrees above the horizon, but also directly over the stack of a power plant about three miles away. Passage of the starlight through small regions of rising hot gases from the stack apparently caused the scintillation. Another observer in this same situation described the star as a dancing light which was sending off red and green sparks.

Living organisms from Venus may never visit the surface of the earth. However, it is reasonably certain that earthlings who are not familiar with the varying appearances of planets, the psychological factors influencing those appearances, and the physical factors affecting light from beyond the earth's atmosphere, will forever be enthralled and charmed as Venus and her companions sparkle and dance—and play tag with those who will play.

# Chapter 5

# They Called It "Peyton Place"[1]

It was late at night. John Ahrens and I were sitting in a car on Jefferson Hill, just outside a small village which I will call Halburg, New York, to watch for unidentified flying objects. Such objects had reportedly been seen from here almost every clear night for the past several weeks. Bill Davenport, who was visiting Halburg as a self-appointed UFO investigator and had insisted that the Colorado Project send someone to check out the "fantastic" Halburg UFO sightings, was sitting in another car behind us. He was accompanied by Benny Brauer, a local UFO enthusiast who had become his companion.

Dozens of people around Halburg had reported seeing strange lights in the sky, and two boys claimed to have seen a saucer-like craft hovering over a tavern on Main Street. According to that claim, the younger boy, aged ten, was outside his Main Street home about 9:30 or 10:30 P.M. when he called excitedly to his visiting twelve-year-old friend, who was in the house, that he saw something like a flying saucer. The friend joined the younger boy on the open porch, and together they watched a strange spacecraft sweep down and stop, hovering a few feet above the tavern and adjacent house across the street, about 150 feet away. The craft then tilted toward the boys, and they saw two strange beings inside. Both beings were standing, facing the boys, just behind the divided window of the spacecraft, each half of which seemed to the boys as wide as a car windshield. The strange creatures were dark brown, human like, but their arms and shoulders were bumpy, like a stack of rocks, and they had large hips "wider than people on our planet." The boys could see lights and control panels behind the "funny creatures," which looked like they were frozen at the windows. The spacecraft itself looked metallic, perhaps stainless steel. It was shaped like a squat, inverted toy top, with a pointed antenna at its top. Around its center, beneath the windows, was a row of odd markings or symbols. Around the rim beneath these markings was a row of square lights, alternately red and white, which blinked constantly until a bright light came on inside the craft. The bright light cast shadows of the two funny creatures across the inside of the craft and revealed the presence, behind the creature occupants, of a box with many green, red and white little square lights, as well as colored buttons. The box-like bottom of the craft also bore red, white and green flashing lights, but these were large, like landing lights of some sort.

The boys watched the object for one-half to two minutes before it leveled off and started to move upward. It then disappeared suddenly, like a light bulb switched off. It made no sound whatsoever. A blast of air or wind struck the boys as the object vanished.

The same boys reported seeing another UFO the following night. This one did not get close enough for them to see occu-

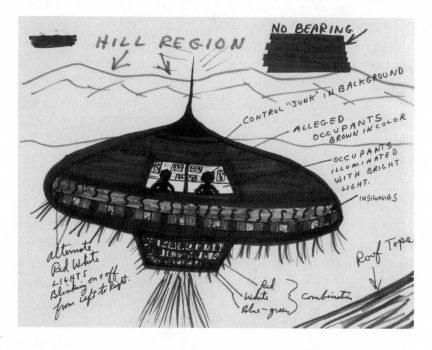

Drawing of UFO as reportedly seen by two boys across the street in a small town in New York state.

pants, but it caused a screaming, wailing noise on their walkie-talkies as it wobbled and circled over their house before disappearing. They later saw other, more distant, objects which they assumed to be like the object they saw near Main Street. At one time, two such objects, one red, the other white, met and touched each other, riding like the two halves of a hamburger bun before separating and disappearing separately. The boys also had watched a UFO follow a jet airplane.

Benny Brauer, a young Halburg man in his early twenties, also reported numerous sightings of strange UFOs. The most spectacular was a daylight sighting in which he and his girl-friend saw an enormous solid silver object in the sky. Benny estimated the object to be half a mile long. It looked like two aircraft carriers silhouetted against a bright blue sky, and, after being visible for about half a minute, it simply disappeared as a jet aircraft came overhead. Benny told a news reporter of this and other UFO experiences in the following manner:

> And Wednesday night we brought a friend of mine up here who never believed it. We sat out here in back and we watched the most fantastic spectacle I have ever seen in my life. We saw some come in low, with red, white, and green flashes. We saw some that just missed the tree tops which were red—bright red— over the top of us, going due North. Every one of those things had a pattern to it—monstrous, glowing globes which had a steady course—like they really knew where they were going. We looked up to the right— way up high was this great big globe, and dropping off from it was a white flasher—like a plane from an aircraft carrier. Then it disappeared, and a jet fighter came through. And a—gad, what can I tell ya? Uhh— one hung over the trees—a glowing globe. And it woke this boy up. A dog was barkn'. He went to the window. And he told me that he thought he was dreamin'. I've got a photograph of the most unbelievable footprint you've ever seen. It's half as big as mine—I take a size ten and a half—ahh, this is half as big as mine, and its got spiked toes—way out—a little, narrow, high instep, and a little teeny heel on it. And it was walking along with a horse's track—off the main highway up here. And this went on last night, too. Ahh . . . what was I going to tell ya? Oh! I went out in the back yard Wednesday night, and over comes this thing with all the flashes on it—no, that was Thursday night—I called the state police, and this trooper came out. He got here about 9:15. He got out of his car and he looked at us

55

with this incredulous look, you know, like we're all insane. I said, "Ya, I know what you're going to say. But will you just stand here a few minutes, will you, please?" He came out and stood there for approximately five minutes, and one came over—a big, glowing one—the kind that go North, you know. I said, "What do you think that is?" He didn't say. His mouth just dropped. At the same time, my girlfriend's sister was screaming around the house, and we all went around the house, including the trooper, and, coming in low, over Route 13, was this brilliant, bright red, glowing object with unbelievably red lights on it. And it just missed the top of the hill and disappeared. At the same time, to our left, came this white flasher, with this tremendous flashing sequence with red, green, and white all over. And that cop, he couldn't say a thing. I said, "You know, I think they are landing on Cooper Hill." That is a desolate, wooded area. You know, there are about a hundred square miles of nothing. He told me, and I quote, he said, "I'm not going up there." O.K. He got in his car and he drove away.

Melody Norton, younger sister of Benny's girlfriend, had given me a list of names, addresses, and telephone numbers of people who had called her home to report UFO sightings. These calls had come to the Nortons, she said, because Bill Davenport had been staying with them and had published their telephone number as the place to report UFO sightings. Bill himself was no longer welcome at the Norton's, he said, because Melody's parents objected to his relationship with Melody. He had been correlating and documenting the various sightings and, he said, had developed a complete dossier on the Halburg "flap." He had already introduced us to Benny Brauer, and had taken us to interview the ten and twelve-year-old boys and Mrs. Barkley, who lived near Cooper Hill and also had reported a UFO encounter. We would investigate Mrs. Barkley's story later.

By 11 P.M., John and I decided it would be useless to remain longer on Jefferson Hill. During the couple of hours we were there, the entire area had clouded over and it was snowing almost constantly. Visibility was poor, and Bill said we would see no UFOs in such weather. I suggested to Bill that he loan us his file on pertinent UFO information, that we might study it at our motel and determine which additional reports seemed worthy of checking. Davenport's current host, Elmo Small, an apparently alcoholic man in his 50s, had appeared on the scene— thoughtfully with hot hamburgers for us. Bill could go back to town with his host, get the dossier and bring it to a tavern near our motel. We could review some of the cases as we warmed up, after the chilling watch, with some hot buttered rum.

Elmo and his wife both appeared with Bill at the tavern. After a bit of social conversation over the cups of hot rum, John and I took our leave, telling Bill we would contact him again before we left the area and return his file of information to him. We thanked him for his cooperation.

Davenport's presence during interviews had proved to be a distinct detriment to our learning the facts involved in the UFO reports. As the two young boys told us of their experience, Davenport interrupted frequently, prompting the boys if details of their story were not as he said he remembered their telling it before. The same thing happened when we interviewed Mrs. Barkley, who said she saw a bright object which left a landing nest in the cattails behind her house. Although it was obvious that Mr. Davenport expected to guide our entire investigation, it was obviously necessary for us to work in his absence. Bill was appalled that we were not including him in our plans for further investigation.

Upon reaching the motel, John and I compared notes on the two principle witnesses in the Halburg flap—Bill Davenport and Benny Brauer. Information Davenport and Brauer had given us about themselves and each other seemed significant in evaluating the UFO reports. Our notes read:

Benny Brauer: About 23 years old. Highly emotional about UFO sightings. Convinced and noisy. In process of divorce, with three children in another state. Has been living with the Norton family, where he has fathered one illegitimate child by Melody's older sister, who is now carrying another child by him. Is now unwelcome at the Norton home, since Davenport said to the family that Brauer didn't love the girl and wouldn't be likely to marry her. Now staying at YMCA. Discharged from Navy, according to his story, because of hardship case since his wife was sleeping with other men in front of children. According to Davenport, Brauer had tried suicide and then been discharged from Navy. Quite unstable. Has been promoting UFOs as prime interest and trying to sell story to *Look* magazine. No job, at times worked at selling encyclopedias.

Has had close association with the neighborhood kids, who have been all worked up about UFOs. A great majority of the Halburg sighting reports appear to have originated from a closely knit group of youngsters whom Brauer influences. Melody Norton's closest girlfriend, Nancy, is an older sister of the younger of the two boys who reported a close sighting of a saucer.

The older boy, aged 12, spends much time at the younger boy's house. His grandmother is a close friend of Mrs. Barkley, who had the saucer nest in her cattails. All the youngsters in the group observe "strange light"

UFOs as a regular activity, apparently with the stimulation and encouragement of Brauer.

Bill Davenport: About 26. Broke, and living off the land. Selling memberships locally, at $5 each, in his "UFO research corporation." Apparently using such dues to make own ends meet. Had been staying at the Norton home, along with Brauer, and obviously was involved with Melody, a high school student. He also is no longer welcome at the Norton home.

The notes made no mention of Davenport's remark, when referring to the little village of Halburg. "That is a living Peyton Place. Wait 'til you see it!" We had seen a bit of it, and thought perhaps it deserved the appellation. The notes also did not include my personal thoughts regarding Mr. Davenport. Because of the nature of his earlier phone calls to us about other UFO cases, before he came to Halburg, I had reached the point of refusing to receive further calls from him. I had lost any confidence in either his judgment or honesty. Other staff members had listened to his insistent pleas that we check out the Halburg UFO sightings, which he considered the most significant close range sightings ever reported. Since most of our information regarding the Halburg sightings came to us through Mr. Davenport, I had been reluctant to agree to this field investigation. Only the recommendation of Dr. J. Allen Hynek, Air Force Consultant on UFOs, who thought the Halburg reports worthy of our investigation, made me withdraw my objections to this field trip.

On his private initiative, Dr. Hynek had attended a four-hour Halburg community discussion of their UFO sightings at a meeting sponsored by Davenport. Dr. Hynek had said he found no reason to discredit the story of the two boys who had a close sighting of a saucer-like vehicle and that other reports, while not too impressive, were numerous enough to warrant our investigation.

Suspecting that Davenport would want to make a triumphant issue of our arrival on the scene of the UFO sightings which he had been "investigating" for several weeks, we chose to avoid the nearest large airport, where he probably expected us to arrive. We flew to LaGuardia, took the helicopter over Manhattan to Newark, where we caught a Mohawk plane directly to the town seven miles from Halburg. We then proceeded to investigate the local UFO situation. When we contacted Mr. Davenport, he told us he had called a press conference at the airport where he expected our arrival, and had to cancel it when we failed to show there. Although I held an expressionless poker face, I could not avoid grinning internally. If the press were interested in our presence, they were welcome to contact us. Our purpose was to learn what the local UFO sightings were all about—not to enhance the prestige of Mr. Davenport or his "UFO research corporation."

Before turning in for the night, John and I looked over the material in Mr. Davenport's folder on local sightings. We discovered, much to our amusement, that a detailed history of local reports, which Davenport had told our staff he was laboriously developing, was copied directly from a single newspaper article. He hadn't even bothered to paraphrase the news reporter's story.

According to newspaper accounts, neighboring counties had been the sites of UFO reports several years previously. In April of 1964, a dairy farmer encountered an egg-shaped metallic object at 10 A.M. There were two occupants, four feet high, who spoke English. They were from Mars. In July of the same year, five children saw a spaceman and his craft two miles from their home. A minister and his wife saw a noiseless saucer-like UFO which flew at helicopter speed and had white lights flashing where its wings would be if it were a plane. Huge crowds had gathered to watch for the UFO the minister and his wife had seen.

The sightings of the current Halburg flap, except for the reports of the two boys and Mrs. Barkley, were nearly all night observations of strange lights in the sky, generally larger than airplane lights and unaccompanied by sound.

Observers included a male high school teacher who saw six UFOs in one evening, a Halburg housewife who saw as many as six bright UFOs in a half hour period, and a few other adults, as well as Benny Brauer and his young cohorts. There also was a report of discovery of a circular area in the neighboring forest in which all trees had fallen or been broken off, as if, the discoverers assumed, a powerful circular vehicle had landed or hovered there.

As I retired for the night, pondering which additional reports we should seek to check out, I wondered what reality lay behind these UFO observations. Were the lights merely airplanes too distant for their motors to be heard, like the one we observed in the early evening while driving on Cooper Hill, across the valley from Jefferson Hill, when Mr. Davenport said "There, that might be one now!" John had watched the moving white light. After discerning appropriately located green and red lights accompanying the white one, John pronounced this vehicle an ordinary airplane, which we were satisfied it was.

The boys' story had been particularly interesting. It was puzzling, however, how a strange vehicle could hover a few feet from the village's only tavern at 9:30 P.M., with three dogs howling weirdly because of the object's presence, and not be observed by anyone other than the two boys. As a news reporter had pointed out, the boys described a vehicle and occupants essentially identical with the one in the opening sequence of the TV show "The Invaders." The described craft apparently left no evidence of its physical presence, so there was nothing to evaluate but the testimony of two young boys. About all we could do to help that evaluation was give the older boy a written test from which his psychological tendencies could be judged. John was prepared to give such a test. We would ask the boy's mother for permission to do so the next day, since the boy was quite willing.

Mrs. Barkley's cattails should also be checked. The "saucer nest" there was now more than a month old, but was said to be visible yet.

Mrs. Barkley, fifty-five, social worker, divorcee, lived in a rural home with sons Lance, twenty-one, and Henry, sixteen. She told us that she had been home alone on a Friday night, after she and Lance had heard a sound like something running through the yard. While Lance and his friend were scanning the backyard with a powerful battery lantern, she heard a bumping noise on the back porch. Lance and his friend found nothing unusual, and went out for the evening. It was about 8:30. She turned the TV set on, and got an unusually jumbled pattern which she couldn't adjust into a picture. She turned the set low and sat down. Then she heard a vicious deep-throated growl from the Labrador retriever, Blaze, tied in the back yard. Her Dalmatian, in the house, stood up, the hair straight on end along his back. His tail was tucked between his legs, he walked stiff-legged, and, like Blaze, began the terrible growling. She had never seen him act like this before.

She went to the kitchen, trying to calm the Dalmatian, and looked out the window at Blaze, who was facing the swamp, growling and carrying on. He seemed very disturbed. She turned out the house light so she could see outside better. Then, she saw a bright light over the swamp, which she first thought was a hand light held by a coon hunter. Suddenly, she realized the light was not a flash light, but was something different. It was very bright. She watched for ten or fifteen minutes, gradually

62

realizing she was observing something very unusual. The light was hovering, off the ground, over the swamp, about fifty yards behind her house. The light varied in brightness, but never disappeared. It was like a halo, uniform throughout, and huge—at least five or six times as wide as a full moon.

Mrs. Barkley decided to investigate the strange light. She turned the house light back on and got the battery lantern her son had used earlier. Stepping onto the open back porch, she pointed the lantern in the direction of the strange light and flipped the switch on. As the beam reached out into the swamp, the strange light vanished—suddenly and completely. After trying to calm Blaze, who remained restless, she went back into the house. She thought, "Well, maybe that was Swamp Gas." Yet, she had an eerie feeling.

When her boys came home later that night, she told them about the strange light. She took a good bit of kidding from the boys, and said, "No, I didn't see any green men!"

She awoke early Saturday morning, still puzzled and curious. Before the boys got out of bed, she bundled herself up and went down to the back swamp. There, exactly where she had observed the light, the cattails had been squashed to the ground in a circular area the size of her living and dining rooms combined. The downed cattails were swirled around in a clockwise pattern. The surrounding cattails stood erect and normal. Winter had not set in.

Mrs. Barkley didn't check for footprints or vehicle landing leg imprints. "I just stood there. I felt awed, with a strange feeling which lasted a day or two afterward. Something had been there. I wasn't seeing things!"

Mrs. Barkley had impressed us as a sincere and intelligent person. She thought she had observed a spacecraft of some kind, though she didn't imagine it necessarily to be from another world. She thought more in terms of China as its origin.

I thought it strange that, after making such a remarkable discovery in the swamp, Mrs. Barkley hadn't bothered to tell even her sons about it until three weeks later, after the two young boys reported seeing their spacecraft. When I asked her son Henry, who was present when we interviewed Mrs. Barkley, if he had seen the "landing nest" in the cattails, he told me he had never gone down to look at it. Hmmmmm. Well, the nest was reportedly still apparent, and, while it was too dark to look at it while we were at the Barkley's, Mrs. Barkley had told us exactly where it was and had given us permission to observe and photograph it whenever we wished during the day, though she would be at work and the boys in school. Maybe tomorrow we could drive by her place again and take a look at her cattails.

We'd better check the road conditions before we go anyplace tomorrow, I thought to myself as I lay in bed, pondering the situation. We had nearly got stuck on those slick back roads around Cooper Hill, as our rented car was without snow tires.

John and I would have to talk with a lot of people tomorrow—people who had not seen UFOs, as well as the apparently reliable of those who had. Particularly, though, we'd like to observe the UFOs on Jefferson Hill ourselves, and get photographs and spectrograms of the lights if they were indeed strange.

These thoughts passed through my mind as I tried to formulate plans for the next day. It was mighty late. The next thing I knew I was holding a telephone to my ear and speaking a disgruntled "Thank you" to the clerk whose cheerful "Good morning, it's 6:45" hadn't really made me feel like thanking her at all.

We learned a lot that day about what occurred routinely in the skies around Halburg. An intelligence officer at the nearest air base thought the reported UFOs observed as lights in the sky were ordinary aircraft. There were no Air Force planes operating in the vicinity because it was a high density region for commercial planes, flying at both high and low altitude. The operator of a local charter air service informed us that his four planes, like quite a number of other private planes in the region and some commercial planes, were equipped with a relatively new anti-collision stroboscopic light. The lights, which were mounted on top of the tail fin so they could be seen from nearly all directions, flashed for seven microseconds fifty to sixty times per minute. They had a rated equivalent of two million candle power during the period of their flash. The anti-collision lights could be used at any or all times during a flight, at the discretion of the pilot. The charter planes flew frequently at night, as did other planes equipped with the new light. The operator was certain these lights were the reported UFOs.

The local state police were intrigued by the UFO reports, which had received much newspaper publicity. The trooper who had responded to the call from Benny Brauer told of his drive to Jefferson Hill. There, he found Brauer and several youngsters running about with blankets over their heads, peering from under the blankets to look for UFOs. The trooper observed with them for a time, watching their excitement as they saw "another one." He was pretty certain they were looking at a Mohawk turbo prop.

The assistant manager of the neighboring town's Chamber of Commerce also told us he had spent an evening on Jefferson Hill with Davenport, Brauer, and the kids. While he was there, the others saw three "UFOs," two of which he could identify as airplanes. The plane motors could not be heard at first, and Brauer argued that they were noiseless and, therefore, not airplanes. The sound of the motors was audible before the lights disappeared, however. The third "UFO" he thought was probably a satellite. It was a pinpoint of white light which moved steadily across the sky without changing direction. There was no noise associated with it.

The high school shop teacher seemed to be a calm, rational,

and pleasant man. He described observations of lights in the sky, six in the course of one evening, which maneuvered in a manner which seemed very strange to him. He did not think they could be airplane lights.

When we arrived on Jefferson Hill for the second night watch, the Davenport-Brauer group was there waiting for us. They had "seen one" about 6:30, but now the weather was closing in and it was not likely we would see anything further this night. We sat through a few snow flurries before Davenport came back to our car to tell us we should accompany them to a spot a few miles away where, he had heard, the weather was clear. We stayed on Jefferson Hill a couple of hours, waiting for a break in the weather which never came. We saw only airplanes.

John and I were scheduling our day's activities after breakfast the next morning when a newspaper reporter requested an interview. She was doing a Sunday supplement on UFOs for her city newspaper and wanted to accompany us on our investigation that day. She had a photographer with her.

John planned to administer a psychological test to the twelve-year-old at his school, which he would have to do in private. Otherwise, I could see no reason why the reporter's presence should interfere with our investigation.

As we considered the reporter's request, we got a bit of somewhat startling news. The reporter phoned her office and, during the conversation, learned that we had scheduled a press conference for 2 P.M. at our hotel, with both newspaper and TV reporters to be present.

We decided Bill Davenport must have called this conference for us. We'd have to find out what was being done in our names without our knowledge. I suggested that the reporter and photographer have a cup of coffee in the hotel lunch room while we straightened out our schedule. Then, I phoned the hotel manager to learn what this press conference was all about. The manager only wanted to be helpful. When Mr. Davenport called him for permission to hold the press conference in our room, the manager had suggested we use the Blue Room, and arrangements were all made. Special lighting had been provided for the several TV cameramen who indicated they were coming. Mr. Davenport had said he was calling for me, and the manager assumed the press conference had my sanction.

I thanked the hotel manager for his information, told the reporter she and her photographer could come along as observers if they wished, and joined John for the short drive to Halburg. I hoped the representatives of the press would find their conference with Mr. Davenport and Benny Brauer that afternoon to be worthwhile.

It was snowing lightly, again, as we tramped around the partially-frozen swamp behind the Barkley home, carefully watching for the quicksand that Mrs. Barkley had said abounded there. We searched carefully for any remaining evidence of a landing nest in the cattails. Our feet got wet and cold. We scared up numerous rabbits, and flushed one cock pheasant from his shelter. Stretching our imaginations to the limit, however, we were not able to reconstruct any evidence of the existence of a thirty-foot area of squashed cattails lying in a clockwise swirling pattern.

Lunch consisted of a quickly-grabbed sandwich at the Halburg Inn over which the boys' UFO had appeared. We photographed the buildings and surrounding area from the boys' observation point across the street. While John gave the twelve-year-old his test, I took the news people with me to interview Mrs. Baxter, a Halburg housewife who appeared to have no connection with the Benny Brauer group, but had reported seeing numerous UFOs.

Mrs. Baxter was delightfully refreshing. She had spent many hours watching strange lights through binoculars. She saw as many as six in a half-hour. Sometimes, it was a white light which flashed with heart-beat regularity. Sometimes binoculars revealed a red light beneath a steady white one. One, which came from behind a grove of trees and she thought was very low, but her husband thought was quite high, flew straight like a plane, then made a tight U-turn and retraced its path toward Cooper Hill. She also saw airplanes, which had white, red and green lights and made audible noise.

Mrs. Baxter wouldn't allow pictures with her in them, as her husband opposed anyone knowing that she claimed such sightings. He observed these strange lights with her but thought they were airplanes. She just knew they couldn't be airplanes, not only because they were silent, but because there couldn't be that many airplanes in the sky around Halburg. "Why would there be so many airplanes around a little insignificant place like this?" Mrs. Baxter was quite willing to believe that there were that many flying saucers from other planets around Halburg.

When we returned to our motor hotel, some of the TV and news people were still hanging around, waiting for an interview. Telephone messages from producers of other TV news broadcasts requested more appointments for interviews that evening. One producer was furious. He had sent a photographer to the press conference to get pictures of the scientists from the Colorado Project, and the photographer had come back with pictures of Davenport and Brauer. Damn! Since we had no feud with the press, I agreed to help him salvage something from the situation by making a few comments about the local UFO situation over the telephone, which he could tape record for his news broadcast. He could dub in some standard UFO pictures while he played the comments.

A savory dinner of ravioli at an Italian restaurant where we had agreed to return Davenport's file of information to him helped me keep my cool while Bill talked. He was apologetic about the press conference and acted as if we should consider him a serious and competent UFO investigator. While I resented his victimizing local people, we had gotten a number of good laughs from his antics. It appeared the victimizing was about to end, for his "research corporation" had no money to continue operations. Elmo was now furnishing Bill's shelter, and apparently buying most of whatever meals Bill had. Bill told us he would be leaving in a few days for Canada, both to escape the draft and to investigate Canadian UFO reports, particularly the case in which a man got burned by a UFO near Winnipeg. He said he sold his car to pay his corporation's phone bills, and he and Benny Brauer would go to Winnipeg in Benny's car.

Winnipeg was a couple thousand miles away. I was personally quite familiar with the case he referred to (see Chapter 2). I sat back and listened to his meaningless chatter. I was tempted to give Bill some fatherly advice when he asked me how he should have gone about the Halburg investigation differently. I decided, however, that it wasn't worth the effort.

As we attempted to say "farewell" to Bill Davenport and his side-kick Benny, we learned he had arranged for Elmo to meet him and Benny at our hotel, where they would watch themselves on the 11:00 P.M. TV news on our hotel TV set. Elmo was already waiting for us there. Thinking the message might get through to Mr. Davenport, I said we would return a photograph we had left out of his folder to him through Elmo, and would say "good-by" to him there. Then, we returned to our motor hotel.

We got the photograph and found Elmo to give it to him. In walked Davenport and Brauer suggesting we all go to Jefferson Hill to watch for UFOs, since the weather had suddenly and finally cleared. The suggestion appealed to John, since we expected this to be our last night in the region and it would be, barring new developments, our last chance to see for ourselves what was being reported here as UFOs. I had several appointments with newsmen, however, and since our phone number had been published to enable local people to call us about UFO sightings, I felt at least one of us should stay near the telephone. John left for Jefferson Hill with Davenport, Brauer, and Elmo.

Calls did come in to report a very bright UFO which was still hanging in the sky. The location was that of the bright star Sirius. After my suggestion that it might be Sirius, one of the callers—the high school shop teacher whom we had interviewed earlier—phoned back to agree that he had been looking at Sirius and apologized for the error.

John and the accompanying trio returned to the hotel to find me and two TV reporters outside the hotel, checking the sky for one of the telephone-reported UFOs which turned out to be Sirius. The Dog Star was causing quite a furor. As we all went inside, another phone message indicated a sighting was in progress. Mr. Davenport phoned the woman who had reported this sighting and, after a short conversation, excitedly handed the phone to me. "Here you are, Dr. Craig. This woman is seeing an object hovering near her house. It's spewing out glowing red globs and emitting beams of green, white and red light . . ." I took the phone and listened to the excited woman. Her daughter, audible in the background, also was chattering about the UFO. I tried to calm both individuals, and listened to their description of the object's location. The location again was that of Sirius. I asked the woman if it could possibly be the bright star she was observing, and told her where the star should appear relative to the constellation Orion. She did not accept this as a possibility, but relayed information to her daughter for checking. Then she embarked upon a discussion of other UFO activity she had observed in the past. After this review, I again asked her about the hovering object she originally reported. "Yes, I guess we've been bamboozled again. I guess that is just a star."

70

After our visitors had finally left, John told me what they had seen on Jefferson Hill. When Sirius rose over the distant trees, his companions immediately called it one of the UFOs. They watched it change color, particularly when it was low in the sky, and only some time later agreed with John that this "UFO" was a star.

John also mentioned the nature of the conversation of the group as they drove toward Jefferson Hill. After initial chatter about saucers, persons, and sex, John had to parry a proposition that, instead of going to Jefferson Hill, they all go to a designated place and engage in homosexual activity. The proposer thought that would be a more pleasurable way to spend the evening than looking for UFOs on Jefferson Hill. As John laughingly told me of the situation he had found himself in, we both agreed that Bill Davenport may have been nearly correct when he called Halburg a living Peyton Place.

---

[1] In some true stories, the author changes the names of those involved to protect the innocent. In this case, I have changed all names to protect everyone—without regard to innocence.

# Chapter 6

# Don't Let Anyone Know Who I Am

Mr. X

The statement had been typed, as read over the telephone by a college student in California, and was ready for the project director's signature. It was couched in legal terms, and said that we would not, under any circumstances, reveal the identity of the UFO witness whose experience I was packing my bags to investigate. The college student was one of three young members of a NICAP affiliate group who had discovered the incident. The witness was an apparently successful business executive who was proud of his achievements and had told the students he would talk with Colorado Project representatives about his UFO experience only if strict conditions of anonymity, guaranteed by signed agreement, protected him from adverse affect on his business or family. The statement, as composed, we assumed, by the member of the trio who was a budding law school graduate, did not itself reveal the identity of the man with whom we were making the agreement. We assumed, therefore, that the agreement had no legal status, since the party of the second part was unknown. However, it satisfied those who wanted it and gave us access to a current UFO report of a type we wished to learn more about, one in which an automobile had reportedly been stopped by a UFO. We were quite willing to keep the man's identity secret whether or not we were legally committed to do so. The signed statement went into my briefcase for delivery to Mr. X.

I didn't know who Mr. X was or where he lived, but the students would meet me at the Los Angeles airport that evening and drive me to X's home the next day. It would be about a two-hour drive.

As the plane spanned the distance to Los Angeles, I reviewed what I knew of the reported UFO encounter. I would fill in details when the witness told his story to me directly.

According to the report, Mr. X was driving alone on a lonely back road about 3:30 A.M. He was on his way home from the Los Angeles region. Progress was slow as he drove through patches of fog in the early morning. Suddenly, his car motor went dead, the lights went out, and the radio quit playing. A weird white light flooded the area around his automobile. As he shoved his foot hard on the brake pedal to stop the car, which normally had power brakes, he had a distinct feeling of pressure pushing down on his head and shoulders. A glowing object then moved from above into his windshield view, filling most of it. The object was bigger than the width of the road, and Mr. X estimated it to be fifty to seventy-five feet above him. Its bottom was the orange-red color of the inside of a burning furnace. A ring of lights encircling the object seemed to be rotating, and the whole glowing body wobbled as it hovered. Mr. X was terrified. His heart was

73

throbbing and he had difficulty breathing. After perhaps ninety seconds, the object accelerated at a fantastic rate and vanished into the fog ahead. The car headlights then came back on. Mr. X was able to start the motor again, though for a short while it ran unevenly, as if missing on one or two cylinders, before seeming to run normally.

Mr. X sped from the region as fast as the spotty fog would permit. On reflection, he felt he probably had driven at an excessive speed. He felt he had to get to where there were other people. He desperately wanted not to be alone. He turned off his original route to drive to the nearest settlement, where a milk delivery man directed him to an all-night restaurant.

His fright must have been obvious, for the restaurant waitress who took him coffee asked if he was all right. He told her of his experience, which he had already related to the milkman. After returning home, he realized that, for business reasons, it should not become known that he had reported seeing a UFO.

The college students had learned of the event through a chance meeting with the milkman, and had identified Mr. X through the waitress. After talking with him briefly, they phoned the information to the Colorado Project.

As far as we knew, no one else had seen Mr. X's UFO. That made it a rather weak case, unless I could find additional evidence of the UFO's presence. If the UFO disrupted the car's electrical functioning, this might have been accomplished by a strong magnetic field. Such a strong magnetic field should leave residual effects on magnetic bodies, such as the car. These effects perhaps could be identified.

Engineers with the Ford Motor Company had pointed out to us that automobile body sections, at the time of forming, lifting with electromagnets, and spot welding, take on a definite magnetic pattern, or signature, because the work necessarily is done in the earth's magnetic field. The work-hardened steel retains permanent magnetism, much as a nail does if it is laid parallel with the earth's magnetic field and struck along its length with a hammer. All body parts formed on the same dies will carry the same magnetic pattern. Thus, cars of the same make and model, if made at the same factory, will be identifiable by the pattern of magnetism which will be retained by the metal. This pattern normally remains unchanged for the serviceable life of the car, unless the body is dented and straightened. Ford engineers Frederick J. Hooven and David F. Moyer, who called this effect to our attention, also had supervised the examination of the magnetic pattern of a car which reportedly had been held, while still operating, under the control of a UFO for several minutes. In that case, they had found the original pattern still present.

The failure of automobile engines in the presence of observed UFOs is such a frequently reported aspect of UFO encounters that we found it particularly puzzling, because we could think of no reason for them to do so. A magnetic effect seemed the only logical answer, but we were not sure even that was logical, for there was no information available to tell us how strong a magnetic field would have to be to cause malfunction of such an engine under operating conditions. We felt, however, that magnetic mapping of car bodies could serve as a tool to help answer the primary question, for any magnetic field strong enough to cause electrical system malfunction should be more than strong enough to change the magnetic pattern of the car body. In order to use this tool to learn more about UFOs, we needed cars to study.

That need proved difficult to fulfill. Reports in which cars had stalled were nearly all events which had happened several years earlier, and the cars were no longer available for examination. We watched for current reports in which the claim of automobile stoppage was made. Mr. X's was the first such report to come to our attention, so I was anxious to examine his car for demonstrable magnetic effects.

I had not yet checked the magnetic mapping technique, and did not know how sensitive a magnetometer would be required to measure the residual magnetism of a car. My field kit included an excellent compass, however, and I thought it might be possible to use it for such mapping. I intended to give it a try. If that did not prove adequate, and the UFO report, after initial investigation, still seemed good enough to warrant further work, I would seek Mr. X's permission to borrow his car for a complete mapping with a magnetometer.

My plane, arriving at 8:05 P.M., was met by two of the college trio—a pretty girl and the budding male lawyer. The girl's parents were there also. The third member of the trio, the leader of the group, would meet us on the other side of Los Angeles at the apartment where the girl and her parents lived. We could review the reported UFO incident there and make plans for the impending visit with Mr. X.

By midnight, I was crawling into bed at a motel. Initial acquaintances and preliminary plans had been completed. Mr. X, contacted by telephone, had agreed, after further careful assurances of anonymity, to meet us at his home before 9 A.M. The college trio would pick me up at the motel at 5:30, and we would have breakfast at a famous inn on the way to Mr. X's home.

As we were admitted into the home of the reticent witness, whose name I now knew but was committed never to reveal, I was struck by the presence of a sign on a divider inside the front door. In bold letters, it proclaimed "my name is Nelson Van Brocklin, and baby don't you ever forget it." (I here use a pseudonym.)

X was about 5'7" tall, 160 pounds, black hair, fairly ruddy complexion, perhaps forty-five years old. He accepted the written statement of anonymity and acted particularly relieved when I told him I would be the only project member to know his identity. His name would not be placed on any tapes, reports, or project records, and any correspondence would be addressed to him by me personally in private just before mailing.

Then, beneath the American flag on his living room wall, he spoke carefully of his experience, describing the UFO encounter in detail as I tape-recorded his comments. I assured X that I would erase the name of his associate, whom he had spoken of inadvertently, and check that no other leads to his identity or home location were contained on the tape. The NICAP youngsters were hopeful that they might later get a copy of this tape. As far as I was concerned, this would require only Mr. X's approval.

I asked Mr. X if he would take us to the site of his UFO experience, which was only about fifteen miles away. He was surprisingly reluctant to do so. Probing for the reasons for this reluctance, I found Mr. X was afraid to go back. Even the thought of returning to that spot made him feel uneasy. He said he would never go there alone again. Nonetheless, he did agree to take us there.

Before we left, I wanted to examine the Cadillac convertible he had been driving that eventful night. The NICAP youngsters had previously looked at it and reported strange things about it. The clock had stopped at 3:46, which was therefore assumed to be the time of UFO contact, and had not run again. While the AM radio now functioned normally, the FM gave forth only a steady buzz. His stereo tapes seemed to have lost fidelity. The paint on the hood was strangely pitted, the rear window warped and distorted, and they had measured a slightly higher beta-gamma radiation count on the affected car than on X's second Cadillac.

I checked these observations, taking pictures of the hood paint condition and rear window, and checking for radioactive materials with a Geiger counter. Although the counter showed only normal background readings, I took smear samples inside and outside the cars for more precise counting later. Then, I turned my attention to the magnetic pattern of the car body, and my hosts wondered aloud what I was doing.

I was surprised how sharply the needle of my compass swung about as I passed it over the surface of the car. Readings varied through the full 360-degree range, and sometimes changed as much as seventy degrees over a one or two-inch distance. They were, however, reproducible, and it looked as if my compass would indeed do the job. I noted and recorded the car's orientation with the earth's magnetic field, laid out an arbitrary gridwork of points on the hood, fender tops, and rear deck, measured the positions of these points from recorded reference points so I could relocate the grid points at any time, and determined and recorded the compass reading at each grid point. Since I had no comparison car of the same model and year immediately available, I filed these data away for later reference and climbed in beside Mr. X for the drive to the site where he had encountered the strange object. The college trio followed in their car.

As I surveyed the dash area and asked about the operation of the clock and radio, my attention was repeatedly drawn to the engraved metal tag displayed prominently in the center of the dash board. "This Cadillac custom made for Nelson A. Van Brocklin." Mr. Nelson A. Van Brocklin had already told me he bought the car second hand. I was having the unusual privilege of riding in a custom-made second hand car!

Mr. X Van Brocklin expressed concern about the safety of letting his family ride in the car and about the effects of exposure to the UFO upon his own health. I assured him there was no residual radioactivity present, and suggested he use the car as he wished, but delay having the clock or radio repaired for a couple of weeks in case we should wish to examine them in their present condition. Mr. X had said we could have his car for a day or more, if needed, for further testing.

Before we reached the site, Mr. X told me of the effect of the UFO experience on his religious outlook. "Though I seldom prayed, I prayed to be gotten home safely that night. Seeing this thing and being near it like that—and getting home safely and all—that experience has made me a true believer in—I don't know if you'd call it God exactly—I now feel more intensely a—religious presence."

Mr. X reenacted the experience at the site. As he sat in the stopped car and described what he had seen, he twice paused abruptly, held his head in his hands with his eyes closed, and then asked to be excused for his feeling of illness. I probed gently for more information on points that were discrepant from his earlier account.

After taking photographs of the site, examining the region for any unusual conditions, and measuring some distances, I joined the college trio for the return to Los Angeles. Mr. X asked that we accompany him back to the highway intersection, about 2-1/2 miles in the opposite direction from L. A. This we did, for X didn't want to be left alone here, where his weird experience had its setting.

My three companions had been most cooperative, and, as we drove back to the big city, I explained to them the existence of magnetic signatures on cars, and allowed the girl to copy the raw compass readings I had recorded. I would compare this pattern with that of other Cadillacs of the same model. If they differed, that might indicate that Mr. X's car had been in a strong magnetic field, and further study would be in order. If the magnetism of Mr. X's Cadillac had not been changed since its manufacture, we could only conclude that it had not actually been in a magnetic field strong enough to cause engine or headlight malfunction.

The musketeers were not happy, and I began to realize how great were their expectations. Their initial disappointment that I had not impounded the Cadillac and shipped it back to Detroit for disassembly and complete scientific scrutiny built up to resentment which eventually could no longer be contained.

One of them said, "It seems to me that for the Colorado project not to fully examine every conceivable aspect of the car would be gross negligence!"

I tried to be patient and explain that we indeed were examining every physical aspect conceivable. Electric circuits are not magic. They have physical existence and operate according to physical principles which are reasonably well understood. The same kinds of things which cause them to operate can interfere with that operation. A changing magnetic field could stop or reverse the flow of electric current in a wire. We were checking for evidence that a magnetic field had been present.

The response was, "A group of scientists should be able to think of new physical principles, involving something other than magnetism, which would account for the stopping of automobiles by UFOs!"

It was obvious the youngsters believed that UFOs had demonstrated the obsolescence and inadequacy of current science. I may have been inclined to agree with them if I could prove that a UFO had actually stopped an automobile. Any UFO. And any automobile. I knew I had no chance of doing that, however, solely on the basis of the story of a lone, exhausted, diabetic patient who had drunk two shots of liquor on the long drive from the big city in the wee hours of the morning, and was looking through fog in the direction of a very bright planet—even if that gentleman did have milk with his scotch.

It remained to be proven, of course, that a magnetic field strong enough to stop an automobile engine would permanently alter the magnetic pattern of the car body. A technician, using strong magnets in the national laboratory where he worked, ran some tests on a simulated ignition system and concluded from them that a field in excess of 20,000 gauss, at the coil, would be required to cause malfunction. Since the car body would shield the coil from an external magnetic field, the strength of the external field would have to be considerably greater than this.

I later ran some tests with a 1000-gauss horseshoe magnet on a friend's car in Boulder, Colorado, and showed that 1000 gauss was more than adequate to alter the magnetic pattern of the body permanently. More precise information was not necessary to prove our original assumption, and I did not determine the minimum magnetic field that would alter the pattern. However, this appeared to be a mere few gauss, since the field strength around the magnet I used dropped from 1000 to 235 gauss in the distance of one inch, and changes in the signature pattern were observed for points nearly a foot from the magnet. Such a field is still many times stronger than the approximately 0.4 gauss of the earth's magnetic field, in which the pattern does not change.

I located a Cadillac of the same year and model as Mr. X's on a used car lot in Boulder. After establishing the fact that all Cads of a specific model in a given year were manufactured in the same plant, I got permission from the lot operator to do a bit of research with his used car. I parked it at the same angle to Earth's magnetic field as Mr. X's car had been when I examined it, and located the same grid points as I had used on Mr. X's car. When I took compass readings at those points, I was amazed how precisely they agreed with the readings made in California. Neither car had been subjected to a strong magnetic field.

So we now know that if an automobile should be stopped by a UFO-associated magnetic field, the body of the automobile will retain evidence of such encounter. A simple sensitive compass will display this evidence. And a good horseshoe magnet in the hands of a hoaxer will suffice to confuse the issue.

X's Cadillac had the same magnetic pattern it had when it left the factory. What happened to him the night of November 8,

1967, probably will never be known—perhaps not even by the gentleman himself.

## Major Y

Two photographs delivered to us at Woodbury Hall commanded the attention of all staff members present.

"Look at that! That's the best picture of a flying saucer we've seen yet."

"This photo's a lot clearer than the other one. And it does look authentic, too. The areas of direct sun reflection appear to be properly located for a photograph taken from an airplane. The clouds look right, too. I wonder if the major can prove he took these pictures under the conditions he claims."

"If he can, he has proof that flying saucers are real! That ain't swamp gas."

"Let's look at both photographs and compare the cloud formations in the background. If the photos were taken within a few seconds of each other, the clouds should not have changed noticeably."

"Do the two photos show the same clouds?"

"They do. Look. The saucer has moved from this position in the clouds to—about here. Looks okay! See, the clouds match up. The angle of view has changed in the second photo, but the shapes of these clouds are identical with those over here in the first photo. Only the relative position of the flying saucer has changed, as it should if the story is . . ."

"By golly, maybe we've got something here. Let's get some copies of the slides made immediately, and see what further information we can get to help Bill in analyzing the photographs."

The man who delivered the slides to us had said the retired Air Force officer who took the photos of a brick-red flying saucer agreed to let us make copies of his slides and study them in any

Major Y's Photographs (from slides—the original was a bright orange or red color)

way we wished. He requested, however, that we not reveal his name or associate his name with the photographs. In particular, he wanted no publicity about this incident.

I glanced again over the information we had about the man who claimed to have taken these 35-mm color photographs through the windshield of a C-47 he was piloting before his retirement from the Air Force.

Age 44. Married. Three children. Served in an enlisted status, USAAC, 1943-46. University education. Pilot training after re-enlistment in Air Force. Awarded wings in 1950. Assigned to Strategic Air Command in 1954, piloting B-47s. Served with SAC until retiring, late 1966. Rank of major. Now has responsible civilian job. Reputation irreproachable.

One could not ask for a more credible witness. Mature. Reputation of level-headedness and reliability. Trained observer. Sixteen years an Air Force officer. Pilot. Five thousand hours logged in the air. And he had photographs to prove that he saw a red saucer-like object, flat-bottomed, with a dome on top and a dark band which looked like windows around the dome.

We appreciated the chance to examine the photos, and respected the photographer's desire for anonymity, though such desire under the astonishing and fabulous circumstance of successfully photographing a real flying saucer would not ordinarily be expected. If the major saw this UFO while he was in the Air Force, he was obligated to report it at the time. He had not. Were there other reasons why he wished his name kept secret? Perhaps we could learn such reasons when we talked with him. We assigned him the designation Major Y and deleted his name and address from all official records.

The information which had accompanied the slides revealed the circumstances under which the photographs purportedly had been taken. It read:

In July, 1966, Major Y took off in a C-47 on his last official Air Force flight. He had taken his camera along, hoping to get pictures of mountains in western Utah. The camera was a Viotlander 35mm, with built-in light meter, with synchronized needles to mark proper exposure. The camera was loaded with high-speed Ektachrome (160 ASA), set at about 500 speed, and focused for infinity.

Major Y was in the plane's left seat, as pilot, and was flying along at a true air speed of 150 knots. He had the camera in his lap, ready for quick snapshots, and at about 11 A.M. was near a reservoir southwest of Provo, at about 10,000 feet. Sky conditions were mostly clear with high cirrus clouds. Y's co-pilot, Charles, also now retired from the Air Force, was busy with a navigation problem, computing their estimated time of arrival at Reno.

Y said the UFO in pictures he took appeared suddenly off their wing, as if flying in a great arc around the C-47, to look the plane over. He picked up the camera from his lap and quickly snapped the first picture, which appears blurred. He then moved his camera, quickly swinging it to the right. The UFO disappeared for an instant behind the plane's compass, mounted above the instrument panel, in the center of the windshield. As the object appeared in the clear again, Y took the second picture, this one without blurring. He said the whole sighting was only a few seconds in duration, and he is sure his co-pilot did not even look up in time to see the UFO.

In appearance, the UFO in the pictures is of circular shape, flat on the bottom, and rounded on top, with a central raised portion in the middle, top. In color, it is an orange or brick-red. A change in flight attitude seems to be apparent from a more down-tilted position in the first photo, to a more level position

85

in picture No. 2. A bright reflection, or a light, is apparent on the raised central portion in the second picture. Projections of the pictures may reveal additional detail.

The pictures were beautiful. And the man who took them was apparently of the highest reliability. There were, however, disturbing weaknesses in the story. One was his failure to report his sighting, as required by Air Force regulations. These photos were taken a year and half ago. Why had he not let their existence be known to other than a few of his close associates during all this time? Did not the co-pilot, seated right beside him in the C-47 cockpit, either see the UFO or know the pilot had not only seen but actually photographed this fabulous object? If the pilot hurriedly snapped pictures through the cockpit windshield, would not parts of the framework of the windshield show at the edges of the pictures? There was no evidence of the windshield apparent in either photo.

Adding to the difficulties, the numbers stamped on the slide mountings were not consecutive. In addition to the processing date of December 1966, the mounting of the blurred slide carried the number 14 and the second slide number 11. Had the pictures actually been taken in reverse order, and two additional pictures taken between the two we had? If so, where were the other two pictures, and what did they show? Would it have been possible for the pilot to snap more than two pictures during the few seconds he said the UFO was visible?

Perhaps Major Y could furnish satisfactory answers to some of these questions. I made an appointment for Dr. Norman Levine and me to visit him at his home. We both were anxious to learn more about these particular photographs.

We were not familiar with the cockpits of C-47s. Norm called Frontier Airlines to learn if they had a DC-3 available for our examination at Stapleton Airport in Denver. The DC-3 is the passenger version of the C-47, so the cockpit and windshield structure would be the same. Frontier had one at the airport, and welcomed our inspection of it. We arranged to make this inspection on our way to interview Major Y.

Somewhat to my surprise, we found that it would be quite possible to take photographs from the pilot's seat, shooting in the directions the photos of interest were supposedly taken, without having any part of the windshield framework in the field of view of the camera. The photographs could not be condemned for absence of such framework. That question was satisfactorily cleared. We continued our journey to talk with Major Y.

Mrs. Y met us at the door of their beautiful home in a Denver suburb. She stayed within voice range during the entire interview, and gave strong support to her husband's story regarding details of film processing and authenticity of the pictures. When we pointed out that photographs of objects like the one in Y's slides were quite common, but nearly always proved to have been faked by one of several common methods, she belligerently defended the photos. "These pictures certainly have not been faked," she told us. "There may be lots of fake pictures, and these pictures may not be the best, but I know they are honest pictures of what they show."

Mrs. Y seemed offended that the authenticity of the photos would be questioned. Norm calmed her a bit by commenting that, since many people would presume fakery when they saw such a picture, the photographs would have to be defensible against such accusation if they were to be of any value in our study of UFOs. Major Y swore that his photos were of a real flying saucer seen under the conditions he was describing.

His description followed closely the information we already had. He had turned control of the C-47 over to the co-pilot and readied his camera to take pictures of the mountains ahead. He was holding the camera in his lap when the unknown object appeared at about his ten o'clock position. He quickly photographed the object, wound the camera with a single lever stroke, and got a second picture of the object as it accelerated upward and to his right. The object sped out of the field of view. Further observation of it was blocked by the cockpit ceiling. It had been visible only a few seconds. Major Y just had time to bring the camera up to his eye, snap a picture, wind the film, and snap the second picture.

"Did the co-pilot see the saucer?" we asked. The co-pilot was busy with computations, and did not look up in time to see the object.

"Did you tell him what you saw and photographed?" With this question, I was testing for consistency in the Major's account, for he had already told me, during the telephone conversation when I made the appointment for this visit, that he told the co-pilot he had just taken a picture of something and the co-pilot's response was a disinterested "That's nice." Y then had said that the co-pilot didn't know but that he had photographed the left wing of the plane, or something of that sort. Now the Major was saying he asked the co-pilot if he saw the object he just photographed, and the co-pilot said he did not. According to this account, the co-pilot should know that the pilot photographed an unidentified object at the time. Yet no one got excited about the event and no one reported the incident upon landing.

Why had the incident not been reported to the Air Force's Project Blue Book? The major knew that people were ridiculed for reporting such things. Also, he had been piloting the plane without authorization to do so. He had been removed from flight status after fifteen years of piloting and was on this flight originally as one of several passengers in the back end. He had traded positions with the pilot so he could keep in practice, since he was anticipating a commercial pilot's job after his impending retirement.

"Where and when did you have the film developed to see if

you indeed had photographs of the object you saw?" we asked. He told us he left the film in the camera until the roll was completed several months later. There were some pictures already taken on this roll of film before the UFO sighting. After the UFO shots were taken in July, the roll was finished during September and October. It was developed in early December through the camera shop at a local discount store.

Major Y couldn't recall what the early pictures on the roll showed, but the later ones were taken on their drive across the Rocky Mountains after his retirement from the service. To finish the roll, they had taken pictures of a big October snowstorm in the Denver area.

Major Y was aware of the discrepancy we had noted in the slide mounting numbers. He gave this little import, however, stating that, for some reason, all the pictures from that roll were numbered out of order. We asked if we could see other pictures from the same roll, and the major asked his wife to see if she could find them.

After a few minutes, Mrs. Y appeared with ten additional slides. She said these were from the same roll, but she could not find the others. She must have sent them to her sister. Slides which were numbered 1 through 8 showed scenes of the post-retirement drive across the mountains. Numbers 9 and 10 were of the October snowstorm. We particularly wanted to see slides carrying numbers 12 and 13, since the UFO pictures carried the mounting numbers 14 and 11. No additional slides were to be found, however.

Major Y was positive these slides were from the same roll of film as the UFO shots, for they were all process-dated December, 1966, and his family did not have another roll developed until sometime in 1967. This was confirmed by Mrs. Y who said she and her husband were together when they picked up the pictures which included the UFO shots. Their son was home on

89

leave from the Marines at the time, and the three of them were the only ones to see the UFO pictures before the major stashed them away in a drawer. To avoid ridicule, they never mentioned the pictures to their young daughters and had even yet told only a few close associates about them.

With Y's permission, we took the ten additional slides with us for further study. The numbering discrepancy seemed to me a serious one, but perhaps something could have gotten fouled up in the sequence of mounting the slides and stamping numbers on the mounting frames.

I felt there was another detail shown in the pictures themselves which was inconsistent with the major's story. According to his account, the plane was heading southwest to west at the time of the sighting, about 11 A.M. The clear picture was taken with the UFO in about the twelve o'clock or one o'clock position from the plane. In studying the UFO image on the clear photograph, however, I had concluded that the position of the bright spot, if the brightness were due to specular reflection of sunlight as it appeared to be, would require the plane to be headed in a direction between east and north, which was just about opposite from the direction the major said he was heading. I could have been wrong in the analysis, however.

Other weaknesses in the major's account of the incident, such as his casual manner of treating his seemingly fantastic experience and failure to report it, did not seem logical to me. However, there perhaps were extenuating circumstances which may have made such behavior rational. Anyway, human behavior is not always noted for its rationality. If we found there was indeed some foul-up in numbering of the pictures, allowing reconciliation with the major's account on this point, the pictures would be worth Dr. William Hartmann's time in photographic analysis.

The major had been cordial, and apparently stable and sincere. Why would a mature man of such high reliability perpetrate a UFO hoax? He wanted no publicity, had not tried to sell his photographs, and offered full cooperation in having his pictures studied and analyzed by the Colorado Project.

As soon as we got back to Boulder and the project offices in Woodbury Hall, we removed Major Y's twelve slides from their mountings to examine the frame numbering on the film itself. Each half-frame is numbered at the edge of the film before it leaves the factory. While stamping of numbers on mountings during processing might conceivably result in an unlikely mixing of the sequence, the numbers on the film itself certainly would tell the actual sequence in which the pictures were taken. Alas, these numbers showed the same sequence as indicated on the mountings. The mountain trip and snowstorm pictures were in the order that the Y's said they were taken. However, the UFO pictures had been taken after the snowstorm, which was several months after the major's retirement. They were not taken by him from a C-47 while he was in the Air Force—nor was one slide taken immediately after the other. Any hopes that these pictures could be used to support a contention that flying saucers inhabit Earth's skies had been quenched even before the photos themselves had been analyzed.

There seemed to be an understandable reason why Major Y desired that we not let anyone know who he is. But why would *he* try to pull such a hoax as this? We probably will never know the answer to that question.

I tried to arrange another meeting with Major Y, wishing to observe his responses when gently confronted with the confirmed evidence of fakery. The underground grapevine apparently was functioning, however, for the meeting, which he first agreed to, was never consummated. The original appointment was canceled with trivial excuses, and alternate dates similarly rejected. "I'm very busy with yard work—putting up a sun-dial, doing concrete work, planting things. This is a bad time to take time out to talk about this."

I finally attempted to get his response to the evidence of fakery over the telephone. I explained the frame numbering system used by film manufacturers.

"This discrepancy has us very puzzled," I told him. "We cannot justify detailed photographic analysis unless we can clear up this discrepancy. I wanted to get your response to this situation."

The major was speechless for several moments. ". . . I don't know how to answer that. I didn't even know there were numbers on the film—they must be covered up by the frame!"

After a long pause, he went on. "Maybe I was wrong about those pictures being on the same roll—I've got stacks of pictures lying around here. . . . That snowstorm was not the same snowstorm that I thought it was. . . . I don't know why the two pictures are not numbered consecutively. Perhaps I turned the film-advance lever so hard that the film went on past the next frame."

The major did not pursue this last suggestion after I pointed out that not only had two frames been skipped, but exactly two frames were missing, an unlikely coincidence even if the camera had malfunctioned.

Although I thought the probability that Major Y would tell us how his pictures actually were made was vanishingly small, I turned the torture screws a little tighter. With tongue in cheek, for I knew these pictures were not appropriate for that type of photographic analysis, I implied that analysis would tell us just how far from the camera and how big the object photographed actually was. I explained that detailed analysis was expensive, however, and we didn't want to spend the money unless we had an apparently authentic UFO photograph. The major did not seem anxious to have the analysis done. "Maybe we'd just as well forget it, and not spend that kind of money on this because of the strange aspects you mentioned."

Major Y had commented earlier that he had waited eighteen years to get a picture of these things, and then when he did there were so many odd things about the picture that people would not believe it. He was quite ready to write these pictures off as failures. "I guess I'll just have to wait another eighteen years and get another picture."

Eventually we returned the major's slides to him by registered mail. The letter of transmittal read, in part:

In view of the discrepancies we discussed in our telephone conversation, I am forced to conclude that the photographs were not made under the conditions originally claimed. Because of these discrepancies, the pictures cannot be used by us to support claims that the object photographed was other than an ordinary object of earthly origin, tossed into the air. If you have other helpful information, please phone me at the number given, or write me at the University of Colorado. In any case, your name will not be used in any records or discussions of these photographs.

Major Y had appeared to be the most reliable of witnesses. His claims of past experience were confirmed in his military records. There was nothing on file in his medical records to cast doubt on his veracity. His present and past associates considered him honest, reliable, and credible. He remains among the set of anonymous people who have not photographed a real flying saucer.

# Chapter 7

# Watch the Pendulum

Reports of sightings of unidentified flying objects number in the thousands. Most of these are eye-witness accounts of something seen, or thought to have been seen, by one or more persons. The observed object left no physical artifact, no calling card, no alteration of the environment which could be studied either to determine the nature of the visitor or to establish that a real visitor had actually been present. With such reports, one is left with only the mind or minds of the witness or witnesses to study. Since a majority of the reports are of this nature, the reality behind them had to be evaluated with strong dependence upon man's limited knowledge of his own mind, as elucidated by professional psychologists and psychiatrists associated with the project's studies.

Was the reported sighting of a flying saucer the product of a vivid imagination or hallucination, or was something physically real actually observed? If physically real, was the observation properly interpreted by the observer? These questions were constantly hounding us. When one observes any physically real object, the perception of that object takes place in the observer's mind. The human mind is well known for its ability to deceive itself. Even mature minds which normally are capable of distinguishing outer reality from their own internal mental creations have frequently been observed, particularly under conditions of fatigue and isolation from other people, to lose that capability. Hallucinations are as real to the persons experiencing them as perceptions of objects which other people would call real. How, then, is one to determine, when listening to the testimony of someone who says he saw a flying saucer, whether or not a saucer was present in the physical world? One might do this, with an acknowledged degree of uncertainty, through results of psychological tests on the observer.

In the process of our investigations, we had encountered numerous cases in which an external reality was observed, yet the mind of the observer so distorted the information available to the sense organs that the observer believed he saw something entirely different from the object which actually was there. It was such distortion which caused the planet Venus to be reported to us as a saucer-like vehicle with rows of windows around it, and which imparted motion to stationary objects. Unless one can establish the presence and identity of the misinterpreted object, reports which involve such are extremely difficult to evaluate from the testimony of the observer. Psychologists sometimes find certain observer tests, such as one called the Thematic Apperception Test, or the famous Rorschach Test, to be helpful in such cases. Often, however, unless one already knows what object or phenomenon was present, the accuracy of the observer's description remains uncertain, and an investigator cannot determine whether or not the observer saw what he thought he saw.

When many different observers are involved, the likelihood of gross misinterpretation is still present. I have already discussed a UFO case (Chapter 4) in which law enforcement officers in about fourteen different communities spent the early morning hours of several days chasing the planet Venus. The suggestion by other officers that this bright object was a UFO which had been observed to do such things as chase police cars undoubtedly affected the manner of perception of the object by new observers. Those observers perhaps would have seen the light as a star or planet in the absence of such suggestion. History furnishes numerous examples of more wide-spread effects of the functioning of crowd psychology. Dr. Mark W. Rhine, Assistant Professor of Psychiatry at the University of Colorado Medical Center, referred to one such incident in his contribution to the official report of the Colorado Project. That incident was the London panic of 1524 in which thousands left the city to avoid a great flood which a fortune-teller predicted and which, of course, never occurred. While this incident did not involve a misinterpreted object external to the human mind, it exemplifies the frequently encountered operation of hysterical contagion—the same kind of contagion which causes multiple observers to see stars, airplane lights, or glowing earth satellite debris as intelligently-controlled spacecraft from other planets.

If different witnesses to an event report independently of each other, and one witness's perception of the event could not have been influenced by the interpretation of the others, agreement of the testimony then more reliably indicates what was actually present. One must yet be alert toward self-deception or mass deception. Furthermore, most UFO reports, unfortunately, do not involve multiple independent witnesses. So, we were unavoidably faced with the problem of getting the most reliable information possible from eye-witness testimony, often from the only witness to the reported event.

96

Project psychologists wrestled with the problem and gave selected tests to individual witnesses in some of the cases we studied. After considerable staff discussion of what else we might do to get all the information which could conceivably be useful in determining whether or not a strange flying object had actually been observed by a witness, we decided to determine if techniques of hypnosis could be of value. This was outside my field, but it seemed to me an effort of desperation. I would be involved in the selection of test individuals, however, since these would likely be people I encountered in field investigations of UFO sightings, and natural curiosity made me intensely interested in the details of any hypnosis efforts. The hypnosis would be done, of course, only by qualified personnel under conditions not hazardous to the witness, and with the full cooperation and consent of the witness. The disturbing uncertainty in conclusions drawn from eye-witness testimony alone made even this effort seem worthwhile.

"The Interrupted Journey" by J. G. Fuller, for instance, about an alleged UFO incident which preceded the Condon study, was published both in book form and as a two-part series in *Look* magazine. Hypnosis was used in this case to establish the "truth" of the testimony of the witness. The merits of such use of hypnosis are highly questionable. As Professor Rhine writes in the official Condon report:

> Hypnosis has nothing to contribute to the routine evaluation of the creditability of the eye-witness. While it may occasionally be useful as a source of information, it cannot be used as a way of *proving* that the witness is telling the truth. Sometimes hypnosis can aid in bringing to conscious awareness material that has been repressed. But persons who cannot distinguish their fantasies from reality will, under hypnosis, only reveal

97

more of the same fantasies. Their production under hypnotic trance will demonstrate only that their reports are "real" to them, even though they may not in fact have any basis in objective reality.

In spite of limitations of expected benefit, we proceeded with plans to give hypnosis a chance to perform. We considered various witnesses, some of whom we knew to have trapped themselves in unintentionally fraudulent claims, and some who told stories of experiences that were still puzzling. We selected a small-town police officer who had reported a close encounter with a flying saucer while he was driving alone on patrol duty. As part of his testimony, he indicated there was a period of about twenty minutes, while he was near the UFO, that he could not account for in his memory. If his related experience were real, perhaps hypnosis would allow events of that twenty minutes to be brought out from behind a subconscious memory block.

The patrolman was a twenty-two-year-old Marine veteran. On the night of his unusual experience, he had been working a fourteen-hour shift, starting at 7 P.M. He said that he looked at his watch as he turned his patrol car around on the state highway at the edge of town to check what he thought was a stalled truck on a county road just off the highway. It was 2:30 A.M. As he turned onto the county road, he switched the headlights to bright and stopped his police car. The red blinking lights he had thought probably were from a stalled truck were actually coming from a saucer-shaped object hovering about six feet above the road some forty feet ahead of the patrolman. The object was as wide as the roadway. Its surface appeared like polished aluminum. As the patrolman's headlights struck the object, it lit up brilliantly and started rising, emitting a siren-like noise. Light glowed from inside it, revealing a row of seven evenly-spaced oval windows in which red lights blinked on and off. He no-

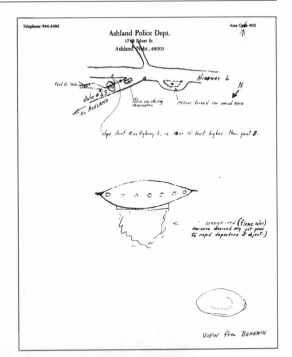

Sketch of UFO by police officer who claimed observing it.

Photo by Jerry McElroy

"The pendulum swung on."

99

ticed a cat-walk around the outside of the object, beneath the windows.

The object rose gradually, with side-wise fluttering, and emitted a flame-like material from its underside. The patrolman opened the car door, stuck his head out, and watched the object move slowly overhead, then accelerate rapidly and shoot upward out of sight.

When he checked the clock at the police station, to which he returned directly, the patrolman was astonished that it read 3 A.M. He felt it could not have been more than ten minutes since he turned back to check the blinding red lights. He suspected that perhaps he had not been conscious during a period of about twenty minutes while he was in the presence of the strange saucer. He still felt weak, sick, and nervous after reaching the police station.

Was this testimony an outright lie sparked by subconscious need for attention and importance? Was it hallucination, perhaps brought on by exhaustion and loneliness? Was a physical object like the one described actually present? No independent observations or physical evidence could be found to support the patrolman's account. His police chief was certain the account was neither the product of fabrication nor of hallucination. If it were real, what happened in the unaccounted-for twenty minutes? Perhaps hypnosis sessions, plus a full battery of personality tests, could answer all these questions.

The patrolman was seated in one corner of a room at Colorado University's testing and counseling building. He was watching a pendulum bob swing rhythmically and repetitiously on a string held by a professional psychologist a few feet away. The psychologist was writing in his notebook, recording both his own questions to the patrolman and the response to each question, as indicated by nodding or twisting motions of the patrolman's head. The patrolman had been instructed to use one of four specified motions to indicate "Yes," "No," "I don't know," and "I don't want to say."

The psychologist proceeded with his questioning of the presumably hypnotized witness.

"Did you experience a UFO sighting on December 3, 1967?"

"Yes."

"Is there more information available?"

"Yes."

"Is there more subconscious information?"

"Yes."

"Are the recollections of the event accurate?"

"Yes."

"Are there some details which are not accurate?"

"No."

"Is there a discrepancy in time between the sighting and the end of the sighting?"

"Yes."

"Am I aware of what happened?"[1]

"Yes."

The pendulum swung on. I couldn't tell if the patrolman was actually in a trance state or was putting on an act of cooperation. I sat back and, with others who were present, quietly observed the proceedings. The patrolman's boss and mentor, the police chief, sat near the patrolman, scribbling copious notes as the pendulum swung and the questions were asked and slowly answered. The pendulum kept swinging.

After the session was over, an observing psychologist told me he felt the patrolman had been in a "medium trance state." No strong effort had been made to take him to a deep trance level. Although it was never obvious to me that he had reached a state of trance, new information had indeed been presented. The patrolman had revealed that, during the UFO observation, a white blurred object, apparently an intelligent organism, came from the UFO and approached the car. He had some sort of mental communication, or "conversation," with this object, which somehow prevented his calling in on his police radio and prevented his drawing his gun to shoot at the UFO. The communication regarded the activities and purposes of the UFO occupants. From such communication, the patrolman learned that the craft was propelled by a type of electrical and magnetic force, that it operated from another galaxy, its occupants were friendly and were here to prevent earth people from destroying the earth.

These "revelations," of course, were typical UFO lore. The pendulum-swinging psychologist questioner was a genial professor from a neighboring university. He readily admitted a bias due to his belief that spacecraft from extraterrestrial sources, controlled by intelligent beings, are conducting an intensive survey of the earth. He could draw no firm conclusions regarding the source of the revealed information.

The psychologists hit the hapless patrolman with a full battery of tests—Rorschach, Thematic Apperception, Sentence Completion, Word Association, Wechsler Adult Intelligence Scale, and Minnesota Multiphase Personality Inventory. Results of these tests would be useful in our evaluation of the UFO report.

As the police officers left to catch their plane for home, I hoped they could slip quietly back into their jobs and gradually forget the UFO incident. The patrolman had told us that, after seeing the UFO, but before coming to Colorado, he was bothered by a ringing in his ears, and sometimes awakened at night to find himself choking his wife or handcuffing her ankles or wrists. It seemed that if he could accept the incident and turn his attention back to normal police duties, he might avoid a personal disaster.

My hopes did not survive my next telephone conversation. The reporter, who called from a city near the patrolman's home town, wanted my verification of information the patrolman and police chief had phoned to him from Colorado regarding the hypnosis session and new information which it had revealed. The policeman had arranged for the reporter to meet them at the airport as they arrived home, so they could give the newspapers the full account.

A week later, Jim Wadsworth accepted a telephone call from a law student who lived in a city near the patrolman's home town. Three weeks after the patrolman's experience, and in nearly the same location, the student had observed an odd row of colored lights in the distance as he was approaching a highway underpass while driving alone at night. He stopped the car momentarily to look at the lights. He arrived home to find it an hour later than he knew it should have been. He did not know what happened to the lost hour. As he prepared for bed, he had a feeling that "they" were still with him, that they had communicated, wanting him to go on a trip with them. He felt an impelling friendship with them, and "told" them he would go but wasn't ready yet. Afterward, he found it impossible to concentrate on his law studies and couldn't sleep nights. He considered seeking psychiatric help but wanted to contact our project first, for he was concerned that psychiatry might interfere with our investigation of his experience. He had driven to the neighboring town to talk with the patrolman whose experience, which the student's wife had read about in the newspapers, seemed similar to his own. Even the aftereffects of the experiences seemed somewhat similar.

I overhead some of Jim's conversation, and he later began to fill in some of the details. I couldn't help interrupting.

"The police chief did *what*?"

"The chief tied a rock to the end of a string, and started swinging it like a pendulum in front of the law student and asking him a lot of questions."

I burst out laughing, but stopped short. The vision of the police chief swinging the pendulum as he tried to hypnotize the uncooperative new witness, which initially struck me as being hilarious, seemed, on second thought, to be a scene of a tragic comedy.

Many years after the Colorado Project, claims of contacts with alien beings were still reported, seemingly with increasing frequency. In his book *Abduction: Human Encounters with Aliens*, published in 1994, Dr. John E. Mack suggested that hundreds of thousands of Americans believe they have been abducted and transported to alien spaceships. Dr. Mack, a psychiatrist and professor at Harvard University Medical School's Cambridge Hospital, had interviewed more than a hundred "abductees," and came to believe their experiences were quite real. He used hypnosis in his professional efforts to help abductees overcome the trauma resulting from their reported strange experiences.

In no "abduction" case, however, has there been any physical evidence that a spaceship had actually been in the vicinity. Without such evidence, and without convincing demonstration that the hypnotist is truly testing the patient's suppressed memory, rather than testing his or her imagination or responsiveness to suggestion, contactee reports reside in the realm of fiction. Perhaps when more is learned of the human mind and the nature of "reality," such reports might be viewed in a different light.

---

[1] His wording, I think, was to place the question in the mind of the hypnotized witness and eliminate the questioner-witness separation which would result from phrasing the question, "Are *you* aware of what happened?"

# Chapter 8

# The Will to Believe—Or, I Suspect the Society Editor Is Still Laughing

## Ubatuba

The Ubatuba magnesium samples were the most renowned pieces of flying saucers in existence—at least, it was claimed that they were pieces from a flying saucer. One of them was in the possession of Coral and Jim Lorenzen, founders and co-directors of the Aerial Phenomena Research Organization (APRO), headquartered in Tucson. Jim and Coral had agreed to let us analyze the Ubatuba magnesium; however, they considered the sample too valuable to be trusted to the U.S. mails. It would have to be picked up by personal courier and hand carried wherever it was moved. After all, fragments of extraterrestrial flying vehicles were extremely rare and almost impossible to acquire. One simply could not chance losing them or allowing them to be destroyed in the process of analysis.

Ubatuba is a town on the coast of Brazil. It was near this town that a disc-shaped flying object supposedly was seen to explode and scatter its burning fragments into the shallow water along the beach. I had read an English translation of the account of the event, supposedly as printed in the society column of O GLOBO, a Rio de Janeiro newspaper, 14 September 1957:

We received the letter: "Dear Mr. Ibrahim Sued. As a faithful reader of your column and your admirer, I wish to give you something of the highest interest to a newspaperman, about the flying discs. If you believe they are real, of course. I didn't believe anything said or published about them. But, just a few days ago, I was forced to change my mind. I was fishing together with some friends at a place close to the town of Ubatuba, Sao Paulo, when I sighted a flying disc. It approached the beach at an unbelievable speed and an accident, i.e. a crash into the sea, seemed imminent. At the last moment, however, when it was almost striking the waters, it made a sharp turn upward and climbed rapidly on a fantastic impulse. We followed the spectacle with our eyes, startled, when we saw the disc explode in flames. It disintegrated into thousands of fiery fragments, which fell sparkling with magnificent brightness. They looked like fireworks, despite the time of the accident, at noon, i.e. at midday. Most of these fragments, almost all, fell into the sea. But, a number of small pieces fell close to the beach and we picked up a large amount of this material which was as light as paper. I am enclosing a small sample of it. I don't know anyone that could be trusted to whom I might send it for analysis. I never read about a flying disc being found, or about fragments or parts of a saucer that had been picked up; unless the finding was made by military authorities and the whole thing kept as a top-secret subject. I am certain the matter will be of great interest to the brilliant columnist, and I am sending two copies of this letter—to the newspaper and to your home address."

Mr. Ibrahim Sued's column continued: From the admirer (the signature was not legible), together with the above letter, I received fragments of a strange metal. . . .

According to the Lorenzens, their disc fragment was sent to them by Dr. Fontes, a Rio M. D. who, because of his interest in flying discs, had contacted the society editor and had been given the three fragments the editor received. A chapter of one of Mrs. Lorenzen's books tells, in Dr. Fontes's words, of his obtaining the fragments from the newspaper society editor:

> I phoned him that same day and asked for a meeting to discuss the matter. He agreed. I arrived at his apartment four hours later. There on the table, I saw the samples sent by the unidentified correspondent—three small pieces of dull-gray solid substance that appeared to be a metal of some sort. Their surfaces were not smooth and polished, but some quite irregular and apparently strongly oxidized. Their appearance suggested they might be, if really metallic, pieces of fragments disintegrated from a larger metallic mass or object. . . .
>
> The material was light, definitely lighter than aluminum—almost as light as paper. Amazed, I told Mr. Sued I had some friends with scientific backgrounds who might be called in to investigate the samples. He said he knew nothing about UFOs and was even convinced they did not exist. He was not curious about the samples and I could take them.

This story of the origin of the Ubatuba samples was even more nebulous than most UFO accounts. The illegibility of the signature on Mr. Sued's letter made the account particularly sus-

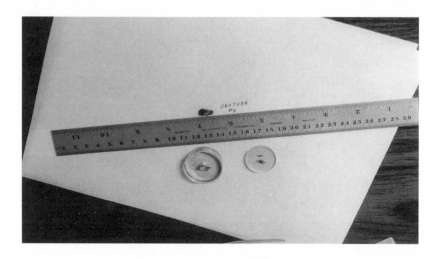

Picture of the invaluable sample of magnesium said to have been from Ubatuba, Brazil.

The "Ubatuba" Magnesium

picious, for it prevented any checking of direct witnesses to the claimed event. In a hoax situation, this dead end for investigators would be most convenient. Did Mr. Sued actually receive a letter from a fisherman who witnessed the explosion of a strange disc? Did he receive a letter from a practical joker who wanted to have some fun? Did he compose his own letter?

According to Mrs. Lorenzen, the witnesses to the explosion incident were never located. Dr. Fontes and a friend had "canvassed the beach area" around Ubatuba, trying to identify and locate the witnesses. They succeeded only in locating a fisherman who recalled that a group of vacationers from an island town had talked about such an incident and had displayed pieces of a gray substance.

So, the story of the exploding disc of Ubatuba was never to be verified, and we had no means of associating the metal fragment the Lorenzens possessed with an observed UFO, even assuming absolute honesty and integrity on the parts of Mr. and Mrs. Lorenzen and Dr. Fontes.

Except for one claimed fact, I would have considered this case too weak to warrant further attention. That claim was that analysis of the fragments, done expertly at the Mineral Production Laboratory of the Agricultural Ministry of Brazil, had shown the metal to be magnesium of a purity greater than it was possible to achieve by earthly technology. If that claim were true, the origin of the samples would indeed be of special interest.

Since the Lorenzens were willing to lend us their sample, we could check the claim that it was more free of trace impurities than the purest magnesium metal produced at that time in earthly metallurgical laboratories. Norm brought the sample from Tucson, and I made arrangements for the analysis.

Eventually, I was on my way to Washington, D. C., with the Ubatuba sample in my brief case. I also carried a comparison sample of purified magnesium metal which I had obtained from

Dr. R. S. Burk of the Dow Chemical Company in Michigan, the company which produced most of the nation's magnesium by extracting it from sea waters. Since I assumed we would be looking for extremely minute quantities of impurity elements in samples which were essentially 100% pure magnesium, I had chosen to use neutron activation analysis, a method so sensitive with most elements of interest that it can detect the presence of quantities smaller than a thousandth of a millionth of a gram. We could use just a tiny sliver off the sample for such analysis and not disturb or damage the major portion of the irreplaceable Ubatuba fragment.

The laboratory I was taking the sample to was the National Office Laboratory, Alcohol and Tobacco Tax Division, Bureau of Internal Revenue. This seemed a strange place to go for analysis. However, I had been convinced that the best neutron-activation analyses in the country was being done there. They had the facilities and equipment and, equally important to me, the personnel had no special commitment regarding the presence or absence or nature of UFOs. Mr. Maynard Pro, Assistant Chief, Research and Methods Evaluation, had agreed to supervise the analysis, every step of which I would personally monitor in detail. Neutron activation analysis involves irradiation of the sample with neutrons to make it radioactive and, by a process known as gamma-ray spectrometry, measuring the energies and quantities of radioactive emission. The neutron irradiation, in this case, would be done by sticking the tiny sample, enclosed in a plastic container, right down in the guts of a nuclear reactor, where it would be struck by billions of neutrons each second. We would use the reactor at the U. S. Naval Research Laboratory. The quantities, energies, and half-lives of the induced radioactivity would tell us not only what elements were present in the original sample, but how much of each was there.

I arrived at the laboratory to find Mr. Pro anxious to help.

As his assistants finished up other work and photographed my samples in preparation for the analysis, Mr. Pro gave me a tour of his lab. I began to realize why the Bureau of Internal Revenue operated such a facility. Neutron activation could so accurately measure trace impurities that those fellows could examine a drop of drinking "likker" and tell what still it came from—even if it were a small moonshine operation in the hills of Tennessee—providing, of course, they had a comparison sample from that still. They had recently been doing some work on paintings. By analyzing a quantity of paint too small to be missed from the work of art, they could determine if the painting was authentically of the seventeenth century, for example, or done relatively recently and made to appear aged.

I was puzzled why the authenticity of paintings would be Bureau of Internal Revenue business. It was. Rich Americans were buying cheap imitations of the old masters in Europe, bringing them to the U. S., claiming they were authentic and worth many thousands of dollars and deducting the thousands from their income tax as they donated the paintings to some art museum.

Mr. Pro showed me how they exposed a somewhat similar fraud when they analyzed an imperceptibly small bit of paint taken from a postage stamp. An enterprising individual had claimed his stamp had been misprinted at the press and was extremely valuable as a collector's item. It had a couple extra stripes on the picture that similar stamps did not have. The stripes were shown to have been added by the entrepreneur.

In one corner of the lab stood equipment for determining the minute quantity of the tritium isotope of hydrogen in water samples. The equipment was now idle. It had been used to check the age of imported wines, for tritium analysis can reveal when the water used in the wine fell as rain. Importers had learned, presumably to their sorrow, that they could no longer get by

111

with false claims regarding vintage wines, so there was no longer much call for such analyses.

We analyzed the Ubatuba magnesium and looked at the results. It was not nearly as pure as the Dow product, which had been produced upon request for "at least twenty-five years." The Ubatuba sample did contain surprising quantities of a couple elements, but the composition could easily be duplicated by "earthly technology," and Dow had produced experimental batches like it many years before the Ubatuba event.

The claims that the Ubatuba magnesium was of unusual purity simply were not true, so arguments based upon that claim were completely invalid. If a Brazilian society editor had originally intended a bit of fun with his readers, he probably got his full measure.

Later, I came upon a bit of information related to the Ubatuba sample which I thought to be significant. It was a report of results of spectrographic analysis of that same sample, done in 1958 at one of the best of our national laboratories, apparently at the request of APRO and through the personal interest of laboratory scientists. It showed the sample to be "not at all pure in the spectrographic sense," with impurity concentrations higher than expected in commercially pure magnesium. The reason this information interested me then was simply that Mrs. Lorenzen had the results of that analysis as well as those supplied from Brazil by Dr. Fontes in her files when she wrote her book. Yet, after devoting most of forty pages to presentation of analytical results supplied by a gastroenterologist from technically undeveloped Brazil, she wrote off the results obtained at a leading U.S. analytical laboratory, by a Ph.D. chemist who specialized in spectrographic analysis, with a single paragraph. After stating that "a technician" did such a test and displaying the results, she discarded those figures with the comment ". . . it was not possible to determine whether the detected impurities were in the electrodes or in the sample. The impurities, however, are those normally found in the standard carbon electrodes."

The U.S. laboratory results, of course, did not support the desires of the author. Like all human beings faced with issues involving ethical, political, or religious beliefs, she chose, from the information available, that which supported her desires— and the desires of her readers.

The blind desire to believe can and does lead a person into absolute absurdities. When writing their book *UFOs? Yes! Where The Condon Committee Went Wrong*, David R. Saunders and R. Roger Harkins had access to early results of the neutron activation analysis of the Ubatuba magnesium. After listing four "expected" conditions of ultra pure terrestrial magnesium in an effort to show that the Ubatuba "fragment" (which was not ultra pure and may not have come from Ubatuba) was not of terrestrial origin, Saunders and Harkins continued:

> As you can see, therefore, the impurities present are not the kind that count—from the standpoint of terrestrial metallurgy, then, the sample can be said to be 100.0 percent pure, because there is nothing in it by accident.

All I can say to this kind of chattering is "Wow!"

## Robots At Cisco Grove

We scratched hard to find some physical evidence to support witness testimony that strange objects were observed in our skies. Coral and Jim Lorenzen, on a visit to Boulder, mentioned that the Air Force had in its possession a metal arrow point which reportedly was bent on impact with a robot from a flying saucer at Cisco Grove, California, 5 September 1964. Why should we not get the arrow point from Wright-Patterson Field and analyze any bit of material that clung to its tip? Perhaps we would find that the robot was made of some material foreign to earth technology.

Since we were scratching hard, I asked Air Force personnel at Wright-Patterson to send me the arrow point for examination, if they had such. Then I listened to the tape recordings of interviews of the witness by both Air Force and NICAP personnel. The story also had been presented in Mrs. Lorenzen's book *UFO Occupants*. The witness, a bow and arrow hunter, had gotten caught by darkness before he could relocate his camp and hunting companions. He climbed a tree, saw a moving light in the darkness, thought it might be a helicopter, got down and built fires to attract attention. He re-climbed the tree to watch the light come closer, make a half circle around him, become a big glowing light hovering perhaps fifty yards away, with three flat objects equally spaced behind it which shone only by reflected moonlight. He observed something drop from one of these objects and heard a crashing through the brush. Then, he spent the whole night in the tree in an ordeal with odd, white-suited "beings" of which he saw as many as seven in the bright moonlight, and a metallic "robot" with glowing eyes like flaming silver dollars. White smoke from the robot's mouth, when the robot was under the tree, caused the hunter to choke and gasp for breath, pass out temporarily, and come to with dry heaves. Convinced that the robot was out to get him, the hunter tried shooting it with the three arrows he had, along with his bow, in the tree. At the range of only twelve feet, and shot at full force, the arrows pushed the robot against a rock, but ricocheted away without lasting damage to the robot. As each arrow struck, electric arc-like flashes occurred between the robot and the arrow. The hunter then tried to drive the robot and two white-suited

114

beings under his tree away with fire, lighting his cap and then each item of his outer camouflage clothing with book matches and throwing the flaming cloth down by the visitors. He succeeded in setting temporary small brush fires beneath the trees this way. This held the visitors back a while and caused the original glowing object to move high in the air, where it remained the rest of the night. The hunter soon ran out of matches and climbed higher in the tree. He tied his belt around his chest and the tree to keep from falling if he lost consciousness again, and he spent the rest of the night in a repeated sequence of shaking the tree to cause the two little men in white to move back from attempting to boost each other up the tree trunk (the trunk was farther around at the base than a human adult could reach, and the lowest branch was about twelve feet from the ground), passing out temporarily as the robot's "smoke" came up through the branches to him, becoming conscious, then sick, and looking down to see the white-suited ones resume their effort to boost each other into his tree, shaking the tree, and starting all over again. Near daybreak, a second robot joined the first. As the two robots faced each other about three feet apart, arcs like electric discharges flashed between them. The smoke from both robots together caused the hunter to lose consciousness for a longer period, perhaps a half hour. When he came to this time, it was daylight and all visitors had vanished. He got down, looked around, and picked up the canteen he had thrown down and one arrow, which lay on the top of some brush where it had ricocheted from the metallic robot. He then hastened from the area and resumed his search for camp.

After listening carefully to this story, I no longer had any enthusiasm for analyzing the arrow point. I was puzzled why civilian "investigators" would present this story as an unsolved UFO mystery.

But perhaps I was far too skeptical. A hunter probably could

Arrow head from Blue Book—Cisco Grove September 5, 1964 UFO Case

get to that twelve-foot high first branch (twice), carrying his hunting bow and arrows, which the little white men were unable to boost each other to. And, although my belt would need to be nearly ten inches longer than it is merely to go around my chest, let alone also around a tree, perhaps this hunter had a big stomach and the top of the tree was small. I didn't know what kind of material his camouflage clothing was made of—perhaps it was more flammable than most. Also, the ephemeris showed that the moon was new at 4:35 A.M. on 6 September 1964, so it would have set just before sunset on September 5 and there would have been no moonlight that night. Perhaps someone had made a mistake on the date of the experience, for the hunter said he climbed the tree in the dark before the moon came up and could later see distant white-clothed little men in the bright moonlight.

So, I examined the bent arrow point I received from Project Blue Book at Wright-Patterson Field. It had been bent by a blow from the side, rather than by impact with a hard, solid target during flight. Since there was no perceptible material clinging to its still-sharp tip, I was not able to determine what the hunter's robot was made of from analysis of that material. I returned the arrow point to Project Blue Book. I don't know what they did with it, but it's their baby. If Colonel Quintanilla ever reads this, he will know I was happy to give it back.

## Snippy's Ascent To Heaven

The phone rang insistently as callers from California to Connecticut and abroad asked for confirmation and further information about the horse in Colorado which had been mysteriously killed, its neck strangely sliced, and the flesh stripped completely from its neck and head by somebody or something from a UFO.

The story, as we had received it, was that Snippy, an Appaloosa horse, was found dead on the ranch near Alamosa, Colorado, where he was pastured. Snippy had been missing for two days and was the object of a search by the rancher. When the rancher found Snippy, the horse not only was dead, with no tracks about, but the bleached bones of his head and neck, eerily denuded of skin and flesh, lay intact and still attached to the rest of the carcass. The cut at the horse's shoulders was so sharp and smooth that it could not have been made with an ordinary knife. There was no blood remaining either in the carcass or on the ground.

The conditions of the carcass seemed so strange to the rancher that he returned to the site the next day with his sister, who had owned Snippy, and her husband. UFOs had been seen frequently in the area before Snippy's death. The exposed bones had turned a bright pink, and a strange sweet odor pervaded the atmosphere. Searching the area around the horse, the trio found fifteen circular marks which appeared to be "exhaust marks" and a circular region about twenty feet in diameter in which the brush had been squashed to within ten inches of the ground. Near this region, Snippy's owner found a piece of the horse's flesh wrapped in a piece of the skin. She picked it up to find it extremely sticky, so she dropped it. Her hand began to

117

burn and turn red and continued to burn until she washed it.

On another check of the area, the searchers found more flattened brush and six indentations, each two inches across and four inches deep, forming a circle three feet in diameter. The searchers were convinced that Snippy's death was not by natural causes and was directly related to UFOs seen in the area. Snippy's owner, however, sought in vain to have authorities check the incident.

Two weeks after the discovery of the dead Snippy, a forestry official with a civil defense Geiger counter checked the area and found the exhaust marks and squashed brush regions to be radioactive, as was some of the material picked up in the vicinity of the dead horse. The bones had burned black. It also had been learned that the rancher's aged mother had seen a large object pass over the ranch house on the day the horse was believed to have disappeared. She said she didn't have her glasses on at the time and was unable to tell just what it was.

The story of the bizarre death of Snippy hit the newspapers and also was brought to our attention nearly a month after the event. New details appeared. A dark, sticky, tar-like substance had been seen on the ground beneath the horse's neck. Speculation was rampant. Word of Snippy's demise traveled more swiftly than the lightning which the local sheriff had said probably killed the horse. It was said that the Snippy story even made headlines in *El Ahram*, the Cairo daily newspaper.

I had taken the phone call which informed the Colorado Project of the incident. After listening to the story, I recommended that we sit tight and watch developments from a distance. It seemed to me I could nearly smell that horse, dead now nearly a month, all the way from Alamosa to Boulder. I was not inclined to take the report seriously, for members of this ranching family had reported UFO sightings previously and were quite aware of the existence of our project. Yet the horse's owner, who "sought

118

in vain to have authorities check the incident," had not mentioned a word of this incident to us—before or after she finally broke the story in the *Pueblo Chieftain* newspaper, for which she also happened to be the Alamosa correspondent. Had there been an honest desire to learn if Snippy had been the victim of probing unearthly visitors, I felt we would have been called in immediately after the discovery of the weird condition of the carcass.

Watching developments from a distance did not prove feasible. Public interest in the Snippy story was too intense, and clamor for official inquiry and comment became demanding. I sidestepped a suggestion that I go to Alamosa to investigate the Snippy case, partly because I was standing by for a possible flight to the state of Washington where UFO sightings reportedly were in progress at the time, and partly because, having grown up on a ranch, I thought I knew what investigation of a month-dead horse would reveal. Fred Ayer, a nuclear physicist on the project staff, volunteered to check Snippy and the multitude of vague UFO sighting reports in the region.

Additional discoveries were made before Fred got to Alamosa, and the newspapers had new fuel with which to intrigue their fascinated readers, most of whom apparently wanted it to be true that Snippy had been done in by visitors from outer space. A "prominent Denver pathologist and blood specialist," who wished to remain anonymous, had performed an autopsy on the Appaloosa horse, Snippy, and found mysterious absence of expected contents of the brain cavity, spinal column, and abdominal cavity. He told the Associated Press that absence of organs in the abdominal cavity was completely unexplainable, as there was no sign of entrance into the horse's body. The absence of abdominal organs and brain did not surprise the pathologist too much, however, for he had read of similar incidents in other countries. He was most puzzled by the absence of any material

119

in the center of the spinal column. Support to the belief that the horse's death was UFO-related was provided by the fact that after the pathologist returned to the ranch house, he and the entire ranch group stood on the porch and watched two unidentified flying objects pass over the house.

Fred Ayer reported that the claims of high radiation counts in the area were false, and the vicinity around Snippy was so thoroughly trampled by the several hundred curious people who had been there that investigation of "broken bushes" was not worthwhile. He called for expert assistance in examining the carcass, and Dr. Robert Adams, chief of surgery at the outstanding College of Veterinary Medicine at Colorado State University, agreed to conduct this examination.

Dr. Adams found evidence on the badly decayed carcass that the animal had suffered from a severe infection in the hind quarters that was adequate to cause the animal's death. The throat of the dying animal probably had been cut with a knife in a final human act of mercy. The absence of nervous tissue from the brain and spinal cord and viscera from the abdominal cavity was the normal and expected condition several weeks after death, for, as Dr. Adams pointed out, these are some of the first tissues to degenerate.

In spite of this finding and the lack of substantial evidence that Snippy's demise had anything other than earthly causes, the belief that the horse had been the victim of mysterious beings from the unknown was too appealing to some people for them to be willing to give it up. Four months later, a newsletter of the NICAP Massachusetts Subcommittee, which has as its chairman one of the most level-headed and capable of UFO investigators, carried the following additional data on Snippy:

NICAP has informed the Chairman through the Affiliate/Subcommittee Newsletter that several curious aspects have evolved from university studies of the "Snippy the Horse" case (see pg. 4, the U.F.O. INVESTIGATOR, Vol. IV, No. 2, October 1967). These aspects include: The horse's bones have turned to dust, portions of the horse's flesh were cooked, that the animal's tail glows in the dark, and that a black goo-like substance from underneath the carcass which turned to white powder contains unspecified living organisms.

Although strangeness, credibility, and detailed knowledge of UFO events all seem to increase proportionately with geographic distance from those events, I was rather astonished to read of these weird developments on Snippy's remains—for just the prior evening, I had seen a TV news item showing Snippy's full and firm skeleton as it had been reassembled for display in Alamosa by veterinarian Dr. Wallace Leary. During the reassembly, Dr. Leary had found two bullet holes in the right thigh and left pelvis which seemed "very probably related" to the infection Dr. Adams had noted. At last report, Snippy's skeleton was still a prime tourist attraction in Alamosa.

## Three Thousand Pounds—In the St. Lawrence River

Mosquitoes by the hundreds were chewing us up as we looked at "the mysterious chunk of hardware" which then rested in the yard of the home of an officer of the Royal Canadian Air Force. The officer was a member of the Ottawa New Sciences Club. The club secretary and her husband had graciously driven me from my hotel in Ottawa to the Colonel's home to see the mysterious metal and talk with club members.

The chunk of metal, said to weigh about 3000 pounds, had been moved from the point where it had been discovered in shallow water of the St. Lawrence River about twenty miles upstream from Quebec City. The founder of the Ottawa Flying Saucer Club, now known as the Ottawa New Sciences Club, had concluded that there were many micro-meteorites embedded in the surface of the chunk of metal and, therefore, it must have fallen to Earth after spending a long time in outer space. He had speculated that the metal had been part of a very large space ship that had met disaster after entering our solar system. The gentleman who drew these conclusions was Mr. Wilbert Smith, a capable electrical engineer who headed Project Magnet, a UFO investigation project which, during the period 1950–1954, enjoyed some degree of official Canadian sanction. His opinions, in view of his record of scientific achievement, were not to be taken lightly. Because of belief in his speculation, numerous chemical analyses had been carried out, and widespread interest had been shown in the object.

The chunk of metal was not homogenous, consisting of irregular layers of differing composition. Analyses by the Canadian Arsenals Research and Development Establishment (CARDE) and by the Mines Branch of the Department of Mines and Technical Surveys had shown it to be high-maganese austenitic steel. These analysts judged it to be of terrestrial origin, probably foundry waste.

Those who believed the metal was something far more significant to the human race than foundry waste did not accept this conclusion. Their own investigators checked the original story printed in a Quebec newspaper, which identified the chunk of metal as one of two fragments of a fiery object which fell out of the sky, accompanied by a tremendous sonic boom, between 3 and 4 A.M.. on 12 June 1960. They had been unable to locate anyone in the vicinity of the "fall" who had either seen the fiery object or heard the sonic boom. The metal had merely been found in the river by beachcombers who, because of the size of the chunk, were unable to haul it away and sell it for scrap metal, as they did its smaller "companion." The local people with whom they spoke all knew about the "rusty old iron," but none supported the idea it fell from the sky. The "foundry waste" conclusion of CARDE, which picked the chunk up for investigation after receiving word of the discovery of a massive part of a space capsule, did not deter believers of the Ottawa Flying Saucer Club, who clung to the contention that the chunk of metal had a very mysterious nature and source. The colonel had gotten the metal from CARDE and, with some difficulty because of its weight, had transported it to his home where it now was under our visual scrutiny. The Spring 1966 issue of the club's newsletter, *Topside,* discussed the mysterious chunk of hardware at Ottawa:

On the outside property to the Headquarters of the Ottawa New Sciences Club, there lies a large piece of metal—an unidentified object which has so far baffled all attempts at positive identification and over which an aura of mystery hangs as to its exact composition, purpose, origin, and most of all, the unusual circumstances surrounding the finding of this large chunk of hardware in the St. Lawrence River of Quebec. This piece of metal measures about 4 ft. by 6 ft. and is roughly oval in shape, somewhat like an inverted mushroom, i.e. flat on top and roughly hemispherical on the underside. A plug or post about 9" in diameter, at 90 degrees to the flat surface, penetrates the centre of the mass and extends through top and bottom surfaces. A smaller protuberance, which may be the remains of a 2-1/2" pipe, appears out of the flat surface near the plug. The weight is estimated at about 3000 pounds. The weight is made up of layers of material which evidently have been subjected to very high temperatures and pressure.

123

The material is ferrous, extremely hard, and resistant to all attempts to cut or dismantle it. It is faintly magnetic until melted when it seems to acquire approximately the magnetic permeability of mild steel.

After telling of the history of the find and giving results of CARDE analyses, the *Topside* story continued for pages, casting doubt on the CARDE conclusion that the piece of metal was foundry waste, and arguing that its origin was still mysterious. The author clung to the belief that minute inclusions near the metal surface may well be micro-meteorites picked up during a long sojourn in space.

Two years later, the Winter 1968 *Topside* continued the arguments which, I thought, contributed little to the knowledge of UFOs as such, but revealed significant information about the desire to believe in the reality of the presence of Space Brothers. There were several pages of discussions of numerous and repeated efforts to analyze the metal and arguments that certain aspects of various analyses were mysterious. The conclusion was that the mystery of the unidentified hardware remained unsolved, although there appeared to be even stranger indications that the metal may be of extraterrestrial origin.

As I looked at the "mysterious metal," my hosts offered to get whatever samples I wished to take from it. The chunk did look to me for all the world like ordinary foundry waste. They brought a sledge hammer, with which we knocked off a small protruding piece which I placed in my briefcase for reasons that were not entirely clear, for it seemed the material had already been analyzed adequately. While I had little immediate interest in the sample, I was keenly interested in learning why the club members clung so tenaciously to the belief that this metal might have been part of a space ship. Was it merely because that belief had been held by the late Wilbert Smith, whom they regarded with such high esteem? I welcomed the invitation into the Colonel's house, away from those voracious mosquitoes, to learn why club members refused to give up the space ship idea in the face of contradicting evidence. The Colonel made this quite clear.

"We were told, through a medium," he said, "that this was part of a space ship twenty miles long and three miles in diameter which was destroyed (by meteorite collision or other catastrophe) and was derelict in space. The people 'topside' wanted to clear the derelict from space because man was getting interested in flying around there, and they didn't want it to cause mishaps. They sent segments to Earth, Mars, and other planets to get rid of them. These pieces on Earth so originated."

Their faith in revelations received through a spiritual medium during seance obviously was stronger than their faith in man's knowledge of nature as obtained through the methods of his science. This fact did not surprise me, for, consciously or subconsciously, Western Man has traditionally accepted divine revelation as the most certain source of knowledge. What puzzled me was the repeated demand for scientific analysis and use of arguments of scientific vein to refute undesired scientific results. Eight years after the CARDE analysis, the group was still seeking additional analyses, and the club secretary suggested I might get additional information from Dr. Eric Smith, Chief, Metal Physics Section of Canada Department of Energy, Mines, and Resources. Dr. Smith had samples of the metal and was awaiting completion of installation of new equipment from Japan, with which he would conduct thorough tests and analyses.

When I later contacted Dr. Smith, he said he indeed planned to analyze the material, but he wouldn't be at all surprised if it came from the Sorel Iron Foundries, Sorel, Quebec, more than fifty miles upstream from the site where the material was found. He said production of high-manganese steel is one of the specialties of this foundry, and it is standard practice to dig a hole in

The "mysterious" piece of metal found in the Ottawa River. New Science Club members considered it a part of exploded flying space vehicle.

sand and dump surplus or non-specification molten material into it. A plug often is inserted so the accumulated mass can be grasped for moving by a crane. Such waste is not utilized or recovered because of its uncertain composition. Dr. Smith said, further, that large chunks of such waste are known to have been buried around a foundry of the Sorel type. His description of the material matched the chunk of metal in the Colonel's yard precisely.

The Colonel and his friends were quite aware of previous analytical results, and probably also were aware of Dr. Eric Smith's expectations. This had little influence on their belief, however. The Colonel expressed to me his feeling that, while his chunk of metal does have all the characteristics of waste from a foundry when viewed in the realm of three-dimensional physical existence, "when viewed in a wider framework, the interface of this dimension with other dimensions, which parallel the physical, it well may be part of a space ship."

While I readily admit the limitations of present-day science, it wasn't, and isn't, clear to me why this kind of argument couldn't apply to any object on earth, including the Colonel's shoe. The "mysterious chunk of metal" was a fetish. Why, then, the insistent demand for repeated physical and chemical examination of something whose ultimate significance was considered to reside in psychic or spiritual realms?

I visited with the Colonel and his associates long into the evening. The Colonel did most of the talking. The conversation failed to provide hints as to why anyone should expect metallorgraphic examination or chemical analysis to bridge a gap between physical and psychic aspects of reality, whether they be parallel aspects or existent in the same unity. Perhaps my knowledge of parapsychology was too limited, and I simply did not comprehend the Colonel's thoughts in sufficient depth to appreciate their value. Man seemingly still has much to learn about interactions between the material world and the mental or imaginary. The impressive success of current physical science, however, belies the existence of certain kinds of direct interaction of psychic and physical events. The Colonel told me of the club founder's efforts to build a device which would detect the presence of a mentally-directed "tensor energy," an energy which could alter gravitational effects and influence the motion of airplanes and other physical objects. Mr. Smith believed this type of energy was not tenuated by distance and was used by the "space people." According to the Colonel, Mr. Smith had created an experimental mechanism which, during one operation, successfully picked up indication of the existence of "Tensor Energy" in specific areas around town. Once the equipment was shut down, however, its detection function could not be resur-

127

rected "because we are not conditioned to control this type of energy."

Any student of elementary mechanics would recognize, of course, that if the motion of objects could be influenced by mental powers possessed by man, or by any other being commonly present in the environment, there would be apparently "magic" and unpredictable changes in an object's motion due to application of those powers by unknown beings, and the science of mechanics would not exist. The fact that rocket ships can be sent to the moon, and computers can be programmed to predict accurately the future positions of rocket ships, planets, and other objects, testifies to the absence of arbitrary, mentally-directed forces which act on physical objects.

As best I could, I tried to follow the Colonel's thoughts. Certainly psychological considerations had deep significance in flying saucer phenomena. Perhaps flying saucer observations, or reports of observations, could furnish some enlightening new knowledge regarding an association between material and psychic realms. Although I wasn't certain I was even asking the right questions, this conversation seemed to be an interesting mental exercise. Nonetheless, I considered both such questions and their answers to be beyond the scope of my assignment of evaluating purported physical evidence that flying saucers have visited Earth. My cryptic memorandum for project files ended with the simple comment, "No further project consideration of the 'mysterious chunk of hardware in Ottawa' is anticipated."


## Space Brothers "Topside"

Checking the "mysterious" hardware in the St. Lawrence River resulted in my reading back issues of *Topside*, the publication of the group originally called the Ottawa Flying Saucer Club.

The messages contained therein seemed directly in line with expectations of famed psychologist C. G. Jung, one of the founders of psychoanalysis.

Jung, who expressed his view in his book entitled *Flying Saucers: A Modern Myth of Things Seen in the Skies*, considered UFOs a significant living legend emerging from a vital human psychic need and a situation of collective distress and danger.

In his view, belief in UFOs as extraterrestrial manufactured vehicles fulfills a general psychic need for a savior acceptable to technologically-oriented societies.

The UFOs can, of course, function as effectively—perhaps more so—in this capacity if they don't exist (in the physical world) than if they do. If they don't exist, believers are in the clear, for the non-existence of such vehicles can never be proven—by scientific or any other means. If they do exist, then that existence could be proved upon acquisition of appropriate evidence. If—alas for our UFO brothers and the fondest dreams of believers—an extraterrestrial saucer should be so unfortunate as to be captured by man, not only would its existence be established beyond doubt, but also something of its nature, and the nature of its creators, would be determined. Human imagination would then no longer be free to create that nature according to desire, and disillusionment is the likely result—as it was when man learned that the moon, planets, and stars were made of ordinary earthly stuff rather than of the quintessence.

Members of the Ottawa Flying Saucer Club were by no means unique in their beliefs regarding the role of flying saucers in human affairs. I have encountered similar attitudes frequently in various parts of the United States as well as Canada, and I suspect such views are common elsewhere. People who express such views include a significant number with scientific backgrounds, and with training in techniques of discerning fact from fantasy. The founder of the Ottawa Flying Saucer Club, Mr.

Wilbert B. Smith, held a master's degree in electrical engineering and a responsible position in the Canadian government. He was the author of several technical papers and a half dozen patents. He considered himself competent to study and report on phenomena of a scientific nature and attempted to apply standard scientific methods to his investigations of flying saucers.

Mr. Smith based his initial conclusion that UFOs were extraterrestrial vehicles on testimony of witnesses and physical evidence which he accepted as valid. His views regarding the nature and purpose of saucer occupants, whom his club members referred to as Space Brothers Topside, however, were revealed to him in a series of communications with, in his words, "intelligence claiming to be extraterrestrial."

In 1963, *Topside* published a collection of Mr. Wilbert Smith's writings. They included the following:

> Furthermore, when the material given to us through the many channels is all assembled and analyzed, it adds up to a complete and elegant philosophy which makes our efforts sound like the beating of jungle drums. These people tell us of a magnificent Cosmic Plan, of which we are a part, which transcends the lifetime of a single person or a nation, or a civilization, or even a planet or a solar system. We are not merely told that there is something beyond our immediate experience; we are told what it is, why it is, and our relation thereto. Many of our most vexing problems are solved with few words; at least we are told of the solutions if we have the understanding and fortitude to apply them. We are told of the inadequacies of our science which is at once simple and yet more embracing than the mathematical monstrosity which we have conjured up. We have been told of a way of life which is Utopian beyond our dreams,

and the means of attaining it. Can it be that such a self-consistent magnificent philosophy is the figment of the imaginations of a number of misguided morons? I do not think so. . . We may summarize the entire flying saucer picture as follows. We have arrived at a time in our development when we must make a final choice between right and wrong. The people from elsewhere are much concerned about the choice we will make, partly it will have its repercussions on them and partly because we are their blood brothers and (they) are truly concerned with our welfare. There is a cosmic law against interfering in the affairs of others, so they are not allowed to help us directly even though they could easily do so. We must make our own choice of our own free will. Present trends indicate a series of events which may require the help of these people and they stand by ready and willing to render that help. In fact, they have already helped us a great deal, along lines which do not interfere with our freedom of choice. In time, when certain events have transpired, and we are so oriented that we can accept these people from elsewhere, they will meet us freely on the common ground of mutual understanding and trust, and we will be able to learn from them and bring about the Golden Age all men everywhere desire deep within their hearts.

Mr. Smith's statement could well be entitled "Christianity Revisited." The Christian beliefs are retained intact—free will; cosmic law; divine revelation; special position of Man in the universe; concern of God for Man; a mediator that is both God and man; benevolence of the mediator; willingness and ability of the mediator to help those who have faith; even the promise of a second coming of the savior and of a return to the Garden of

Eden (Golden Age).

Dr. Jung's observation that flying saucers provide a savior acceptable to technically-oriented societies is especially well illustrated in various *Topside* articles and in verbal expressions of Ottawa New Sciences Club members, who were fully confident that our Space Brothers Topside stand watch over us, ready to save their Earth brothers from self-destruction.

Christians traditionally long for a Second Coming of Christ, yet many realize that, in today's cultures, a human child born in a manger—or in a mansion—of whatever color, sex, or parentage, about whom special holiness is claimed, would not be recognized or accepted as a Man-God. A human being traveling about the globe proclaiming to be the Christ would face not only rejection and shunning but possible incarceration in a "nuthouse"—unless he arrived on Earth in a great ball of fire, or in a flying saucer!


## Line Statistics: The Evidence (Properly Treated) Can Support Any Predilection


The UFO "cases" displayed above are presented here to illustrate the responses of human minds which are governed by the desire to believe in the reality of flying saucers. The ready rejection or alteration of undesired information, weighting of desired information far beyond its merit, acceptance of contradiction without concern or question, and eager consumption of rumor as fact are direct consequences of The Will to Believe. Such responses, however, are by no means limited to the UFO field, for they are encountered daily in all areas where human predilections are involved.

Irrational responses growing from the will not to believe in UFOs could as well be illustrated. For example, in 1956, a detailed analysis of UFO movies taken six years earlier in Great Falls, Montana, was submitted to the Air Force by Dr. R. M. L. Baker, then with Douglass Aircraft Corporation. The analysis involved instrumented measurements and model mock-ups of sun-reflection situations. Although the lengthy report of the analysis contained a single hedging admission that there was similarity in appearance of airplane reflections with the images visible on the film, the report dealt primarily with data which tended to rule out airplane reflections as the correct identification of the UFO images. The gist of Dr. Baker's report was that the UFO images did not appear to be caused by any objects commonly present in our skies. Yet, the writers of Air Force letters and classified memoranda latched upon Dr. Baker's one hedging remark and treated it as if it expressed the results of his study. They did not hesitate to state that "an extremely able and very detailed analysis performed by the scientific laboratory of one of America's largest aircraft companies" concluded that "aircraft reflections might possibly look like images on the film." Thus, with no mention whatever of Dr. Baker's arguments against this conclusion, they used reference to his work to give the prestige of scientific analysis to their belief that the two objects filmed were ordinary aircraft. Whether or not either Air Force or Dr. Baker's conclusions were correct, the tactic is that of the propagandist. Our desires and illusions continue to determine what we see in the world around us—and what we believe of the testimony of witnesses.

# Chapter 9

# The Inexplicable Observations of a B-47 Crew

The Colonel's voice was quivering perceptibly as he related an encounter, ten years past, with a huge glowing object which paced the B-47 he commanded. He obviously had been deeply impressed by the experience and was puzzled and concerned about what he and his crew members might have seen. The fact that he had such an encounter had been revealed somewhat incidentally at a Colorado Project meeting of air base UFO officers when he asked Major Quintanilla to look, after his return to Wright-Patterson Air Base, at the Project Blue Book files for a report of an encounter with a strange object which he himself had experienced about the 18th of September, 1957, while on a flight over the Gulf of Mexico and southern U.S. Although they had reported the event at the time, the Colonel and his crew had never been told what it was that toyed with them for over two hours. It was brightly visible and also emitted radar waves such that it must have generated fantastic energy, unbelievable for any air-borne source. The Colonel was very curious to know what it was, and was anxious for Major Quintanilla to dig this information out for him.

The fact that no report of the incident was present in Blue Book files only served to deepen the mystery. I had taken a personal interest in the case, and, over a period of several months, had sought, through all conceivable channels and with the cooperation of numerous Air Force information officers and other personnel, to locate any report of the UFO incident and data which the Colonel said had been recorded on the flight and picked up by Intelligence personnel when his plane landed. At times, I had found myself as interested in determining where the information was and why it was not in Blue Book files as I was in the contents of the information. After several months of patient effort, however, I had added up the score of what I had learned. It added up to zero, zilch. I had uncovered no evidence whatever that any report of the incident had ever existed. In hopes of opening up new leads to elusive filed information, as well as getting details of the experience itself, I had come to Malstrom Air Force Base in Montana to start over again on this investigation.

I was sitting in the office of Lt. Colonel Lewis D. Chase, Chief of the Operations Division at Malstrom, and Colonel Chase was recalling the experience, which he had pondered many times in the past ten years.

Occasionally, I interrupted the Colonel with a question. The blaring noise of jet planes just outside the building did not bother him, though we occasionally had to pause to await its abatement.

The UFO he was telling me about did bother the Colonel, and he was obviously shaken as he recounted the event to me.

Colonel: We had taken off that night on a combined gunnery, navigation, and what we call a—we had a special type of airplane with a special crew in the back and part of the mission was theirs. We took off from Forbes, flew down over the southwest Texas coast—Almagordo I think is the island—and to a gunnery range there in the Gulf of Mexico. After the gunnery mission, we went out over the Gulf of Mexico on a night celestial mission. This is a practice for the navigator. Then we coasted in, as I remember, at Biloxi, Mississippi—we came back in over the continent. At this point, we terminated the navigation mission and started the Raven mission—this monitoring of electronic signals by our crew in the back. We have what we call a Raven One, a Raven Two, and a Raven Three on the crew. Each man works a different frequency spectrum band.

The number Two Raven at that time was working the frequency band that a radar of the type FTS-5 would operate. As we approached the coast, he picked up a signal that was equivalent to what he thought was an FTS-5. Now, this is a very large ground installation type of radar signal. Our equipment is passive—we listen. However, there was one thing strange about this signal—it was moving up-scope! Well, needless to say, an FTS-5 type installation always moves down the scope, regardless of what direction the aircraft is going. If it's a ground installation, it moves down scope on you. The operator told us later he wasn't too concerned about it and thought, "Well, I've got 180-degree ambiguity in the equipment." Thinking that piece of equipment was not operative, he changed his frequency band. They do this by changing black boxes.

Well, we flew inland up as far as Jackson, Mississippi. That was a turning point, and then we were to work due West toward the Fort Worth-Dallas area because there are quite a number of GCI type installations out there our boys could work against, practicing cuts and things of this nature. Just after we made the turn at Jackson, I saw this real bright light out ahead of us that looked as though it was coming toward us at about our altitude. We were flying at about—knowing the B-47 and the fact that we had now been out about five hours—probably around 35,000 feet. He looked as though he was at the same level. So I called the crew and told them to stand by, that we might have to take violent elusive action. "Make sure your seat belts are fastened, 'cause I might have to go up or down in a hurry." Well, this light— I don't know—at an impossible closure rate, this thing came from where it was to right across the nose of the airplane. I didn't have any time to react at all. That's how fast it was. It went out to about the two o'clock position, and all the lights on it went out. So, sign of the times, the co-pilot and I started an interchange. I asked him, "Jim," I said, "Did you see that?" He gave me some remark like, "Well, I did if you did!" He wasn't going to admit anything. Then one of us made the remark that it must be a flying saucer. You know, we were laughing about this on the interphone. When the guy in the back end heard this, he took the piece of equipment he had been working and returned to the frequency where he had picked up this thing moving up-scope. So pretty soon he called me and he says, "Major Chase, it's out at your 2 o'clock position." Now, he can take azimuth, you know, and he can interpret the characteristics of the type of signal. Sure enough, he picked up the same thing he had before, now at our 2 o'clock position, and holding on the same azimuth. Now mind, we're moving at about 425 true air speed, and he stays at this 2 o'clock position!

Craig: And could you still see it visually?

Colonel: Oh, no. No, this was at night and all the lights are gone now. The only thing we have is this piece of equipment on him, in the back. So, I thought, well, I'll try something, you know. So I reached up and pulled the power back on the airplane— slowed way down. Oh, maybe a hundred knots. He stayed at exactly the same azimuth—2 o'clock. So, then I speeded back up, only this time I went to max speed. Same thing. Stayed there. So I called the center and I told them, "Something up here, but I'm not sure what's going on. I'd like to go over to ground control radar to see if we can get any confirmation on what we are picking up." Of course, we are on a flight clearance plan with the center and we've got to stick to that flight plan unless the center relieved us—which, of course, they did. They said, "You're cleared over to GCI frequency to work with them. Call us when you're done." So, I went over to GCI and, of course, picked up the net from the Fort Worth-Dallas area. We were headed toward Fort Worth-Dallas now. I called them and they said, "Roger, we have you. We have the both of you on the scope!"

Craig: By "the both of you," did they mean you and the target?

Colonel: Yes. Myself and the target. And they gave me at this time ten miles range. Now, they can also range me, where we can only azimuth. So, again I go through the procedure, when he calls the ten-mile range, of the slow up, the speed up, and everything, and they keep calling, "ten mile range." Regardless of what I do, it stays at ten miles.

Craig: Did you try turning?

Colonel: No. Not this time. I guess we were fifty to seventy-five miles from the Fort Worth-Dallas area, coming in like this between the two cities. At this point, the guy in the back called me and said, "Lew, they are starting to move up scope on us." Now, whatever the source of energy or whatever it was, it was moving ahead of us.

Craig: Was it still about ten miles away?

Colonel: It stayed exactly ten miles. It changed its position to in front of us and kept that range. Now, I don't know whether that has significance or not, but the range stayed ten miles even when we moved up.

Craig: Which specific radar installation was giving you this information?

Colonel: Well, I wouldn't know the specific tower, but they are pretty well spotted in there. In fact, they could follow me all the way from there, all the way back home.

Craig: Was there a particular control base, though, which was giving you this information? I don't know how they were organized at that time.

Colonel: I don't know either, Dr. Craig. I can't answer the question of just who. We had a frequency to call GCI, and we talked with them a lot because we worked with them.

Craig: You don't know the frequency, of any way I could . . .

Colonel: I don't remember that any more, but that information isn't hard to come by. ADC could give you that information.

Craig: Okay.

Colonel: Okay. Well, after he got out directly ahead of me, then all the lights came on again. He's now right dead ahead of me. GCI is tracking him for us at ten miles. So, then, I floorboard the thing again to max and take off after him. Now, a light at night—this was just a huge red glow. That was all it was at this time. It appeared to me that he'd stopped dead. Now, I'm going as fast as that B-47 will go, but all of a sudden the closure rate is tremendous. Just as I got almost over him, the light goes out, GCI loses him on the ground, and I lose him on my equipment.

Craig: You were over him this time?

Colonel: Yes. Like I say, we were at this high speed and it appeared to me he'd stopped and we passed over the top of him. But, just as we got up close to him, the lights go out. I started to turn immediately to the left, but it takes you thirty miles to turn that thing when you're wide open, because of the small wing lift that it has. Just about the time we got about half way around the turn, my boy in the back called me and says, "I have him again. From our position, he should be just West of Fort Worth, around

139

Mineral Wells."—I think that's the name of the little town. So I called GCI, and they said, "Roger, we have him. We have him on the scope again." So, as I came around, about half way around the turn, we picked him up with the lights on again. Only now down at a lower altitude. I told GCI that I estimate him to be at about 15,000 feet. I said I'd like to go down on him and they said, "Roger. We have the traffic in the Fort Worth area cleared out. It's clear to go down."

They were talking with the center at the time. I didn't know this at the time, but they were trying to get fighters off. So, I started to dive down at max air speed and it looked to me as though he was stationary. Again, I can't tell because my speed is so high. I don't know whether I'm just closing on him that fast or what the case is. But, I estimate that I got down to 15,000 feet, and—I guess at about five nautical miles—the lights go out, he goes off my scope, and he goes off the GCI. He's completely gone.

Now, at this point—I've been out for a while now. Playing around with the jet, it's been eating fuel pretty fast. So I look down at the gauges, and I figure, "Okay, I've got to start back for Forbes if I'm going to get there." So, using the excess speed that I had, I pulled up to 20,000 feet and started north of Fort Worth toward Oke City. Just used the speed and climbed to 20,000 feet and asked the center for that altitude and they said, "Roger. You can use that altitude." Well, I hadn't any more than leveled off when my boy in the back calls me and he says, "Lew, we've got company. Behind us this time—behind us." So, again GCI confirmed this. Well, they told me they were trying to launch fighters in the area. We're pulled up now and we're headed at a pretty good speed toward Oke City. Well, they passed me off from one GCI site to another as we went up the line—and he stayed, according to their scopes and my azimuth, directly behind us at ten miles.

Craig: He liked that ten mile range!

Colonel: Yes. So we went on up. We crossed Oke City. And, just as we got to Oke City, my boy in the back tells me, "His signal is fading out!" And they lost him on GCI. So, right in the Oke City area is where we lost him.

Then, of course, we went on in and landed at Forbes and Intelligence people met us at the aircraft and talked with us—picked up—we had wire-tape recorders that we could record what went on—and picked up that—and I don't know what else they picked up from our boys in the back.

Craig: This wire recording would have been your conversation during the event?

Colonel: Yes.

At this point in the recounting, the commander of the base dropped in to convey his regards and assured me that if there were any privilege he could extend, or any accommodations or transportation I desired, he would certainly see that they were furnished. I appreciated his friendly, cooperative attitude, which was typical of that shown by top level officers at various air bases I visited while working on the UFO project. I thanked him for the offer as he hurried off to keep a chopper from interfering with the honors ceremonies that were then in progress on the field.

Some information I wanted was still missing, so Colonel Chase and I sat back down and talked for another hour or more. I probed for details that might help me locate the wire recordings and the reports which were presumably written subsequent to the event. I also probed for more details that might help illuminate the nature of the strange visitor.

A check of flight records revealed that the event must have occurred between midnight and 3 A.M. on 19 September 1957. The first light, which the Colonel had initially thought was that of an aircraft before it shot past the nose of the plane, was pure white. However, when the strange source later moved ahead of

141

the B-47, it was a solid red, steady glow. It was huge—not a small ball of fire like the "foo-fighters" seen by World War II pilots. The Colonel thought it was more the size of a barn than the size of a basketball. He saw no shape to the object, just an apparently symmetrical red glow.

The six crew members were now scattered about the world. The two with whom I was most interested in talking, however, co-pilot Captain James McCoid and No. 2 Raven operator Captain Frank McClure, now Majors, were both on active duty at Offutt Air Base in Nebraska, and I could get in touch with them later.

Colonel Chase didn't know what air base fighter craft would have been scrambled from and couldn't remember where he sent the lengthy Intelligence questionnaire he and his crew filled out some time after the event. After talking recently with Major Quintanilla, the Colonel did not think the report ever got to Blue Book. There were no leads here for me to follow. Although he didn't recall doing so, the Colonel was certain he also would have had to send a written report of the event to his commanding officer at the time, for his mission had not been completed as originally planned. Perhaps such a report would be recorded in the Wing history.

The Colonel felt that Majors McClure and McCoid probably would be able to tell me more than he could about what happened to the wire recordings and other information picked up by Intelligence people when the B-47 landed. I hoped this would be true, since I had to have new leads if I were ever to locate such information.

Before I had a chance to talk with Majors McClure and McCoid, a group of ten outstanding scientists who specialize in research related to plasmas (gases in ionized condition) met with us in Boulder to consider the possibility that localized atmospheric plasmas could be responsible for a significant number of UFO reports. An editor of *Aviation Week and Space Technology* had claimed that many UFO reports could be so explained. Since the UFO that Colonel Chase had encountered was a glowing mass without sharp boundaries, displaying some characteristics similar to the "ball lightning" type of plasma phenomenon, we chose Colonel Chase's report as one of those to be heard by the group. His UFO had, of course, according to his account, displayed behavior difficult to explain in terms of any known phenomenon. It traveled faster than airplanes. It emitted visible light, but not constantly, and also apparently emitted, as well as reflected, 2800 megahertz radar waves. It vanished and reappeared inexplicably, and in pacing the B-47, it displayed behavior indicative of intelligent control.

After hearing this UFO report and other somewhat related ones, and discussing UFOs and plasmas for several hours, one participant asked if there were more reasons for relating the UFO descriptions to known characteristics of plasmas than there is, at this point in our knowledge, for relating them to extraterrestrial space ships. A leading plasma scientist , who desires not to be quoted when he makes such statements, responded in the negative, stating that on the basis of the sightings he thought the space ship explanation more probable than the plasma. It was obvious that he felt there must be a third choice some place, yet his dilemma brought forth good-natured merriment.

Majors McClure and McCoid met my plane as it arrived in Omaha. The day was Veterans' Day, an official holiday. They wore their uniforms nonetheless, so I could recognize them in the airport crowd.

Major McCoid had returned only that morning from a short tour of duty in Europe. I was startled at his youth and found it difficult to believe that this young officer, now apparently about thirty, had been co-pilot of the B-47 during the UFO event ten years previously. The event was etched deeply in his memory, however, as it was with Major McClure, who was Major McCoid's senior by at least ten years, and Colonel Chase. All three crew members had been profoundly impressed by that fantastic and puzzling experience a decade earlier.

The two officers drove me out to Offutt Air Force Base, which served as headquarters for the Strategic Air Command. Since this was a holiday, no one would be on duty at the Operations Building, and we could talk there without interruption.

A dozen large aircraft could be seen lined up on the field as we approached the Operations Building. Some of these were to be flown later that day. These were fully-equipped command ships, and one of them would soon take off, with an officer of General rank aboard, to relieve a similar command ship then in the air. The Strategic Air Command kept one general officer airborne at all times. If a nuclear attack wiped out everything below, this air-borne general still could give the order for retaliation.

I hesitated as the two officers started to enter the building. I was still scanning the sky, but seeing now only in imagination that isolated command ship which, to me, symbolized man's collective insanity. I shook my head to clear the cobwebs within and followed Majors McClure and McCoid through the door of the Operations Building.

Major McCoid, who had been co-pilot, and Major McClure, No. 2 Raven operator, gave an account of the 1957 incident which agreed in its principal features with that given by Colonel Chase. Some points were vague or uncertain in memory after the passage of ten years. They were most impressed, however, by the way "it" had disappeared suddenly, to reappear elsewhere. It seemed to have instant relocation capability, with no evident track between its point of disappearance and point of reappearance. Their account indicated two additional instrumented observations of the "object" which the Colonel hadn't mentioned.

144

McClure recalled that when he picked up the image after the joking comments about flying saucers on the intercom, the navigator, Tom Hanley, had tilted the antenna of his radar unit up and was actually tracking it with his radar. When Hanley gave the crew a bearing to the target, it exactly coincided with what McClure had.

McClure: Colonel Chase and Major McCoid were visually tracking this thing and I was able to get DF [direction] readings from it. Now, as I remember, the ground site would say, "We've lost the target." You two people would say, "It's out." They couldn't see the light they saw before. Hanley—all this happened simultaneously—he would remark, "I've lost my target." And my signal would go out in back, all like that. Just like you threw a switch and it all went off. Then, it would appear at another place, just seconds later. Oh, I could track movement when it went by us. I originally picked the signal up behind me. It went up to the right side of the aircraft and then it just hovered out there, out in front of us. Then we lost it, and then it turned up on the other side of the aircraft and moved clear around us, as I remember. But we would lose it from time to time.

Craig: But when you lost it, did all four people lose it at the same time?

McClure: Two different people were tracking on radar sets, two people were watching it visually, and I was watching it electronically. And this would all happen simultaneously. Whenever we'd lose it, we'd all lose it. There were no buts about it. It went off!

The second electronic image not previously mentioned was on the scope of No. 1 Raven operated by Captain Provenzano. This receiver covered all frequency ranges and showed the same image McClure observed. The third Raven unit was operating in a lower frequency range than the thing of interest was emitting. Its operator searched in vain for a signal to tie in with what everyone else was seeing.

My hopes of locating some original data on this incident were laid to rest with finality when Major McClure said they recorded no data on that flight. The officers explained that this was not a normal training mission in which Raven No. 2 data would have been wire recorded, and films would have been made of the display on the scope of Raven No. 1. This was, instead, a mission for equipment shakedown prior to deployment of plane and crew to England scheduled for the night of September 20. They fired their guns over the Gulf and all that, but since the object of the flight was just to see that everything worked right, they had taken neither film for the Raven No. 1 camera nor a magazine for the wire recorder aboard. There were no such data for the Intelligence people to pick up at the end of the mission.

The officers verified that the returning plane had been met by Intelligence representatives, who were given whatever information was available regarding the mission. I had already tried in vain to locate reports even they may have submitted. Apparently, no UFO report of the incident had reached Project Blue Book. The crew never heard any more about it. There is no reference to the incident in the history of the 55th Strategic Reconnaissance Wing of the Strategic Air Command, to which the B-47 was assigned at the time of the incident. Did reports of the incident go into special, still secret files? After pondering this question in relation to all my experiences in pursuing this case, I felt I had no good reason to think so. Did Intelligence people have knowledge of something men had put in the air, with which the B-47 crew was not familiar, which they determined to be responsible for the strange observations from the B-47? If this were the case, no report of a UFO should have been submitted to Blue Book. This was an ECM (electronic counter-measures) plane, flying during a period of involved activity in anticipation of the USSR satellite effort. It was two weeks before Sputnik I. Radar chaff, at least, probably was in the air. Yet, we had insufficient information to answer this question, and I saw no possibility of getting the additional information necessary for a satisfactory answer.

What did the B-47 crew encounter? Was it something ordinary, misinterpreted as a result of extraordinary weather or other conditions? Was it an unusual and unknown physical phenomenon in the atmosphere? Was it an extraordinary "thing" under unknown intelligent control?

I continued to wrestle with that primary question. The weather must have been clear, for Colonel Chase said he could see lights of towns below and McCoid said he remembered seeing burn-off flames at refinery plants in Texas. (McCoid said the thing he saw in the sky appeared somewhat similar to the burn-off flames, but there was no confusing the two.) Weather data for that day and time of day over Fort Worth showed a light temperature inversion at an altitude of 34,000 feet. The project's radar propagation consultant, Mr. Gordon Thayer, analyzing the weather data, felt that intense temperature inversion over localized areas at that altitude, capable of giving strong reflections at both radar and optical frequencies, was possible, and might, though this seemed improbable, account for certain aspects of the observations. Such accounting would be in terms of optical mirage of an airplane with landing lights on, distant city lights, and echoes or reflections of ground radar emissions. The "instant relocation" characteristic makes one support reflections rather than direct observation. The fact that the "thing" apparently gave off the same radar frequency as the ground radar installations (2800 megahertz) makes one suspect a ground radar relationship. Things did become confused at the time, and, on thinking it over, Major McClure felt that, after they got over

Dallas, the ground site signals did get mixed up with the signal they were especially concerned about. The original signal of concern, however, could not have been direct reception of ground radar, for it moved too fast on the scope and moved up-scope; had he been receiving reflections of ground radar, he would have expected stronger direct signals on the scope also, and there were none. The reported observations just would not fit into ordinary explanations in spite of certain situations which indicated they might.

Are we left with only the extraordinary conclusion, or do misinterpretation of observations and vagueness of memory open the door to explanation in terms of the ordinary?

The B-47 crew encountered something that seemed indeed extraordinary to them. They had a feeling it was interested in them, but they couldn't gain an advantage over it. It seemed to be under intelligent control, and had weird behavior characteristics. They do not know what it was. And neither do I.

In 1969, after completion of the Colorado Project and publication of the Condon Report, Dr. James McDonald pursued information about the B-47 case in the Air Force archives at Maxwell Air Force Base, Montgomery, Alabama, where the Project Blue Book files had been sent for preservation. To my surprise, he succeeded in locating the B-47 case file in the archives. The file contained the detailed report the plane crew remembered submitting to Air Defense Command shortly after the incident.

The Air Force claimed that all Blue Book reports were declassified in accordance with Air Force directives before deposition in the archives. Dr. McDonald found that this report had been classified during my search for it; however, that fact should not have kept the people I had asked for it from revealing its existence and making the classified report available to the Colorado Project and to Colonel Chase, upon the request he made to Blue Book.

The best recollections of the B-47 crew, and checks of their personal flight logs, had set the probable date of this UFO encounter at 19–20 September 1957, and it was a report of an event on these dates that I had requested from various sources. Dr. McDonald found that the correct date of the event was 17 July 1957, and Blue Book had received summary information on the incident from Air Defense Command on 25 October, more than three months after the event.

According to McDonald, the B-47 case is now carried in the official Blue Book files as "Identified as American Airlines Flight 655." Flight 655 may have had some involvement with the reported UFO incident. I can imagine, however, what Colonel Chase and the rest of his B-47 crew must think of this "explanation" of their puzzling experience which stretched over hundreds of miles as they played "tag" with something strange to them for about an hour and a half.

Beyond this "identification," the file McDonald located shed no further light on the nature of the radar-emitting ball of light the plane crew reportedly observed.

My immediate reaction, upon learning that Dr. McDonald had located the report of this incident in Air Force archives, was to wonder if the negative word to me was a result of indifference, incompetence, or intentional deception. Efforts to locate the intelligence report had been made at our request by Aerospace Defense Command Headquarters, which reported that neither intelligence files nor operations records contained any such report. Our inquiry directed to Strategic Air Command Headquarters had elicited a response from the Deputy Commander for Operations of the Air Wing involved. He said a thorough review of the Wing history failed to disclose any reference to a UFO incident on 19 September 1957. After a moment of reflection, however, I found it not really surprising that the report was not found, when the B-47 crew identified the date two months

149

and two days from the proper date. Blue Book reports were filed by date and location of the reported event, and Blue Book personnel might also be forgiven for telling Colonel Chase they had no report of his puzzling experience. For one to expect military personnel making a search of this type to display the brilliance and desire that Dr. McDonald applied to the effort would be unrealistic.

# Chapter 10

# Cloak and Dagger Work

The largest civilian organizations of flying saucer enthusiasts both freely expressed conspiracy theories stating that someone is conspiring to hide the truth about UFOs from the American people. One of these groups claimed that the upper echelons of the Air Force were the conspirators, while the other group felt it was the ubiquitous CIA keeping the UFO truths even from the Air Force itself. Since I considered anything possible, I watched, as we studied the UFO question, for any firm evidence of a secrecy conspiracy. Pursuit of such evidence, of course, itself had to be done secretly. This chapter deals with encounters related to that pursuit.

## A Clandestine Meeting at an Airport

I hesitated as I hung up the telephone. Multitudes of people were milling about the phone booth I occupied at a major west coast airport, yet at the moment I felt strangely alone. A tingling sensation made a fleeting passage up my backbone. If the claims I had just heard were true, and some section of the Air Force or other agency had vital information that was being withheld even from the official investigation project which the Air Force itself financed, then this project which I was working on had been established as a sham activity to reassure a deceived public that it was not being deceived by its own government. The implications were distressing. I wondered how I would handle the situation if the evidence I was about to receive proved genuine.

I had just agreed to meet a man I shall call Mr. Sheets at another west coast airport in less than three hours. After several weeks of effort, I had finally made telephone contact, and it sounded as if I might have hit a jackpot. Mr. Sheets not only could tell me about the pictures he claimed had been stolen from the Air Force, but he had acquired copies of the photographs which he would transfer to me if I would meet him this afternoon at the airport nearest his office.

I had never met Mr. Sheets, and, had he not been a reputable physicist with a large aeronautical company, I probably would have passed off as idle rumor his claims of knowledge of photographic proof of the existence of flying saucers. When someone of his apparently established technical competence and reputation for achievement makes such a claim, he must at least be given ample opportunity to produce the evidence. I was willing to protect identities of anyone involved in surreptitious removal of photographs from Air Force files or in getting those photographs to members of our project.

Mr. Sheets had apologized for not responding to my letters, and, indicating he had just acquired the copies of the photographs of interest, told me he had been about to contact me when I phoned him. Now he would meet me at the airport, which I could get to quickly through the coastal airline shuttle service, and would have the pictures with him. I could recognize him by the color of his suit and the flower in his lapel.

The shuttle plane landed, but I saw no one who fit the description in the waiting room just inside the terminal. I decided to check the waiting room of an adjacent wing. As I walked in that direction, I noticed a man some forty paces away who fit the description. He was coming directly toward me.

"Are you Mr. Sheets?" The question had already been asked by eye contact and raised eyebrow. The casual verbal question on close approach served only to confirm the assumed answer.

I wanted to get as much information about the photographs and their source as Mr. Sheets could or would divulge. He said he had a commitment to drive his daughter to some early evening function, and could not spend more than a few minutes with me at the airport. He suggested the airport bar as the most suitable place for us to talk.

We selected a secluded table away from the bar and ordered a drink. After the waitress left with our order, Mr. Sheets handed me three photographs. Although our eyes had not yet fully adjusted to the relative darkness of the room, I could see that the photographs showed solid vehicles of flying saucer type suspended in the air. Two photos seemed to be of the same object in different positions as seen between trees in a distance. The object had a relatively flat bottom, smoothly rounded dome on top, and a definite row of windows encircling its center. The third photo showed a less distinct object in the distance beyond a pickup truck which appeared in the foreground of the picture. It seemed to be a different object than that shown in the other two photos.

Where were the photos taken, and by whom? Mr. Sheets said they were obtained by a friend of his from a third person, known to the friend, whom he could not at this time identify to

"Secret" photos of flying saucers said to have been stolen from the Air Force. (taken from a slide)

me. This third person, who could not afford to have his identity known for obvious reasons, had himself taken the UFO pictures while he was in the Air Force, sometime within the past five years. The pictures had been confiscated by the Air Force, but at the time of his separation from the service, this person, resenting denial of the privilege of retaining copies of the photographs he had taken, made some copies which he secretly took with him. The original 35-mm slides were said to be in custody of the Air Force at White Sands, New Mexico.

Mr. Sheets agreed that vague information of this type gave us little to work with. If we were to break into this case, we had to have definite information which we could verify and support. Exactly when and where were the pictures taken? By whom? Under what circumstances? Precisely where were the originals

154

filed? We would take any necessary steps to protect an informer's identity, but we could present no case without such information. Mr. Sheets felt he probably could get more information of the type we needed, for which I would contact him later.

Meanwhile, the photographs themselves not only showed impressive solid objects, but because they also included tree tops and other identifiable objects, they also appeared amenable to analysis. Was it actually a large object in the distance as it appeared, or was it a double exposure, suspended model, or other hoax? Our photographic specialist would have to render that judgment, and I carefully placed the pictures in my briefcase for later delivery to him. Since I could get no further information about the photographs at this time, I took advantage of the opportunity to visit with a local school teacher who had first-hand knowledge of numerous UFO sightings in Mexico.

Returning to Boulder, I told the family closest to me about the UFO report I had gone to the west coast to investigate. I also mentioned that I had flown to another city to pick up some photographs which were claimed to be real pictures of flying saucers. Jerry, aged fifteen, glanced at them and immediately recognized them as pictures of a UFO he had seen in *True* magazine. He went upstairs to his room and returned with the magazine in hand. He was right. The magazine showed a slightly different view of the same object. The next morning, I showed the pictures to the project staff at Woodbury Hall. Those who were not so new to the project as I was at that time recognized them as some of the photographs said to have been taken by a Mr. Villa. Three sets of claimed UFO photographs were available commercially from various suppliers, seven to thirteen in a set, and our office had copies of these. We checked an advertising flyer from the project files. There were the same photographs, all in Villa set No. 1.

It was to be several months later before I visited Mr. Villa,

155

who said he took his UFO pictures near Albuquerque. It was, however, already very doubtful that the pictures I received at the west coast airport would be useful as proof that flying saucers inhabit Earth's skies. It was already quite certain that they were not stolen from Air Force files, and were not evidence that some section of the Air Force was keeping UFO secrets from the American public.

## Disappearing Photographs and Men in Black Suits

Conspiracy claims are so frequently heard, and so frequently supported by purported specific case evidence, that one is disposed to give them some thought. Are such claims merely an expression of individual and mass paranoia? How much of the "case evidence" is valid? Is there a real possibility that one of the conspiracy theories is true? If it were true, would the probability that an outsider could discover and establish that fact be greater than zero? How might he accomplish this?

I, myself, could not answer these questions. Most Americans, having confidence in the honesty of those who control their lives, would simply write such claims off as paranoid reactions. The Orson Wells "Invasion from Mars" episode of 1938, however, had shown that control of mass hysteria could be a major problem if an outer space vehicle landed on Earth and the fact that it had landed were known by the public. Perhaps such a situation would come under the category of situations in which certain governmental personages would consider falsification to be justified—following the attitude expressed in October 1962 by Assistant Secretary of Defense Sylvester that governmental falsification was all right if the results were good. Believing this to be the case, some members of one of the civilian organizations expressed to me their belief that the real purpose of officially establishing the Colorado Project was to furnish a means whereby the fact of extraterrestrial visitation could be revealed to the public in a non-disastrous fashion. The government might thus be saved from eventual forced admission that it had intentionally deceived its own people. Whatever were the facts regarding extraterrestrial visitation, this belief regarding the Colorado Project was certainly erroneous.

On the other hand, it was apparent that if any conspiracy actually existed, some individual working with the project would be privy to it. Thus, if one of us wished to investigate the "conspiracy theory" he had two strikes against him at the start. As a member of the project, he presumably had access to whatever pertinent information he reasonably desired. However, his efforts in behalf of the project were known to the other active project members, and through them, to the project's chief Pentagon contact. If he were about to acquire information which was forbidden to him by a Pentagon-related agency, that agency would be aware of which door or crack in its defense was being assaulted, and could react accordingly.

We had one strike left, however, and could examine some of the "specific evidence" that somebody was withholding the UFO truth from the American people. This type of evidence generally took the form of claims that official agents had mysteriously confiscated photographs of UFOs, or that two mysterious men in dark suits visited UFO witnesses not only to confiscate photographs but also to warn witnesses not to talk with anyone about what they had seen.

The case of Mr. Sheets above seems typical of claims that the Air Force has, in secret files, photographs of known extraterrestrial vehicles. Several other reports implied that unknown objects frequently are seen around our missiles after they are launched, as if someone were checking them out. A most interesting report of this type was printed in a textbook, *An Introduc-*

157

*tion to Astrodynamics,* by Dr. R. M. L. Baker. In a section of the text dealing with anomalistic aerial phenomena, Dr. Baker reported that ". . . three Navy cameras and two Air Force cameras were viewing the launch of a Thor-Able Star (015, project A-4/01019). Just after the second stage was ignited, three of the cameras showed an object as bright as the second-stage flame, moving 'straight up' the film frame at about one third degree per second."

After presenting arguments that this bright object was not an optical illusion (lens flare), an artificial satellite, aircraft, birds, insects, or balloons, the author comments, "Certainly a triangulation study could be completed using the films since there were simultaneous views from two sites and the second stage of the Thor-Able Star could be used for reference for both position and brightness. At this writing, the author does not know of any such analysis, the outcome of which could possibly establish the natural source of the peculiar image."

Various sources produced a variety of other claims involving photographs of unidentified objects and official secrecy regarding them. I made a mental list of such claims in anticipation of an opportunity to investigate them.

The most widely publicized movies of UFOs, taken by Mr. Mariana in Great Falls, Montana, in 1950, had been loaned to the Air Force for analysis. Mr. Mariana claimed the first part of the film, in which the two objects could be seen most clearly and which showed them to be spinning oblate solid objects, had been cropped off and never returned to him. Furthermore, he claimed to have a letter from the Air Force admitting the cropping.

Three original Polaroid photographs of a solid UFO in the shape of a short cylinder with a rim around its bottom, taken near Santa Ana, California, in August 1965, were said to have been picked up by two men who flashed North American Air Defense Command identification cards at the home of the photographer-witness. The two men "borrowed" the original prints. Neither the prints nor the NORAD representatives have been seen or heard from since.

A school teacher's daughter in California, in a personal letter to another teacher, told of sighting and photographing several unidentified flying objects in Nebraska a month earlier. "My original negatives disappeared while in the hands of a newspaper in Lincoln, Nebraska."

A man, whom I will call Mr. Frasier, took five pictures of an object of the type he and numerous associates had been observing frequently in the night sky during a period of several months. The color slides he obtained showed a bright object. One of the slides showed the object to be disc-shaped, with a dome and tail. Mr. Frasier loaned the five pictures to a friend, Mr. Carlson, who worked at a TV station and wanted the pictures to be used on a television documentary program about UFOs which was planned at his station. Several weeks later the documentary had not been presented, and Mr. Frasier asked Carlson to return the pictures. Mr. Carlson informed him confidentially that the picture which showed the clear image had been picked up by an Air Force officer who left instructions that the matter not be pursued. Mr. Carlson also volunteered the information that the station would deny this had happened and say only that the picture had been lost. This prediction was confirmed when Mr. Frasier requested return of his pictures from the station management.

An airline pilot in Australia reportedly took pictures during a UFO sighting on 28 May 1965. The sighting was witnessed by the entire crew. "When the plane landed, the films were confiscated by the Australian Air Force."

A civilian UFO buff gave us the name and address of one of twelve witnesses of a UFO incident near White Sands Proving Ground in June, 1963. A fifty-foot diameter disc, coin silver in color, circled the Twin Buttes radar antenna site slowly in broad daylight at a range of 150 feet. Ninety feet of 35-mm movie film were shot of the object. The Air Force confiscated the film two days later.

The list of disappearing photographs continued to grow. Several of these films, if they actually existed as claimed, would independently serve as convincing evidence that flying saucers exist as a physical reality. Could we possibly locate and examine any of the unreleased or "confiscated" film? Could the claims, some of which came from highly credible sources, be verified? Would the existence of a conspiracy be revealed by verification of one or more of these claims of film confiscation?

Whatever the outcome of an investigation, such film, if it existed, was crucial to a reasonable evaluation of the entire UFO question. We had to satisfy ourselves that such film did or did not exist, and, if we thought it did, leave untried no possible path to its discovery and examination.

The first step was to get as specific information as it was possible to obtain about those instances which seemed to merit investigation. Perhaps, operating covertly or overtly as the situation seemed to demand, we could trace confiscated film, if it existed, from its point of disappearance to its current place of storage.

I contacted Dr. Baker, whose book revealed the existence of the peculiar bright image on tracking film of a missile launched at Vandenberg AFB. Dr. Baker had also done a detailed analysis of the Mariana movies from Great Falls several years previously. Perhaps, as well as giving us more information about the missile-associated UFO, he also could give us some clue to help determine whether or not some of Mariana's film had been kept by the Air Force. Dr. Baker was enthusiastically cooperative. I telephoned Dr. William Hartman in Arizona, who was doing photographic analyses for the project, to see if he could join Dr.

Baker and me for a conference about UFOs in Dr. Baker's office in California. He could.

Dr. Baker reviewed his work with the Mariana film. If any cropping had been done, however, it happened before Dr. Baker acquired the film strip with which he worked. The amount of film originally present could not be discerned from any information he had available.

Dr. Baker could give us the time and date of the missile launching and location of the cameras. The movies which showed the peculiar bright object were taken about noon on 5 December 1963. Although the film was Air Force property, it was not classified. Dr. Baker had been shown the movies by an excited UFO enthusiast who had a part in developing the film. This man said they expected something particularly interesting on these films because radar returns had indicated the presence of an unknown object. Dr. Baker recalled seeing only an almost undefined white dot on two of the films. Film from the third camera, however, showed the unidentified object, just after second stage ignition, with about the same brightness as the second stage "bird." While the bird itself left a contrail, there was no contrail associated with the unknown object.

Since Dr. Baker had furnished specific information, including a firm date, project number, and camera sites, we probably could locate the films of interest, if they hadn't been destroyed on some routine schedule, and could check the peculiar unknown on the films. I telephoned the Public Information Officer at Vandenburg AFB and asked if he could help me locate these films. He was a graduate of the University of Colorado, and was most anxious to help. The next day he called me back and gave me the voucher number under which the desired films could be found in the central film depository in Dayton, Ohio. We got the film, which was examined later by Bill Hartmann. Classified tracking data and information on the film told him the exact position of the missile and of the unknown image at specific known times. The image which moved across the film field was simply the planet Venus, which only appeared to move because of the changing field of view of the tracking camera.

As Dr. Baker had suggested in his text where the existence of this image was first revealed to the public, analysis "could possibly establish the natural source of the peculiar image." It did. And it left us, in this case, with no UFO.

Review of the Mariana case, however, had yielded some indication, in early Air Force correspondence about the movie film, that the original film actually was longer than the segment which was analyzed by Dr. Baker. Therefore, as I went about the country on other UFO investigations, I kept asking questions about Mr. Mariana's film. Various people in Great Falls firmly believed part of the film had been removed by the Air Force. There had been no actual recording or measuring of film footages loaned to and received from the Air Force, however, and the claim that not all the film was returned could not be verified. The Air Force had denied the claim and denied now having any part of his film. Mr. Mariana could not locate the letter he said he had received in which the Air Force admitted removal of part of the film. If a more distinct portion of Mr. Mariana's movie, showing extraordinary rotating flying objects, did or does exist, it clearly was not to be acquired for our study—and we could not prove that it had ever existed.

Among the other claims of photograph confiscation, there surely were some that would hold up under investigation, and perhaps lead us to useful and interesting UFO evidence.

Since we had copies of the Santa Ana photographs, location of the originals was not extremely important. The original photographs were desired for analysis, however. If the claim that two men permanently "borrowed" the originals was true, the men would necessarily have been impostors, for this type of activity is not NORAD's cup of tea. There would be no way of tracing those photographs.

As for the vanished fifth picture of Mr. Frasier's set, interest in it also vanished after further investigation revealed that this group's "UFOs" were actually military aircraft engaged in practice night aerial refueling operations. It seemed doubtful that a photograph of this operation would show a disc-shaped object with dome and tail, and extremely doubtful that such a picture had been confiscated by representatives of any conspiracy.

I did make telephone contact with the man, whom I will call Mr. Clark, who reportedly witnessed the odolite filming of a fifty-foot disc which circled the Twin Buttes antenna in broad daylight at a distance of 150 feet. Needless to say, I was extremely anxious to locate and see that particular ninety feet of 35-mm film. Even verifying the existence of such film would be a significant achievement. If the film did exist, I would need specific information, such as Dr. Baker had given us in the Vandenberg case, if I were to initiate an attempt to trace the film.

I telephoned Mr. Clark at home in the evening, hoping he would feel more free to talk about his experience in the environment of his own home. He indicated I was asking about a touchy subject. He wouldn't put anything in writing and would rather not talk about the incident because he and all other witnesses to the incident had, upon request, signed statements immediately afterward which said, in effect, that they had not seen anything, and it was understood that anything they had seen would not be mentioned. When I stated that I only wanted to verify the correctness of information I had already been given, he said it was true that he was at the Twin Buttes radar site and watched a UFO make two circles around it. Mr. Clark had not actually seen the moving pictures, but assumed they existed because "they" said they had taken pictures. He said the pictures would have been taken by the regular operator of the odolite camera which

163

was used in tracking missiles. Missiles were being fired from Pecos to White Sands, and being tracked as they came over this antenna station. The UFO he and the others at the station observed was a saucer of about fifty-foot diameter, flying at about 1500-foot altitude—or about level with the station, which is on a peak. The saucer was about 1000 yards away, and circled the antenna twice. This happened at 2:30 or 3:00 in the afternoon. It was not a conventional object and certainly had no wings.

Mr. Clark gave information hesitantly, and sounded quite nervous about discussing the subject. He said he did not want to get involved in any inquiry, for he had signed a statement pledging secrecy. I thought perhaps he could give me more specific information if I would visit him personally sometime when I happened to be in his city, providing I assured him his name would not be associated with any information he divulged. I asked if he would be willing to talk with me sometime under these circumstances. He refused to make a commitment to do so, and spoke of planning to go on vacation soon. I could think of several possible reasons for such evasiveness.

I next phoned Mr. Clark about six weeks later. I was still interested in his claims, although our first conversation had changed the distance of the flying saucer from 150 feet to 1000 yards and the firm knowledge of the purported incident had been left in an incomplete state.

Mr. Clark had expressed the belief that officialdom was keeping a lot of UFO information secret. With this in mind, I opened the second conversation with the comment that we had been assured by the Air Force that we could have access to any information they have, and we wanted seriously to test that assurance. To do so, we had to know specifically what information to request and therefore needed detailed information about the UFO filming incident we spoke of earlier.

Mr. Clark responded to this approach. After my assurance that his name would not be associated with any investigation, he spoke freely of the incident. However, he did not remember the date it happened—not even the year. He was not involved in the missile tracking, but was running some special antenna-response tests for the aircraft company for which he worked. There were probably seven other witnesses, all working on the tracking of missiles. These people had charge of the equipment and cameras, and would have turned film over to the Army routinely after the work was completed. Mr. Clark then said that he, himself, did not actually sign a statement that he would not reveal information about this UFO incident. Others, he said, did sign such a statement, and he was asked not to mention the incident to anyone.

Attempting not to reveal my concern that the Army now had the film which was reportedly confiscated by the Air Force, I asked about the Army involvement. This antenna was operated by the Army, sometimes with Navy participation, according to Mr. Clark. He did not know names of any commanding officers or other witnesses. I then brought into the conversation the earlier claim that the film had been confiscated by the Air Force. This left Mr. Clark mumbling about some vague connection with the Air Force, and resulted in the statement that he doesn't know who obtained possession of the film.

By the time this conversation was finished, I could only conclude that, again, the vanishing film existed only in the minds of men.

Obviously, I would never make much money as a detective. I'd certainly hesitate to accuse any agency of confiscating UFO photographs and keeping them secret from the public on the basis of evidence I had been able to muster about secret photographs.

## Air Force Secrets

Since we were members of an official group charged with determining the facts about UFOs, we were frequently told about supposedly secret events which the unauthorized informer would not have mentioned under other circumstances. Loyalty to the flying saucer commitment was seen frequently to be stronger than loyalty to other gods, including country and employer.

One UFO buff, a technically trained man working with the space program, frequently gave us "leads" to undisclosed information he thought we should check out. We must, of course, not let his name be associated with any investigation for obvious professional reasons. Most of his tips did not survive initial scrutiny. One project member, however, attempted to pursue one of the tips.

The man knew of the existence of a prior top secret study of unidentified foreign objects flying over the United States. The study was funded by Air Force Intelligence and carried out by Harry Diamond Laboratories. The results of the study were never disclosed. We should have been, and were not, informed of such a study. Why were we not told about it, and what were its findings? The man knew the contract for the study did exist and the study had been carried out because he himself had been interviewed to work on the project. Although he did not take the job, he could tell us when the study was made and who was in charge of the project.

Norm tried the frontal attack. He sent a letter to the chief of the laboratory branch which purportedly had made the study of foreign objects, requesting information about results of the study. He received a courteous reply which stated that that office had no information on the subject. The reply also contained the suggestion that perhaps he was referring to work of another group which resulted in an unclassified report titled "Investigation of

Satellite-Related Ionospheric Anomalies."

The Diamond Laboratory may not have made a secret study pertinent to the UFO question. If it had, I saw no reason to expect a reply different from the one Norm received.

There were times when I wished I could don a cloak which would make me invisible and do a little sniffing.

One such time was when an informant sent word that on 9 February 1968 at about 10:00 A.M., an alert against a UFO was received at Dow AFB, Bangor, Maine. According to this information, jet interceptors were rolled out, armed with rockets, and taxied to the runway. They did not take off. This was one of several UFO alerts at the base that month. Air pursuit was considered useless because the UFO was too fast to be caught by a fighter plane.

When I phoned the UFO officer at Dow for further information, he informed me that he knew of no such alert. However, this base was operated by the Strategic Air Command, which had no fighters. The officer thought it quite possible that Air Defense Command (ADC) personnel, who operated some fighter craft at the base but were stationed on the other side of the field, could have a UFO report and not tell SAC about it. He agreed to check the ADC unit and inform me by return call what he could learn about the existence and cause of an alert on 9 February.

His return call the next day told me what he had learned. The 75th Fighter Defense Squadron had received an alert on 9 February 1968 and fighters were rolled onto the runway ready to scramble. This action was taken on orders from higher headquarters, the 36th Air Division at Otis AFB. The alert to scramble was said to be definitely not against a UFO, but any other information regarding the cause of the alert would have to come from Otis AFB.

Further inquiry through the Pentagon regarding the cause of the alert at Dow AFB on this date, brought the response that there was no alert on 9 February 1968 for units of the 75th Fighter Defense Squadron. The 57th, based in Iceland, did have a scramble that day, and probably our information sources had confused these two squadrons.

While I felt that any scrambles that day probably were not against any object more exotic than a straying foreign aircraft, the information we received was simply not consistent. In the absence of some independent source of information, we had no means of determining whether or not there was an alert at Dow AFB and, if so, whether or not it was in fact triggered by the presence of an unidentified flying object of a type which should have been of interest to our study.

Another instance in which conflicting bits of information were received from an air base was even more frustrating. Rumor told us that six UFOs had followed an X-15 flight at Edwards AFB, and there probably would be moving pictures of the event. The date was 1 September 1967. Official information sources at the base denied any UFO incident on that date or within a month of that date. There was no X-15 flight that day, so details of the report, at least, were erroneous. Yet, when we checked the rumor source, we found that our informer's information came originally from a source within the base which should have been reliable. Informed of the denial, this person, whom I will call Mr. Caplan, insisted that there was a UFO event there on 1 September. I finally made telephone connection with Mr. Caplan who was, by this time, on temporary assignment elsewhere than at Edwards AFB. I was told that, although he did not see the phenomenon himself, the report of it came to his desk and was turned over, without action on his part, to the Director of Information, Colonel Smith, who was the only person at the base who could discuss it. Mr. Caplan did not know what action was taken or what decision was made about the event.

The suspicion that official lines of communication may not

be conveying the full truth to us in this case was bolstered by the extraordinary elusiveness of Colonel Smith. When I tried to reach him by telephone, he was on another line, in a meeting, and away from the base for the day. The return calls which his secretary promised never came through. Were we being given the run-around? Was there really a UFO encounter at Edwards AFB on 1 September? At this point, we could not be certain there wasn't.

We notified our Pentagon contacts about the unusual lack of cooperation we encountered in attempts to clarify a situation at Edwards AFB. This resulted in a telephone message from one of Colonel Smith's assistants. The message was left at my desk when I was at a meeting across campus. There was no UFO event at Edwards on 1 September 1967.

Under the circumstances, this cryptic message was not adequate to convince us that the earlier information that a UFO sighting did take place was indeed erroneous.

Mr. Caplan returned to Edwards AFB after his extended absence. I suggested to Bob Low, who was traveling to Los Angeles, that a little undercover work might let us know what, if anything, actually happened at Edwards on 1 September. If, while he was in the vicinity of Edwards AFB, he could learn where Mr. Caplan lived and contact him at home, Mr. Caplan might be able to talk with less restraint, and the whole situation, be it cover-up or error, might be clarified. I thought that once Mr. Caplan was back on the job, he might have checked out the report of interest to see what became of it or what its true significance was.

Mr. Low returned from California with the exasperating news that he had not learned Mr. Caplan's home address, but he had been able to contact Colonel Smith and Colonel Smith told him there was no UFO event . . . I didn't need to listen to the rest of the sentence. I knew how a poker player would feel if someone turned up his hole cards before the hand was played.

Was the calling of Colonel Smith at this point simply an

inept move? After considerable pondering of alternate interpretations, I prefer to think that it was.

I acquired Mr. Caplan's home phone number and called him one evening to ask if, after his return, he had learned any more about the event we spoke of earlier. He said he hadn't, for he was told to stay out of that.

"Who told you to stay out of it?"

"Colonel Smith. They said it was their business to put out any information, and I said 'that's fine—no problem.' So I just forgot about it."

"Yes. That's another aspect of our problem. You see, we called Colonel Smith, and we were told by him that there was no event at all. That just didn't give us confidence that we were being dealt with as we are supposed to be."

"As I say, he just told me very briefly to stay out of it, so I have."

"I can see that you have no choice. Do you personally feel there is any reason why we should be interested in this event?"

"Well, as I say—I can't even say anything. You know what I mean. I'm sorry—it's just one of those things. No comment."

Was there actually a UFO incident at Edwards AFB on 1 September 1967? I doubt it. But, even yet, I cannot be certain.

Occasionally, information that was given to me in secret involved military situations which were appropriately kept under security classification. Dealing with such situations was touchy, for, if there were indeed a UFO pertinence, that aspect was my business. Yet, I initially agreed to work on this project with the stipulation that I would not accept any classified information, for I wished the freedom to speak openly about any part of the UFO investigation in which I participated. If an investigation led to a requirement for access to secret information, which seldom happened, I turned the case over to another member of the project and accepted his judgment regarding the extent of UFO pertinence in the case.

In one such instance, the integrity of a major weapon system was brought into doubt by a failure which rumor attributed to the presence of one or more UFOs in the vicinity. It is easy to understand why the information that such a failure had occurred would be closely guarded, for if a potential enemy knew that a major defense system could be made inoperative, the deterrence value of that system could be lost.

In this instance, the ability to launch a flight of ten Minuteman missiles near Malstrom Air Force Base in Montana had been lost. Recipients of the report that a UFO had been sighted over the area were certain the UFO was responsible for destruction of the control system. Upon receipt of this secret information, I arranged a trip to Malstrom, ostensibly to talk with the chief of the operations division, Lieutenant Colonel Lewis D. Chase, about his earlier UFO encounter (see Chapter 9). Discussion of Colonel Chases's experience was one reason for the trip, but the timing was due to the very secret Echo Flight incident.

After Colonel Chase and I had exchanged pleasantries in his office, I asked him about the Echo incident. The Colonel caught his breath, and expressed surprise that I knew of it. "I can't talk about that." As we then talked about his earlier UFO experience, he looked out the window and noticed a small group of men talking with each other near the entrance to a neighboring building. He pointed the group out to me, and told me that was the off-site team investigating the incident I had asked about. If I needed to know the cause of this incident, I could arrange, through official channels, to see their report after completion of the investigation. Later in the day, as he showed me around the base, Colonel Chase did, in fact, introduce me to Major James H. Schraff, who headed the investigating team. We did not tell the major that I knew of the incident he was investigating.

Although local newspapers carried stories of UFO sightings

171

which would coincide in time with Echo, Colonel Chase had assured me that the incident had not involved a UFO. Since Colonel Chase was the last man I would doubt when he conveyed this information, I accepted the information as factual, and turned review of Major Schraff's report over to Bob Low, who had received security clearance to read secret information related to the UFO study.

When Bob phoned Colonel Hippler, our Pentagon contact for the Colorado Project, about the Schraff report, Hippler told Bob he would try to get the report, but he suspected the report was going to be classified too high for us to look at it. He told Bob he thought interference by pulses from nuclear explosions probably were involved. Hippler and other officials were appalled that we knew of this incident. They perhaps would have been even more chagrined if they had known how soon after the incident happened in Montana that word of it and the coincident UFO sightings reached me—from a source on the East Coast. The only type of information that seems to travel faster than the speed of light is rumor attached to a UFO.

On 20 March 1989, more than twenty years after the Echo Flight Incident, an Associated Press release announced Air Force acknowledgment that a few of the Minuteman 3 nuclear missiles in one squadron at Malstrom Air Force Base had accidentally been rendered impotent in 1986 during an annual changing of launch codes. The Air Force reportedly said those missiles could not have been used in 1986 if war had broken out, and the most likely cause was inadvertent personnel error. According to the report, procedures for loading new codes into the missiles had been overhauled and there had been no repeat of the incident.

## Of Kooks And Paranoia

Wherever I went on UFO investigations, I found different individuals and groups of individuals referring to each other as "kooks" and regretting the fact that kooks were associated with their serious interests in flying saucers. One civilian organization even notified us that it had its own undercover agent checking into some of the "kook" groups.

It was obvious, of course, that some of the people with whom I visited required little or no evidence as a basis for belief, and that others were taking advantage of that situation. Stories of trips on flying saucers, physical contact with "men" from outer space, and telepathic contact with outer space intelligences were related to me at various times. Often the people relating these experiences apparently were convinced, in their own minds, that the experiences were real and their accounts true. Internal incompatibilities or contradictions in the accounts were accepted without concern.

Perhaps these people have psychiatric problems. Yet we all have our hang-ups, on one subject or another. Are the miraculous tales related by these people fundamentally different in nature from those which millions of Americans find admirable on Sunday mornings?

A large organization of UFO believers which traditionally subscribed to the Air Force conspiracy theory included, in its leadership and advisers, retired military officers, acting business executives, scientists, engineers, and others whose judgment is generally considered sound and reliable. Some had held such positions as Air Force Public Information Officer or executive officer of the Central Intelligence Agency (CIA) itself, and had been concerned with UFOs in one way or another while in those positions. One would not expect such men to accuse the Air Force of hiding the truth without grounds for the belief. Are their

173

grounds valid? Is this a problem of paranoia or is it justifiable concern?

The U.S. Government did succeed in keeping the development of atomic bombs secret even from the people who were doing the work of purifying the enriched uranium and plutonium of which the bombs were composed. I remember conversations in 1952 with women at Oak Ridge, Tennessee, who worked on the chemical processing of weapon-grade uranium-235. In the early days of this work, they were making the ingredients of the first atomic bomb. All they knew, however, is that they were working with "T," and one drop of the solution they processed was worth the price of a Cadillac. Government agencies do keep secrets from the government's people, mostly under the guise of national security requirements. With examples of secrecy readily at hand, is it irrational to conclude that agencies of our government might attempt to hide the truth about UFOs from the public?

Historically, the CIA was known to have been involved with the UFO question. In January, 1953, the CIA had convened a panel of scientists to review UFO information and files and render judgment regarding the nature of the UFO problem. A censored version of the report had been declassified. Although the CIA was involved in 1953, it was not obvious that it had retained a specific interest in UFOs through the 1960s. If it had, and, as the other large organization of UFO believers maintained, if it had conspired to deceive the public about UFOs, the Colorado project would necessarily have been a tool of the conspiracy. When the founders of this UFO organization revealed, at an evening social gathering, that they not only held that position but also believed the CIA representative on the project was to be none other than the project director himself, that suggestion struck me as being comically absurd. Unfortunately, it was absurd, and patently so, only because I knew the character of the director, and not on other grounds. The CIA, established by the National Security Act of 1947 with the stipulation that it would have no internal security functions, was, by 1951, secretly recruiting scientists to "take any job you want, with any university, corporation, or department—just report to us and collect a decent income." Their recruiter said those words to me, in sworn secrecy, when I was about to receive a graduate degree from Iowa State University. The thought that some member of our project could be reporting secretly to the CIA was, therefore, in itself not irrational.

As I pondered the various conspiracy theories, thoughts of secret activities I knew of in this nation, including the work of thousands of agents whom American citizens are paying to build up personal information dossiers on American citizens, entered the consideration. These thoughts combined with others regarding covert military expenditures and activities. I could not help but wonder if a good psychoanalyst would have to judge the society itself as paranoid.

While I could not dismiss the conspiracy theories on the basis of individual or group paranoia, a little thought convinced me that the fact of extraterrestrial visitation, if it were a fact, could not successfully be concealed for long by either the Air Force or the CIA. That conviction was strengthened by the Echo Flight Incident experience of having quite secret information pound upon my own unauthorized ears when a UFO was rumored to be involved in the secret event. I do not believe that human beings with knowledge of an event of such fantastic significance as extraterrestrial visitation would be capable of refraining from revealing that information for long. Dr. Condon had said, when we pointedly asked him if he would reveal the fact to the public if we came up with firm evidence of real extraterrestrial presence: "Well, I guess I'd phone the Secretary of the Air Force and say, 'We got it—what are you folks going to do with it?'" Dr. Condon was once quoted by the press as saying that the discovery of an extraterrestrial being would be perhaps the greatest discovery of all time—one that he would be perfectly happy to make. While he would have been willing to allow the Air Force or others to reveal this discovery to the public in a manner which avoided panic and chaos, would he have been willing to have the information kept hidden for all time, and not receive public acknowledgment of his discovery? Not likely.

Dr. Condon also had given consideration to UFO conspiracy theories. In a letter to Dr. Walter Orr Roberts, then Board Chairman of the American Association for the Advancement of Science, written after completion of the Colorado study, he wrote:

These people [UFO buffs] in varying degrees insist that visitors are coming to Earth in flying saucers from other civilizations. Some insist that this is known to our government and that the truth is being deliberately held back from the public. After careful study I conclude that there is no scientifically valid evidence in support of either proposition. Notice that I do not say that no such evidence will ever be found; simply that none is available now.

One of the most intriguing stories involved in the Air Force conspiracy belief is the tale of the little green men who were taken from the site of a flying saucer crash near Aztec, New Mexico. The aliens' frozen bodies supposedly are kept in Hangar 19, or some other specific location, at Wright-Patterson Air Base. (A similar story is told about a Roswell, New Mexico, site.)

While working on the Colorado UFO Project, I visited Wright-Patterson to review the files of Project Blue Book. I was not so naive as to think that if a tank full of frozen green men were kept secretly in Hangar 19, I would be able to learn that fact by direct questions to the keepers of the secret, or by sneaking a peek into whatever hanger or building in which they were supposedly kept. I was constantly watching, however, for small slips of the tongue or references to information we were not supposed to know about.

What I found at Project Blue Book was little concern by Major Quintanilla, who was in charge of the project at that time, or by anyone else there, about the fact that public reports of UFO sightings were not investigated seriously by a great number of the "UFO Officers," one officer being so designated at each air base. Their interest was intense, however, in details of any report which might have been triggered by a satellite in decaying orbit and burning as it reentered the atmosphere. Blue Book personnel actively searched for pieces of reentered satellite, for the obvious and practical reason of learning what materials of construction the Russians were then using in their satellite program.

As for the little green men, I next became involved in the tale ten years after completion of the Colorado study. We had purchased and moved onto the historic La Boca Ranch, on the western Colorado-New Mexico border. A gentleman who subscribed to the Air Force conspiracy belief appeared at my door, wanting to talk about UFOs. As we talked, and as he looked around the ranch headquarters and the site where the railroad station had been, I became aware that he was surreptitiously seeking confirmation of his belief that the saucer which crashed near Aztec, along with its occupants, had been loaded onto a freight train at La Boca for transport to Wright-Patterson Air Base. I was a bit surprised, but agreed it probably was true, when he pointed out to me that La Boca was the closest active freight depot from the reported site of the Aztec saucer crash.

Although transport of a crashed saucer over unroaded, mountainous terrain to get to La Boca would have been difficult, the gentleman was certain that this is where that secret operation was accomplished. To him, the fact that I—who had

177

played a major role in the Air Force-funded Colorado Project, and was therefore obviously involved in the Air Force conspiracy—now appeared as the resident-owner of La Boca, was certain confirmation that La Boca was where the little green men were loaded into railroad cars.

### Personal Security Investigations

"Why in the world are they investigating Bob Low? That just doesn't make sense."

Dan couldn't answer my question. He didn't know.

Dan had introduced two visitors who showed identification as U.S. Army Intelligence investigators. They said they were up-dating the security clearance of Mr. Robert Low and wished to speak with me about him.

Mr. Low had served as Project Coordinator during the investigating phase of the UFO project. He had completed his project contribution and had returned to his duties as an assistant to one of the vice presidents of the University. At the start of the project, he had been cleared for access to secret information which he might wish to examine as part of the UFO study. But his work on the Air-Force-financed UFO project was already past, and he was not now associated with military interests. Why U.S. Army Intelligence was re-investigating Mr. Low at this time was indeed puzzling.

Assuming, however, that they had cleared their visit with the project director, I agreed to talk with Messrs. Walker and Bettis. Their questions were along the lines of when I first met Mr. Low; how frequently I saw him; who else worked closely with him; when I saw him last; was I on friendly relations with him; did I visit his home for cocktails or parties; did I have reason to question his integrity, morality, or loyalty; how did he get along with his family; did he drink excessively; had he ever traveled outside the U.S.; had he gone behind the Iron Curtain; did he have foreign visitors; did he make any contacts with foreign embassies; what was my opinion of his ability; would I recommend him for positions of responsibility; would I recommend him for the job he held on this project.

We discussed these topics in some detail. During the course of the project, Mr. Low had visited Europe, and knowledge of the places he visited there was available to the investigators from other sources if they needed that information. He had, to my knowledge, also written to officials in Norway and Sweden for information related to our study. He had been visited in Woodbury Hall once or twice by European newsmen, but there had been no obvious traffic of sinister characters into his office.

The visitors paid casual attention to my responses to their questions. The attitude changed when I responded to the question of whether I would recommend Mr. Low for the job he held on this project. "No. But this is a very special and unique situation. For most situations, he may well receive my recommendation." At this point, Mr. Bettis expressed great interest in having me sign a statement to the effect that I would not recommend Mr. Low for this job and wished to probe deeply into the reasons for this. "It's our regulations that any derogatory information must be in a signed statement."

Among the probing questions were several I refused to answer, for I felt that my opinion in these matters was no one else's business. I told Mr. Bettis, however, that any lack of recommendation would merely be based on Mr. Low's reaction to criticism, and nothing more serious.

In previous interrogations of this type, when the investigator would ask, for example, "Is Miss Jones, who was a student of yours and has applied for a job in the Peace Corps, loyal?" I was always tempted to ask, "Loyal to what? Loyal to the principle that a citizen has a right to privacy in his personal beliefs and affairs? Loyal to the principle that a citizen is to be presumed innocent of any charges until he is proved guilty by a jury of his peers? Loyal to the principle that an accused citizen has the right to face his accusers and answer any charges against him?" Since derogatory information in the files, which can be used and often is the real reason a person is not offered the jobs he wants, is not ordinarily revealed to the investigated person himself, that person obviously has no chance to defend himself against it.

I knew, of course, that this was not the type of loyalty the interrogators had in mind. So, when these men asked if I had any reason to question Mr. Low's loyalty, I resisted the temptation to make them question their own loyalty to basic American principles. Assuming they held the usual concept of "loyalty" as some sort of subservient support of current officialdom whether that officialdom's policies are noble, benevolent, and admirable, or deceitful, debilitating, and calamitous, I merely answered the question, quite truthfully, that I had no such reason whatsoever.

I learned later that, the same afternoon these men visited me, they talked with Mr. Low himself. I was surprised to hear this, for in my past experiences with security investigations, I had never known an instance in which the investigators made any direct contact with the person they were investigating.

They asked Low about his contact with foreign embassies. When they read him the Fifth Amendment, he got apprehensive, clammed up, and said he would have to consult his lawyer before answering further questions. They made an appointment to resume discussion the following day, August 6. On the morning of August 6, however, the security investigators phoned Low to tell him they had decided to terminate the investigation.

Since I knew of this call, I was surprised when Mr. Bettis entered my office that afternoon for my signature on a statement about Mr. Low. I read the statement Mr. Bettis had prepared: "I would not recommend Mr. Robert Low for any responsible position with the U.S. Government because of his inability to accept criticism."

The statement had to be rewritten before I would affix my signature to it, for Mr. Bettis' wording reflected neither my actual comments of the previous day nor my true attitude. Mr. Low executed certain administrative duties quite skillfully, and he would receive my recommendation for many types of responsible positions.

On the morning of 7 August, Mr. Bettis left my office for the third time. He now had a signed statement of what he considered derogatory information, innocuous as I insisted the final wording be, for filing with the secret dossier on Mr. Robert Low. I assume the "termination of the investigation" did not prevent new statements from reaching the file on Mr. Low.

As best I could finally ascertain, this investigation of Mr. Low, after the project was essentially over, was initiated because, following our receipt of an unofficial announcement that the Russians were organizing a scientific UFO study somewhat like ours, Low had, while he was in Washington, stopped at the Soviet embassy to discuss the extent of Soviet interest in the problem. Apparently, Low was photographed as he entered or departed the embassy, was later identified and was now being investigated. A newspaper article by William Raspberry, of the Washington Post Service, has revealed, "It is an open secret in Washington that the FBI maintains camera surveillance of the (Soviet) embassy from a building across the street."

This may not be the reason for this seemingly untimely investigation of Robert Low. It is the best guess I can offer. Whatever the reason, the kind of information added to the secret dossier remains the same.

This particular investigation of Robert Low was being conducted by Army Intelligence (ID/Army) under a cooperative agreement with the Air Force and other investigating groups. Security investigations, generally of their own personnel, constitute the biggest workload of the Air Force's Office of Special Investigations (OSI), which itself has more than 2100 agents in forty-one districts around the world, twenty-five of them in continental United States. A similar organization operated within the Navy (ONI). These three military organizations recently had combined their personnel security files, which were kept at Holloman Air Force Base. Although background checks were not run on everyone in the military services, these files contained over sixteen million index cards containing information which is secret from the sixteen million persons whose backgrounds and attitudes were checked. Additional files of dossiers on individual American citizens were maintained by FBI-HQ, FBI-ID, INS, CSC, CIA, HCUA, and the State Department's Bureau of Intelligence and Research (INR). These files are not accessible to everyone, but they are convenient and useful to those who have access to them and are a major asset in a controlled society or police state. I reluctantly used specific information on the background and character of individuals from such files, obtained through the OSI, a couple of times in evaluating reports of sightings of flying saucers.

In a milieu of distrust of official agencies by civilians; guarded trust in our honesty; rampant rumor; imagined and actual secrecy; suspicion, jealousy, and disrespect of civilian for civilian; arrogant treatment of civilian by military; intense emotional commitment; undercover investigations; suspicion of fellow workers; attempted control of investigation results by pre-committed on both sides of the belief fence; omnipresent "security" machinery that had developed a life of its own; disproportionate news reporting; yet gratifying support and cooperation from all sides, we endeavored to give the American public the most honest and straight-forward answer that it is possible to give to the question of what reality lies behind reports of sightings of unidentified flying objects. Although our investigation was essentially open to the public view, I, too, watched for any evidence of the existence of secret information and occasionally touched bases with the cloak and dagger world.

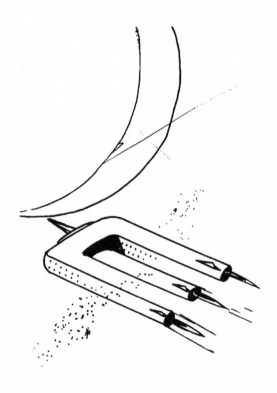

Sketch by Troy Craig

An Air Force officer saw a version of this optical illusion in a psychology textbook and jokingly called it a Russian "BLIVET" or a "BLPFSK."

# PART II

## THE PRODUCTION, CONTENT, AND IMPACT OF THE CONDON REPORT

# Chapter 11

# Mutiny Rebutted

The note was lying on my desk, as Norm had said it would be. "Please report to Dr. Condon's office at 9 o'clock Friday morning." It was signed by Bob Low who, at that time (8 February 1968), still served as project coordinator for the Scientific Study of Unidentified Flying Objects.

I read the note a second time, and looked around at the other desks in the project office at Woodbury Hall, where the major daily activity of the project had been taking place. Two major desks were bare. Cleaned out during my absence of the last several days. Dr. Norman Levine and Dr. David Saunders had been summarily fired by Dr. Condon. Presumably tomorrow's 9 A.M. meeting was to determine whether my services to the project also would be terminated. The whole project was blowing apart!

I had long been aware of friction between some members of the investigation staff and project administration. The investigation staff took incoming calls about UFO sightings and got to the location of each potentially significant sighting as soon as possible in hopes of getting first-hand evidence of what was sighted. Staff members had not liked the attitudes inherent in Bob Low's activities—contracting consultants to do scientific reviews not clearly related to the UFO question—and their dissatisfaction was augmented by newspaper reports quoting Dr. Condon's public remarks about the UFO study, made at academic meetings in various parts of the country. Those remarks had focused on anecdotes about "kooks," such as the man who had messages from the UFO people that a large saucer would land at a certain time at a specified location in Utah, or the distinguished-looking gentleman from the "Third Universe" who, for a large sum of money, would convey to the US Air Force the design and plans for a landing platform which the U.S. must build to accommodate an impending UFO landing.

Although I thought the "kook" reports should be of interest to staff psychologists, they had little to do with the real question the investigation staff was trying to resolve: Had strange vehicles or objects appeared in our skies, as indicated in reports by seemingly reliable observers? If so, were they advanced vehicles created in secret by our own nation or another nation on the planet Earth, or were they, as many people apparently believed, creations of some extraterrestrial intelligence? Some of the active investigating staff, after reading numerous UFO reports and interviewing some of the people who reported strange UFO experiences, considered the extraterrestrial intelligence (ETI) answer to be a serious possibility. At least they felt the evidence had not yet been fully evaluated, the project report had yet to be written, and Dr. Condon's public remarks about the study were inappropriately premature.

The internal conflict had, some two months earlier, reached the point of near rebellion, encouraged, perhaps unintentionally, by two scientists who had vested interests in the UFO question, but had been excluded from participation in the Condon project. Their exclusion was required because the United States Air Force, which had contracted the scientific UFO study, had stipulated that the investigation was to be by scientists who were free of prior commitment or convictions about the nature of UFOs.

Dr. James McDonald, an admirably capable person who held the position of Senior Physicist, Institute of Atmospheric Physics at the University of Arizona, had long been critical of the manner in which the Condon study was being conducted. Dr. McDonald had devoted much time and energy to studying UFO reports. He kept a list of the ten or twenty "best cases" which indicated to him that something strange was observed. He discussed these cases in detail at numerous talks to groups of fellow scientists and to political leaders. Dr. McDonald considered the UFO question to be the greatest scientific problem of our time.

Dr. J. Allen Hynek, Chairman of the Department of Astronomy and Director of Dearborn Observatory, Northwestern University, had been the U.S. Air Force's major scientific consultant on UFO reports for about twenty years. He felt quite embarrassed about his own "swamp gas" explanation of a series of sightings of strange lights in Michigan—an explanation rejected as absurd by the public, and considered a topic of good humor by cartoonists. Dr. Hynek had come to believe, because of the great mass of reports of experiences of strange events which could not be explained easily in terms of misunderstood ordinary phenomena of nature, that something extraordinary, such as extraterrestrial visitation, was indicated. At a talk before a large audience at the University of Colorado during the early days of the Condon study, Dr. Hynek had referred to the UFO phenomenon as the greatest mystery of our age, perhaps the

189

greatest mystery of all time. In my apartment after that lecture, Dr. Hynek expressed the view that it was most important that the Condon project result in the recommendation that scientific investigations of UFO reports be continued in the future. He was aware the Condon study's final report was to include recommendations as to the scope and magnitude of future efforts regarding UFO investigations, without specifying where such efforts would be located in the federal structure. I inferred from Dr. Hynek's remarks that he envisioned an on-going scientific study like the Condon project, expanded somewhat, with himself as its director. If such an organization were to be established, the choice of Dr. Hynek as director seemed reasonable.

Drs. Hynek and McDonald had met with project staff members Saunders and Levine in Denver, rather secretively, in early December, 1967—two months before the Saunders-Levine firing. By that time, they were convinced that Dr. Condon was going to put out a "negative" report and recommend that official investigations of UFO reports be terminated. Those at the meeting decided to form an organization of scientists to promote continued UFO studies.

I learned of the meeting and plans for the new organization shortly thereafter, when Norm Levine asked me if I would join him and other staff members in writing and publishing our own report of the results of the Colorado UFO study—a report that would conclude that extraterrestrial visitation was indicated, and scientific investigations of UFO reports should continue with high-priority funding. He told me about the Denver meeting, and the formation of the new organization. Our "alternative report" apparently would be a major product and foundation of the new organization.

My participation in the "alternative report" apparently was considered highly desirable by the new group, since I had played a major role in the on-site investigations. Norm, with whom I had worked closely on investigations of some of the UFO reports, obviously had been given the assignment of enlisting me into the group. What Norm was proposing, however, was, in my opinion, not mere expression of disagreement with Dr. Condon on the significance of certain evidence. It was a proposal of *mutiny*!

I tried to convince Norm that we really had no irrefutable evidence to support a conclusion different from Dr. Condon's, whatever his conclusions might be. "Oh, yes," replied Norm. "The computer analysis of orthoteny has now shown that there is only one chance in ten to the thirty-ninth power that the sightings did not involve ETI."

Orthoteny. That was the suggestion, originating in France, that if one plotted the locations of all reported sightings on a given day, he would discover that they fell along straight lines. The straight lines would indicate a grid followed by occupants of flying saucers in their systematic surveillance of Earth. If such a systematic survey were being made, and the vehicles were seen and reported, a pattern shown by sighting locations would be apparent only if the "real" sightings could be distinguished from the multitude of sighting reports which stem from other causes. Of course, if only a couple reports of sightings over a given region on a given day remained after application of some process to select the "real" sightings, those locations could always be connected by a straight line. I asked Norm if there had been any selectivity of the reports used in the orthoteny analysis. He assured me that all reports were included.

Then I said, "But we know that most of the UFO reports are triggered by misinterpretations of sightings of bright planets, satellites reentering the earth's atmosphere, weather balloons, and so forth—or they are produced by human imagination, delusion, or psychological need. If all this noise is included in a location analysis, it would do nothing but obscure any pattern

191

of real events."

I gave no weight at all, under the circumstances, to results of a computer analysis for "orthoteny," and I told Norm so. He shifted the argument. "But what about Beverly, Massachusetts?"

The Beverly sighting was difficult to write off as anything other than a real experience with a strange object. I had to grant Norm that fact. He and I had investigated that report together, interviewing the various people who reported participating in this strange experience.

At the heart of the Beverly case, three women reported seeing a strange object at very close range. The eleven-year-old daughter of one of the three had run downstairs in a state of fright after hearing a bump outside her bedroom window about 9 P.M. She had looked out the window to see a football-shaped object with flashing red lights moving in the air. The three women had gone out toward the local school grounds to reassure the girl that nothing to be afraid of was there. According to their account, however, a strange object approached them so close that one woman, who had beckoned the object with her arm, thought it was going to crush her. She described the object as a flat-bottomed metal disc, about the size of a large automobile, with glowing lights around its top. The other two women ran from the approaching object. They reported looking back to see their friend directly beneath the object, which was twenty to thirty feet above her head. The friend had her hands clamped over her head in a self-protective manner. She, too, then ran from the object, which receded and hovered and flew about over the school house.

Norm and I also had interviewed one of the two police officers who had responded to a call about the UFO. The officers had no close encounter with the object, but verified that an extraordinary object, which could not have been an airplane or helicopter, was executing various maneuvers at a low level over the high school.

192

Unless the people involved in this incident had let their collective imaginations run wild, the presence of a strange vehicle, under intelligent control, was certainly indicated. The people we interviewed seemed mentally and emotionally stable, relating an experience which was quite real in their own minds. Yet we had no evidence, beyond the personal testimony we heard, that a real flying saucer had actually been present over Beverly, Massachusetts. People can be, and are, convicted of serious crimes by personal testimony of the type we had heard. But if one is to convince the world that strange, solid objects, controlled by some unknown intelligence, are flying about in our sky, he or she must have evidence beyond common human testimony!

My answer to Norm's question, "What about Beverly, Massachusetts?" was that, while Beverly was an impressive case, it alone would not justify an alternative report claiming that ETI is a reality. If we were to make such a claim, we had to base it upon something beyond what goes on in human minds. We needed to continue searching for evidence to support the human testimony—photographs which show definite objects and which cannot be debunked by the severest analyses; physical samples of substances which can be proven to be of extraterrestrial origin and to have been associated with the observed object; or detectable and measurable physical effects on the environment that can be definitely attributed to vehicles foreign to earthly cultures. Without such evidence, our "alternative report" would convince no one who was not already a believer in ETI visitation.

Besides, I pointed out to Norm, Dr. Condon had assured us that *our* findings and conclusions would be represented effectively in the final report—whether or not they coincided with his own conclusions.

We were aware that, in the absence of overwhelming evidence, an opinion dissenting from Dr. Condon's conclusions would carry little weight. We who might dissent simply did not bear the international reputation and scientific prestige Dr. Condon enjoyed. It was Dr. Condon's conclusion that was awaited by the U.S. Air Force and the world at large. If we were to arrive at different conclusions as a result of our UFO investigations, and those conclusions, together with their justifying arguments, were included in the project report, we really could expect no more.

The suggested mutiny—which I was sure could never have been successful—was one of the reflections passing through my mind as I placed my briefcase on my desk and looked around the empty room. I had a strange feeling of being alone. It was early evening, yet I felt I was the only person in the entire building, or anywhere near it.

I took the sample of Ubatuba magnesium from my briefcase and locked it safely in a file drawer before putting the finishing touches on my trip report. I had just returned from Washington, D. C., where I had taken the magnesium sample for the most accurate impurity analysis that man is capable of doing. (See Chapter 8). I placed the trip report under "Ubatuba Magnesium" in my desk file, without giving it much thought at the moment. Concern over the evident disintegration of the entire project blunted all mental activity. Norm, whom I had phoned before coming to the office, had told me he and Dave Saunders had been fired as a result of a letter Jim McDonald had written to Bob Low, in which it was revealed that McDonald had been shown an office memorandum which Low and Condon thought should not have been shown to anyone outside the project. I looked around and found the copy of McDonald's letter which had been sent to the staff office.

It was a long letter. The fifth page made reference to the memorandum of interest, which had been written by Bob Low on 9 August 1966, during the period Colorado University was

194

considering taking on the UFO project. The memorandum had been addressed to Graduate School Dean E. James Archer and University Vice President Thurston E. Manning. McDonald had quoted the Low memo:

> Our study would be conducted almost exclusively by nonbelievers who, although they couldn't possibly prove a negative result, could and probably would add an impressive body of evidence that there is no reality to the observations. The trick would be, I think, to describe the project so that, to the public, it would appear a totally objective study but, to the scientific community, would present the image of a group of nonbelievers trying their best to be objective but having an almost zero expectation of finding a saucer.

Oh, oh. It was that memo. I myself had run across that memo by Bob Low in the project files. I had been asked to give talks on the Colorado UFO Project at aerospace workshops for teachers in Oregon, and, since I had not been working with the project at its beginning, I had asked Bob where I could find information about the project's inception. He had referred me to the file which contained the now infamous memorandum.

Normally I would not have agreed to give public talks about the project. However, when Pat Cody, Director of Aerospace Education for the Pacific Region of the Civil Air Patrol, threw in a week-end of salmon fishing off the mouth of the Columbia River, I found his offer irresistible. Bob Low was preparing to leave for a trip to Europe, at least partly at project expense, and was not in a position to suggest that I not take advantage of an opportunity to enjoy some good salmon fishing.

Actually, I planned to fish for more than salmon. A trip to Oregon could give me a chance to visit Nick Mariana in Portland, and perhaps confirm claims that the Air Force had removed and kept the best portion of the movie he had taken in 1950 of two UFOs flying over Great Falls, Montana. (See Chapter 10). I considered the Air Force to be quite capable of issuing false information to the public, and thereby attempting to conceal facts of various nature from the citizenry. We had heard that Mariana had a letter from the Air Force admitting it did not return all of his film. The film it did return, which we had examined, showed indistinct objects which could, from that appearance alone, be the ordinary aircraft which the Air Force officially claimed they were. The missing portion supposedly showed shapes and structure that belied the aircraft explanation. If Air Force personnel had pulled some shenanigans with the Mariana films, which were widely claimed to be some of the best UFO photos in existence, that fact would be most interesting—particularly if I could locate the claimed missing frames in Air Force files!

So I had been pondering the dual fishing expedition as I read through the file of early project memoranda and letters, gathering information for the talks to some 1700 Oregon teachers. When I read the Low memo to Archer and Manning, my stomach caught in my throat. It clearly implied that we were involved in a white-wash non-investigation, probably aimed at getting the Air Force off a public criticism hook. Yet that was certainly not my opinion of the project, and when I was hired to work on it, I certainly was not told that I was not to conduct an honest evaluation of the UFO evidence.

Norm Levine was at his desk near-by when I read the memo. I handed it to him, and asked him to read it. After Norm finished gasping, I returned the memo to the file and continued searching for information to convey to the teachers. My own stomach soon settled back in place. While the memo reflected Bob Low's attitude—and, on reflection, was consistent with his actions throughout the project—I knew that it did not represent

Dr. Condon's views. And, after all, it was Dr. Condon's conclusions that would count, not Bob Low's.

The contents of the Low memo became common knowledge around the office. Although we all proceeded with our various travels and tasks, I did not clear the Low memo from the back of my mind until, at a later staff meeting, we confronted Dr. Condon with the question of what would happen if we who were doing on-site investigations of UFO reports were to come to conclusions about the nature of UFOs which differed from his own. We were, at the time, specifically concerned about possible differences regarding the validity of the extraterrestrial hypothesis. Dr. Condon had pointed out that we were completely free to seek out any evidence that extraterrestrial vehicles are or have been visiting our planet, and to pursue our leads in any manner we thought promising. If we could come up with convincing evidence, and could therewith convince him of the validity of the ETI hypothesis, that would be his, and the project's, report.

Now, as I sat at Norm's empty desk in the weird atmosphere of silence in the Colorado Project office in Woodbury Hall, reading Jim McDonald's letter to Bob Low, the memorandum I had purged from the back of my mind was thrust forcibly to attention, inflated to giant proportions. It was being used as a weapon by those who desperately wanted to discredit the Colorado Project. And it was an effective weapon, indeed!

The Air Force was paying about a half million tax-generated dollars for the Colorado study. At lunch with Dr. Condon sometime earlier, I had expressed my personal feeling that the American public deserved as honest an answer to the UFO question as it was possible for anyone to give, and also expressed my personal commitment to see that this was achieved in our study. Dr. Condon's response was, "I feel that way, too, Roy." Was the half million dollar investment, and this unique opportunity to give reliable answers to questions that interested millions of

Americans, now being flushed down the drain? Could the people who wanted no answer different from their own completely destroy the credibility of the Condon report merely by waving before the public eye a memorandum written by someone who was to serve as Project Coordinator? Could the word "trick" in the memorandum be used to make the American public believe it had been tricked into paying for a fake investigation? Would that ill-conceived memorandum which I had run across in the project files cause the project's downfall?

I rechecked to make sure the file containing the Ubatuba magnesium sample was securely locked, and picked up the note from my desk. I pocketed it as I left and closed the office door. Perhaps tomorrow would bring the cleaning out of my desk, too—including the trip report I had just filed therein. The note in my pocket, though it really wasn't needed for that purpose, would serve as a reminder of the hour I was to meet Dr. Condon in his office.

# Chapter 12

# The Writing of the Condon Report

## Continued Disintegration of Woodbury Staff

The elevator lifted me toward Dr. Condon's penthouse-like office in the Joint Institute for Laboratory Astrophysics building. It occurred to me that I had not visited that office before. After working on the UFO project under Dr. Condon's direction for almost a year, I wondered if my first visit to the penthouse was to be for the purpose of being fired. I knew that my summons to the Director's office meant I would be "on the carpet," and the meeting would determine my future role, if any, with the UFO Project.

Kay Shapley, Dr. Condon's secretary, showed me into his office without delay. Bob Low was already there. The atmosphere was tense, and I knew that Dr. Condon and Mr. Low were most distressed about the recent developments involving project staff.

Since they both knew I had been in Washington the previous week monitoring the analysis of the sample of Ubatuba magnesium, the first questions were inquiries into what I had learned.

I explained that the Ubatuba magnesium, claimed by some people to be more pure than Earthly technology was capable of producing, was not nearly as pure as the magnesium sample I had obtained from the Dow Chemical Company. Dow produced high purity magnesium samples years before the claimed explosion and destruction of the flying saucer over Brazil—more pure than the saucer fragment said to have been recovered from that explosion. Since the Ubatuba sample could easily have been produced by earthly technology, I stated, its existence did not serve as evidence that it was once part of a flying saucer.

This information was of interest, but not of great concern under the crisis situation that existed in Dr. Condon's office. The conversation quickly shifted to the topic of concern.

"You know, I suppose, that Saunders and Levine have been discharged from the Project."

"Yes, I have been told about that."

"Do you know why they were discharged?"

"Yes."

"Did you know about the memo that McDonald got a copy of?"

"I knew about it and was quite concerned about its implications until frank discussions with you relieved my qualms about those apparent implications." (Dr. Condon did not mention that he himself had not known that the Low memo existed. This fact was revealed later.)

"Were you there when a copy of the memo was given to McDonald?"

"No. I was not invited to the meeting with Hynek and McDonald. I didn't realize the memo was still an item of concern. I also didn't know that a copy had been given to Dr. McDonald."

200

I did not intend to keep secret the fact that it was I who had first run across the Low memorandum in the project files, and had expressed concern about its implications to Norm Levine. That fact just didn't come into the conversation. The significance of the memo was not in its discovery, but in the way it could be used, and was now being used, in an effort to discredit the entire Colorado Project.

Dr. Condon saw no reason to discharge the third and last of his active senior investigators. It was apparent, however, that the future of the project itself was in question. I was asked to carry on as I had been and try to fill in where the project was left short-handed.

I left Dr. Condon's office more concerned about the project than about my own participation in it. My employment contract with the project was to expire 30 June, so I had only about four months left to work on it anyway. I had already started negotiations to teach a term aboard ship in the "Semester at Sea" program, then operated under the auspices of Chapman College in California. However, I felt personal commitment to the project and urgently wanted to see it completed honorably, giving the public the best answers possible to questions about the existence and nature of UFOs.

Riding the elevator back to ground level from Dr. Condon's office, I thought about how an outsider might think that Dr. Condon, in his distant penthouse, was generally out of touch with the "real" UFO investigations being conducted out of the very active Woodbury Hall office. I knew that this was not the case. When I returned from my first project field trip involving mysterious beeping sounds from nowhere (see Chapter 1), Dr. Condon hailed me at lunch at the University Faculty Club and asked me to sit with him so I could fill him in on the details of the field trip. I knew that my subsequent field work was done with his detailed knowledge and personal approval. He had a

201

distant office, but he knew most of what went on in Woodbury Hall. He did not know about the Low memorandum or our concern regarding its implications.

The project was committed to carrying out on-site investigations of current UFO reports until 30 June, at which time all effort would be shifted to preparation of the final report. A sensational event on the UFO scene would demand attention, of course, but project personnel would pay no further heed to routine reports of UFO sightings after 30 June 1968.

Dr. Dave Saunders was a member of NICAP and the project's "Early Warning Network," a network of people around the country who were specifically designated to phone us immediately about local UFO reports. The Network was largely composed of NICAP members. Saunders' dismissal, and public distribution of the one damnable paragraph which Dr. McDonald had quoted from the Low memo, would undoubtedly result in reduced support of the project by NICAP, the nation's largest organization of people with special interest in UFOs. While we had four months remaining to investigate selected cases from current sighting reports, it was doubtful that we would get early information about many current sightings. As it turned out, some Early Warning Network members decided to continue their functions in spite of reservations they now had about the project's objectivity. News reporters around the nation also continued to phone us about local UFO events.

The number of sighting reports brought to our attention did dwindle, giving me the opportunity to finish investigations of old cases I had started earlier and to work on my contribution to the final report. At this point, that contribution was expected to be a chapter on the physical evidence that strange vehicles or objects had been present in our environment, and some discussion of the case studies I had done on-site.

Bob Low obviously had firm thoughts on what the project's

final report would be like. While the study's conclusions and recommendations would be written by Dr. Condon, Low took it upon himself early in the study to compile "information" to go into the final report. Perhaps he thought that snowing the public with a lot of technical information would create the impression that a truly scientific study had been made. One of Dr. McDonald's items of criticism of the Colorado Project in his seven-page letter to Bob Low in February, 1968 (the same letter that created such a furor because it quoted the 1966 Low memorandum) regarded the sub-contract Low had negotiated with Stanford Research Institute for an up-to-date review and discussion of optical and radar propagation anomalies. McDonald had been told that the SRI contract was for $50,000, and the agreed upon work did not include relating propagation anomalies to specific optical or radar UFO cases. "When I first heard that," he wrote, "I was stunned. My recommendation was to get to a bookstore and buy a $3.00 paper back edition of Kerr's book, and you'd have more solid technical information on propagation physics than you're likely to get out of such sub-contracting."

With three or four subcontracts of this type, including one for a chapter on the history of UFOs and related sightings, Mr. Low was assuring the project a voluminous final report, and he obviously considered it his personal duty to put it all together.

Low's preoccupation with "building the record" for the project's final report did not meet the approval of his administrative assistant, Mary Lou Armstrong. That preoccupation, along with Low's basic attitude toward the project, were strongly criticized by Mary Lou in a letter she wrote to Dr. Condon two weeks after Drs. Levine and Saunders were fired.

Mary Lou brought me a draft of her lengthy letter for review on Saturday, 24 February. Toward the end of the letter, she stated, "I was at the meeting in Denver in early December in which Saunders, Levine, McDonald, and Hynek got together to discuss the possibilities of action that might help to keep the study of UFOs going. In addition, I knew that at that meeting, McDonald received a copy of Bob's memorandum written to Deans Manning and Archer, although he knew the contents of it long before then." Mary Lou ended her letter by saying she was resigning her position as administrative assistant to the UFO project.

Mary Lou's letter was merely putting in writing what she had told Dr. Condon two days earlier. In her discussion of what she perceived to be general working staff dissatisfaction with Bob Low's activities and attitudes, she wrote, "After the last couple of days, I agree that I, and some others, have made a very tragic mistake in not coming to you long before this. But, that is in retrospect and, at the time, I personally did not feel that you would have been as sympathetic to our feelings as you have been."

Sympathetic or not, Mary Lou had been part of the mutiny; her continued employment with the project was not feasible. Dr. Condon accepted her resignation. Another key staff member was lost from the project. Mary Lou no longer would be available to take incoming calls regarding current UFO sightings—or to help prepare the project's final report.

Reporters and writers continued to descend upon Boulder, probing for more material regarding the project and problems within it. One of these was John Fuller, a journalist who had written two articles for *Look* Magazine about a particular reported UFO incident at Exeter, New Hampshire, as well as a book about that claimed incident. Both Mr. Low and Dr. Condon had "no comment" on Mr. Fuller's inquiries. The presence of such individuals, however, made it obvious that the airing of the project's problems in the news media and the campaign of committed believers to discredit the project's objectivity were not about to end.

Dr. Condon had taken so much criticism—some of it grossly unwarranted, and some earned by premature and careless statements about the project made at public gatherings—that he obviously regretted ever agreeing to direct the study. Tough fighter that he was, the limits of his patience and endurance were being tested and strained. I recall his comment after reading one of the many letters received by the project from school children. This letter read, "I am writing a paper on UFOs. Please send me your project." Condon, who thoroughly enjoyed anecdotes and good laughs, said to me, "You don't know how tempted I was just to box up all our files and send the whole damned thing to him!"

While Condon took all the guff from members of the public, I continued my project work, receiving full cooperation and respect from everyone I encountered.

I finally managed to make personal contact with the elusive Mr. Villa, whose sets of UFO photographs were available commercially and had received wide distribution. He told an interesting story of how he knew when to go out with his camera to get more pictures of UFOs. The photos themselves, however, did not warrant detailed analysis by our photogrammetry specialist.

Meanwhile, back at the office, the second shoe was about to drop. The project was receiving rumblings about the article John Fuller had written for *Look* Magazine. On Friday, April 26—the day before *Look* was to reach its subscribers—newspaper columnist Roscoe Drummond phoned Bob Low and read all of the *Look* article Low would listen to. Mr. Low spent the rest of that day in Condon's office.

The *Look* article was sensational and devastating. The cover headline was "Flying Saucer Fiasco," with a sub-heading "The Half-million Dollar Cover-up on Whether UFO's Really Exist." Inside, it was presented as "The extraordinary story of the half-million dollar 'trick' to make Americans believe the Condon

Committee was conducting an objective investigation." Of course, the article was built around the damnable paragraph in the pre-contract memorandum written by Robert Low, and presented as if that memo represented the project as it was being carried out.

On Monday, 29 April, Mr. Low arrived at the office in Woodbury with a copy of the *Look* article in hand. He read a statement to be released to the press, pointing out that he was quoted out of context, and the word "trick" as he had used it did not carry the meaning John Fuller had given it. He then wanted to know if I had been the one who pulled the memo from the files and showed it to other project members.

The *Look* article had said, "A senior member of the staff who was asked to make a speech before a teachers association began looking for specific details on the origin of the project. He was told he might find some information in the open-files folder under the heading 'Air Force Contract And Background'." The article went on to state that it was in this file folder that the staff member found the disturbing memorandum. After all the furor the memo had caused, I assumed it was then common knowledge that I was the one who had first noticed it in the file folder. I was surprised that Bob Low needed to ask the question.

I assured Mr. Low that it indeed was I who had noticed the memo and became concerned about it. I also pointed out that it was he, himself, who had suggested I look in that folder for the information I wanted regarding the inception of the project, just before he left for Europe. If this was new information to Mr. Low, I thought, perhaps I would be faced with another eruption. He said nothing at the time. He was called to Dr. Condon's office, and the two of them spent the rest of the morning and noon hour conferring with legal counsel.

Tension around Woodbury Hall was intense the next few days, but there were no explosions. Bob Low's world had collapsed around him. He had my complete sympathy.

Newspapers around the country had picked up on the condemning *Look* article. In a popular magazine with over 7,750,000 circulation, the article made it obvious that the project's report now would have no chance of enjoying public credibility if Robert Low had a significant role in its preparation. Robert Low had to go. On 15 May, two weeks after the *Look* and multiple newspaper articles appeared, it was announced that Robert Low's duties with the project would terminate on 24 May.

## Picking Up The Pieces

"I've got to have somebody, Roy! " Dr. Condon pleaded as he asked if I would plan to stay with the project beyond my scheduled termination date of 30 June to help get the report in reasonable shape. Dr. Condon was following the advice of friends by looking for a professional editor to assemble and edit the report. However, a person new to the project would sorely need the help of someone who knew the various cases investigated and the details of investigations—particularly in cases for which reports were left incomplete by staff members whose services had ended abruptly. If I would not provide this help, Dr. Condon had no one else to turn to.

Reluctantly, I wrote the administration of the Semester at Sea program and told them that, since I felt an obligation to complete what I was doing and felt it important that I do so, I would not be available to teach on their next cruise. I assumed I'd be able to do a Semester at Sea later. I hated to give up this trip, however, since I considered it an ideal one—from the West Coast, around South America, then to Scandinavia and return to New York.

Editor Daniel S. Gillmor visited the campus on May 15, the

day Bob Low's impending termination was announced. Dan specialized in scientific writing and had worked on publications in Great Britain and France, as well as Canada and the United States. His services were secured for the project with the help of Mr. Gerard Piel, publisher of the *Scientific American*. Dan would start work 10 June. The project was committed to submitting its finished report for review by a special committee of the National Academy of Sciences before the end of the year.

While the dust settled around Woodbury Hall and the office staff got reorganized, I again took advantage of opportunities to put the finishing touches on field investigations I had worked on earlier.

Claims were still being made that the Ubatuba magnesium sample, while found not to be ultra pure as claimed in UFO literature, was nonetheless unique (see Chapter 14). The claims suggested that special crystal structure may have given it the properties desired for space vehicles, and it did contain surprising quantities of strontium. Since the directors of Dow Chemical Company's Magnesium Metallurgical Laboratory at Midland, Michigan, Drs. R. S. Burk and D. R. Beaman, were willing to have their people do whatever microprobe and metallographic examinations of the Ubatuba sample I desired, I headed for Michigan, Ubatuba samples in hand.

Microprobe analysis showed the strontium to be uniformly distributed in the sample. Metallographic examinations done by one of the world's few magnesium metallographic specialists, Mr. Harold A. Diehl, showed large, elongated magnesium grains, indicating that the metal had not been worked after solidification from the liquid or vapor state. It therefore seemed doubtful that the sample had been a part of a fabricated metal object.

A check of the Dow Laboratory records revealed that over the years this laboratory had made experimental batches of magnesium containing various quantities of strontium. As early as

208

25 March 1940, it produced a batch of magnesium containing about the same concentration of strontium as was contained in the 1957 Ubatuba sample.

A fact revealed at the Dow Metallurgical Laboratory that I found particularly interesting was that a specimen of this same Ubatuba magnesium sample had been mounted and examined by Mr. Diehl himself on 14 November 1961. I already knew that the Ubatuba magnesium had been analyzed spectrographically in 1958 by a capable chemist at our Oak Ridge National Laboratories. That magnesium sample may never have been to Brazil, but it certainly had made the rounds in the United States!

Another case on which I wanted to tie up loose ends was the Winnipeg burned-chest case (Chapter 2). Despite promises, the project had not been notified of the finding of the saucer landing site until long after that claimed event, and I wanted to find out what Canadian officials had learned about the case after my Winnipeg trip. A claimed recent visit to the landing site had produced a sample of radioactive soil said to have been taken from cracks in the rock upon which the saucer had landed. The sample was given to the local Royal Canadian Mounted Police, who had sent it to Ottawa for analysis. The Mounties involved were less than happy to be given a soil sample, for the prospector had agreed not to disturb the site in any way, if he ever relocated it, before taking the Mounties to examine it.

The best source of information regarding later developments in this case was Dr. Peter M. Millman, who was Head of Upper Atmosphere Research of the National Research Council of Canada. The study of UFO reports, which had, until the spring of 1968, been handled by the Department of National Defense in Canada, was transferred at that time to the National Research Council. It resided there under Dr. Millman's management.

I visited Dr. Millman in Ottawa to discuss both the burned-chest case and his general attitudes and recommendations regarding investigations of reported UFO sightings. I thought, in the particular case of interest, Dr. Millman could tell me more than he would be willing to put in writing. Through Dr. Millman, I learned that the radioactivity in the soil sample from Winnipeg was crushed pitchblende ore, an ore which occurs naturally in Canadian deposits. We were in full agreement regarding the question of whether or not the radioactive material, said to have been found in cracks in the rock upon which a flying saucer landed, was put there by human hands.

On the way back to Colorado from Ottawa, I stopped at Wright-Patterson Air Force Base, Dayton, Ohio, to see if I could learn anything I didn't already know from Project Blue Book files. My hosts at the air base graciously housed me in their VIP quarters; however, they did not show me the frozen bodies of three-foot tall green Martians they reportedly kept in the Green Room or in Hangar 19 (see Chapter 10).

The chapter on physical evidence was the first that I drafted for the project's report. I had examined all claimed physical evidence brought to our attention, or that we could uncover, including saucer landing nests, occupant tracks, weapon residues, claimed parts of exploded or crashed saucers, "space grass," "angel hair," and radioactive material claimed to have been dumped or deposited from flying saucers. I had even examined a small, fabricated metal part that dropped nearly red hot from the sky onto a person's lawn and turned out to be part of the motor of a neighbor's lawnmower which had been thrown through the air by the rotating mower blade. Some of the claimed physical evidence was analyzed in great detail (see Chapter 8). The chapter conclusion simply said, "This project has found no physical evidence which, in itself, clearly indicates the existence in the atmosphere of vehicles of extraordinary nature. Belief in the existence of such vehicles, if such belief is held, must rest on other arguments."

"Dr. Condon liked your chapter so well that he took it home last night and read it to his wife, Emily," was the cheerful news as I arrived at the Woodbury Hall project office. I was pleased that something seemed to be going right for him. However, I wondered if Dr. Condon would like the other chapters I was working on. Conclusions on some of the field investigation cases would not be so clear-cut and certain as were the physical evidence studies.

Editor Gillmor needed help in more ways than just making sense out of some of the unfinished investigation reports. Dr. Joseph H. Rush, a physicist with the National Center for Atmospheric Research (NCAR) was loaned to the project to evaluate and organize unfinished case reports. We also arranged to borrow, on a short term consulting basis, needed specialists from the local laboratory of Environmental Science Services Administration to apply the Stanford Research Institute discussions of optical and radar principles to specific UFO sighting cases.

Associate Editor Harriet Hunter assumed extra duties as office manager and saw that the work was done on schedule. The edited final report began to be built, section by section.

"If this goes to print as it now reads, it will have to be under your name as author—it won't go that way under my name!" was my reaction to Dan Gillmor when I read his editorial changes to my chapter on physical evidence. He had reworded the introduction to display a cynical attitude which was not mine. The chapter did need editing to remove duplication and awkward sentence structure, but I would not tolerate changes in meaning or intent, and I did not hesitate to let that fact be known. After Dan consulted with Dr. Condon on the minor crisis which ensued, it was agreed that there would be no substantive changes in material submitted without explicit and written okay from the author. Once that hurdle was over, Editor Gillmor and I cooperated on a cordial, friendly basis. His requests for advice re-

211

garding significance or scientific validity of material he was editing were frequent.

During the report writing and editing period, visitors frequently dropped by for various reasons. Several writers for scientific magazines, as well as news reporters, desired interviews about the project. Such interviews were denied, at Dr. Condon's request.

Dr. Condon was strongly inclined to include material in the project report which would correct the errors in UFO writings, including testimony before the House Committee on Science and Astronautics. While he and I had lunch together, we had a long discussion of Dan Gillmor's opposition. Just two days earlier, I had advised Dan against such activity. My opposition was based on the conviction that such sparring would be endless. If one proved six of ten arguments wrong, the opposition would merely drop those arguments and substitute six new ones, leaving us where we started. The situation was similar to pursuing Dr. James McDonald's "twenty best UFO cases," which he told various groups of people were worthy of detailed scientific investigation. As soon as the investigator showed several of the twenty to have no merit, those were simply dropped from the list and replaced with different cases. Since Condon seemed to love a good fight, many of which he had experienced in his past activities, he must have found it difficult to yield to our arguments, and merely let erroneous testimony fall of its own weight. But he did.

Those who were campaigning vigorously for a continuing and intensified role of the federal government in UFO studies were most concerned about Dr. Condon's recommendation for future handling of UFO reports. Dr. Hynek was pushing for establishment by Congress of a UFO Scientific Board of Inquiry which would mount a continuing scientific effort on a "much larger scale than any heretofore." Jim McDonald, on the other hand, lobbied the House Committee on Science and Astronautics to take steps aimed at a "vigorous scientific investigation of the full spectrum of UFO phenomena." He favored multiple grants through existing agencies, such as the National Science Foundation and NASA. Both of these scientists, as well as others with strong commitments for continuous UFO study, feared Dr. Condon's recommendations would close out all options for government financing of UFO investigations in the future.

Before Dr. Condon wrote his recommendations portion of the project report, on 13 September, he called a group of us together to discuss what the project's recommendations should be. The discussion lasted from 10:30 A.M. until 4 P.M. Participants were, besides Dr. Condon and myself, Editor Dan Gillmor, Dr. Franklin Roach, and Dr. Joseph Rush. Dr. Rush previously had written a successful book on "The Dawn of Life." He had both a receptive mind and detailed knowledge of the project studies. Franklin Roach, an astrophysicist who specialized in air glow studies, had been named one of the two Principal Investigators of the project, under Dr. Condon, when the Colorado Project was first announced, but he had resigned in order to give more attention to his regular professional interests. He had returned to Boulder, however, and was writing a chapter for the project report on visual observations made by astronauts.

At the end of our all-day discussion, we did not know what Dr. Condon would write as "recommendations." We were confident, however, that those recommendations would reflect the actual findings of the Colorado Project.

All writing and editing of the project report was finished by the end of October, 1968. It was turned over to the Air Force on October 31, to be reviewed by the National Academy of Sciences and then released to the public. All the pieces were together.

UNIVERSITY OF COLORADO

BOULDER, COLORADO 80302

DEPARTMENT OF PHYSICS AND ASTROPHYSICS

202 Woodbury Hall

1 October 1968

Dear Roy,

The occasion of your leaving the University's Scientific Study of Unidentified Flying Objects should not be allowed to pass without my expressing both my regret that our association in this endeavor has now come to an end and my warmest best wishes for the future. It would really have been impossible for me to function in my capacity as editor of the project's final report without your constant assistance as scientific advisor and your even-handed counsel in matters of high and low policy with respect to every aspect of the preparation of the report. Your contribution of three chapters and many case-reports to the final document are, of course, at the very heart of the report and completely indispensable to it.

Please accept my thanks for all your help and for your tact and good humor on occasions when the going got a little heavy!

Cordially,

Daniel S. Gillmor
Project Editor

Roy Craig, Ph.D.
Department of Physics and Astrophysics
University of Colorado
Boulder, Colo.

# Chapter 13

# What the Condon Report Said

"An automatic best-seller" was *Newsweek* magazine's comment on the report of the Condon Study when it was first announced. Publishers must have thought that, too, for many of them had been clamoring at our door to buy the rights to publish the report. The successful ones must have basked in the knowledge that they had purchased a bag of gold. As the time came for the report to be written, Low's ill-conceived memorandum was being splashed across the country in magazines and newspapers, bringing project credibility into question. The publishers perhaps felt their gold leaking from the bag.

There was really no gold in the sack to begin with. The report could not attract great public interest, for it did not say what a large segment of the public wanted to read: that we had found strong and valid evidence that visitors from alien cultures were flitting about in our skies.

In 1465 pages (963 pages in the re-set Bantam paperback edition), the report covered a multitude of topics. We all have heard a camel described as "a horse put together by a committee." This report did have the features of something put together by a committee—which, of course, it was. Although Dan Gillmor had done a good job of editing, the parts were too disconnected and disparate to be put together into anything with smooth-flowing continuity.

The literature survey and technical discussion of optical and radar mirages, which Bob Low had hired SRI to do, occupied more than 100 pages of the report. Other scientific discussions related to specific UFO observations and, therefore, seemed more appropriate for inclusion. A discussion of problems of human perception and cognition was made vividly real by a detailed description of what numerous and varied observers, from Kentucky to Pennsylvania, reported seeing when they observed parts of the disintegrating Zond IV spacecraft as it reentered Earth's atmosphere on 3 March 1968. Of course, some observers of that event saw a cigar-shaped craft with a row of lighted windows and a fiery tail, even though what they were looking at were point sources of light from burning spacecraft debris.

Dr. Mark Rhine's discussion of psychological aspects of UFO reports also was cogent. He reviewed misidentification of real stimuli, perception of unreal stimuli as real, falsification, and hysterical contagion (the crowd effect). His comment on hypnosis was particularly relevant, since hypnosis had been claimed in some well-known UFO cases to support the validity of the stories related. Dr. Rhine's statement in the report, already quoted in Chapter 7, was, "Sometimes hypnosis can aid in bringing to conscious awareness material that has been repressed. But persons who cannot distinguish their fantasies from reality will, under hypnosis, only reveal more of the same fantasies."

## Case Studies

The section chosen for special comment by Walter Sullivan, science editor for *The New York Times*, in his introduction to the Colorado Study report, was the one containing case studies: "The result has been a series of case histories that reads like a modern, real-life collection of Sherlock Holmes episodes. The cases range from the eerily perplexing to the preposterously naive. The reader is given a taste of the scientific method, even though the cases are often such that they defy anything approaching deductive analysis."

Fifty-nine case studies were presented, and some of them did make interesting reading. Fourteen of them were photographic cases. The interest of the case reports to the casual reader, however, was lessened by changes in the reported locations of most of the events, making them unidentifiable to a reader who wanted to know the outcome of an investigation of a well-published sighting in his own area. For instance, a Los Angeles resident might want to know what the Condon Study learned about the lumber-yard guard who made front-page headlines by reporting shooting at a cigar-shaped flying saucer only 100 feet away while on duty during the night, and picking up the flattened bullets that fell back to the ground after hitting the UFO. That resident would not likely find the case of interest in the report. This case, which occurred during the Colorado Study period, and which I personally investigated, was listed in the report as having occurred in the "South Pacific." Changes in location, like changes and omissions of peoples' names, were made upon the advice of legal counsel to avoid legal actions against the project by individuals who might have felt injured. While the reason for obfuscation probably was valid, that obfuscation did, I believe, make the accounts less interesting to read.

## Studies Made by Project Staff

Details of scientific studies carried out by members of the project staff are described in seven chapters of the report. Social scientists would probably think the studies were unbalanced, since six of these seven chapters involve physical aspects of the UFO report phenomenon. The social sciences accounted only for a survey of public attitudes regarding UFOs. Emphasis was on the physical because Dr. Condon felt that is where it should be if one wanted to determine if any UFOs, other than misidentified natural or man-made objects, had real existence outside the human mind. With that goal in mind, it may be difficult to defend even the attitude survey, for what people believe to be true is of little value in proving truth.

The other six chapters in this section of the Condon report were descriptions of our field studies, photographic analyses, direct and indirect physical evidence, optical and radar analysis of field cases, and Franklin Roach's discussion of observations of unidentified objects by U.S. astronauts. They go into great detail, giving, where appropriate, actual measurement data. For instance, one UFO publication had listed 106 cases in which electromagnetic effects were a significant feature of the UFO report. Forty-five of these involved stalled automobile motors, generally accompanied by headlight and clock failure. We chose to test the magnetic field hypothesis by looking for direct evidence that automobiles reportedly affected by the presence of UFOs had in fact been subjected to a magnetic field that was sufficiently intense to cause motor malfunction (see the case of Mr. X, Chapter 6). The report discussion covers the reason automobiles have a permanent magnetic "signature," the intensity of magnetic fields required to alter the signature, the intensity of fields capable of causing motor malfunction, and actual compass reading data demonstrating the existence and permanence of such signatures.

The Condon report points out that physiological effects of UFOs also are reported frequently, including strange reactions of animals, feelings of pressure, heat, or "prickly sensations," and, occasionally, lapses of consciousness by a human observer. Relative to such claims, the report states:

Our field teams also have noted that strange animal reactions, and even interference with telephone operation, have been claimed in cases in which the UFO was later identified as a bird or a plastic balloon. Such instances confuse the issue, but do not prove that in other cases there is no relation between claimed unusual physical and psychological effects and UFO sightings. However, after careful consideration of these claimed effects, as well as claimed radiation level excursions and unexplained electric power interruptions attributed by some writers to the UFO presence, we found that we had no recorded or otherwise verified instances which establish a relationship between an UFO and an alteration in electric or in local magnetic fields or in radiation intensity.

## Observations Of Astronauts

The Condon report gave special consideration to things seen by astronauts while in orbit about Earth. There were two reasons for such special attention. One was the special qualifications of astronauts as observers, with excellent eyesight, special training in basic physical science, and familiarity with navigational astronomy. Observation from orbit, free of restrictions of ground-based observation, was also an advantage. The second reason for special consideration, however, was the presence on the project staff of Dr. Franklin E. Roach, who not only was designated originally as a principal investigator for the Condon project, but had, in the course of his normal professional duties, participated in the scientific briefing and debriefing of the astronauts on Mercury and Gemini flights between 1961 and 1966.

Dr. Roach discussed objects seen by astronauts which, at the time of observation, were not identifiable by them. He went into vivid detail of conditions of observation, through small windows which inevitably got coated with light-scattering deposits which hampered observation, and quoted taped records in the astronauts' own words as they described unknown sights to ground control. The result was a fascinating account which gave the reader a feeling of sharing the experiences with the astronauts.

Most of the unknowns the astronauts observed turned out to be illuminated flakes of paint or other surface material flaked off the spacecraft itself, materials "dumped" from the spacecraft or vented from on-board storage tanks at craft sunrise, and other man-made spacecraft in orbit, including booster rockets and other debris associated with placing the various craft in orbit.

In Dr. Roach's opinion, three of the multitude of visual sightings of unknowns by astronauts while in orbit had not been explained adequately. He considered these three to be a challenge to the analyst. The one he considered most puzzling was Astronaut McDivitt's observation from Gemini 4 of a cylindrical object with a protuberance. That spacecraft was in free drifting flight somewhere over the Pacific Ocean. McDivitt thought the object was probably some unmanned satellite, and NORAD suggested it might have been Pegasus B, which was 1200 miles away at the time. McDivitt questioned that identification, and Dr. Roach considered it suspect. Astronauts McDivitt and White reported that they were not successful in a serious attempt to see the Pegasus B satellite during a later encounter when Pegasus was only a fourth as far away.

On the same Gemini 4 flight, McDivitt also reported observing a moving bright light at a higher level than the Gemini spacecraft. McDivitt referred to the sighted light as a satellite. However, as far as Dr. Roach could determine, that suggestion was not confirmed by a definite identification of a known satellite.

The third observation which Dr. Roach considered inadequately explained was by Astronaut Borman on Gemini 7. Borman had reported seeing a "bogey" flying in formation with the spacecraft at the start of the second revolution of the flight. There appeared to be hundreds of small particles in orbit with the "bogey" object, and they appeared to be in polar orbit. The booster rocket also was observed at the same time and identified by the astronauts in orbit similar to theirs. While the bogey and accompanying particles had the appearance of fragments from the Gemini 7 launching, such fragments could not have been in polar orbit, as they appeared to be to the astronauts. For that reason, this sighting remained on Dr. Roach's list as unexplained.

When I visited with Dr. Roach in Hawaii in 1987, he mentioned that another astronaut told him during a debriefing that, before he became an astronaut, he made a series of ground sightings of an unknown object or objects in California. The sightings were corroborated by members of his crew. Since they were not made from orbit, however, they were neither reported nor further investigated by Dr. Roach, who suggested I might try to contact this astronaut to learn more about those sightings. The sightings did not seem extraordinary, however, and I did not try to contact the astronaut.

## Visual and Radar Mirages

Gordon Thayer, a radar specialist working with the Environmental Science Service Administration, had been assigned the task of examining cases in the project files in an effort to determine whether or not anomalous modes of propagation of electromagnetic waves (the mirage effect) could account for the visual and/or radar appearances. It was a difficult assignment, apparently made in hopes of tying technical reviews Bob Low had contracted to project investigations. Mr. Thayer concluded that anomalous propagation was the most plausible explanation in nineteen of the thirty-five radar-visual cases he examined.

Some of the sightings Mr. Thayer examined were attributed to man-made devices. Seven were left in the "unknown" category.

## Photo Analyses

Photographic evidence of the existence of "flying saucers" was examined and reported by Dr. William K. Hartmann. His study included both new cases (photos made during 1966–68) and independent re-evaluation of older cases. From those studies, he concluded that most UFO photos are the product of misidentification, poor reporting, or fabrication. Two of the photographic cases he examined remained unidentified after analysis. They were the motion pictures of two bright light sources taken at Great Falls, Montana (discussed also in Chapter 10), and two photographs of a saucer-shaped craft taken at McMinnville, Oregon, in May, 1950. Dr. Hartmann reported the latter case to be one of the few UFO reports in which all factors investigated appeared to be consistent with the assertion that an extraordinary flying object—silvery, metallic, disc-shaped, tens of meters in diameter—flew within sight of two witnesses. However, he noted that, even in this case, the evidence did not positively rule out fabrication.

Dr. Hartmann's general conclusion regarding photographs that remained unidentified after analysis was that none of them conclusively established the existence of "flying saucers" or any extraordinary aircraft or unknown phenomenon. He pointed out that it is always possible to "explain" the observations, either by hypothesizing some extraordinary circumstance or by alleging a hoax, and none of the cases investigated was compelling enough to be conclusive on its own.

The project report does not mention some interesting photographs, said to be of "UFOs," which we ran across in various ways during our investigations. In one case, an observer at the Climax, Colorado, Solar Observatory reported the presence of a saucer-like object in a photograph he had taken the previous evening. He had not seen the object when he took the picture. It just appeared on his photograph. When a project investigator checked with the photographer in Climax, he found the photo was taken through a window. The "UFO" was the image of a light fixture behind the photographer reflected by the window glass. When this was pointed out to the photographer, he readily acknowledged, with a bit of embarrassment, that this indeed explained his mysterious "UFO." Interestingly enough, twenty years after this simple explanation, I noticed this picture of the reflected light fixture printed in one of the sensational newspapers at the grocery store checkout stand. It was presented, of course, as a photo of a real flying saucer.

My own review of all the field studies we did for the project led to the conclusion that I would not recommend official field investigations of routine UFO reports if the intent of those investigations was to determine whether or not an alien vehicle had been physically present. Our experience indicated that, if there were an observation of a vehicle actually from an alien culture, unless the sighting were of a truly spectacular nature, the report of it would be buried in many thousands of similar reports triggered by ordinary earthly or astronomical phenomena. Success in sorting that special report from the others would seem unlikely. One might assume that an actual landing of an alien vehicle or being would create a response so different from the usual UFO sighting report that the event would not pass unheralded.

## Dr. Condon's Recommendations

Dr. Condon's conclusions and his recommendations for dealing with UFO reports in the future, which, as stated above, were the major concern of individuals who desired perpetual federal involvement in UFO investigations, were succinct. His conclusions were simply stated: "Our general conclusion is that nothing has come from the study of UFOs in the past twenty-one years that has added to scientific knowledge. Careful consideration of the record as it is available to us leads us to conclude that further extensive study of UFOs probably cannot be justified in the expectation that science will be advanced thereby."

This is the conclusion Condon's detractors feared. They may have been surprised, however, at his recommendations: "We believe that any scientist with adequate training and credentials who does come up with a clearly defined, specific proposal for study (of UFOs) should be supported. We think that all the agencies of the federal government, and the private foundations as well, ought to be willing to consider UFO research proposals along with others submitted to them on an open-minded, unprejudiced basis. While we do not think at present that anything worthwhile is likely to come of such research, each individual case ought to be carefully considered on its own merits."

Dr. Condon continued, "This formulation carries with it the corollary that we do not think that at this time the federal government ought to set up a major new agency, as some have suggested, for the scientific study of UFOs. This conclusion may not be true for all time. If, by the progress of research based on new

224

ideas in this field, it then appears worthwhile to create such an agency, the decision to do so may be taken at that time."

Regarding the question as to what, if anything, the federal government should do about the UFO reports it receives from the general public, Dr. Condon's comment was, "We are inclined to think that nothing should be done with them in the expectation that they are going to contribute to the advance of science."

The thought that some UFOs might constitute a threat to our national security was treated by Dr. Condon thusly: "We adopted the attitude that, without attempting to assume the defense responsibility which is that of the Air Force, if we came across any evidence whatever that seemed to us to indicate a defense hazard, we would call it to the attention of the Air Force at once. We did not find any such evidence. We know of no reason to question the finding of the Air Force that the whole class of UFO reports so far considered does not pose a defense problem."

Condon then turned to Project Blue Book, the Air Force's special operation for handling UFO reports. "It is our impression that the defense function could be performed within the framework established for intelligence and surveillance operations without the continuance of a special unit such as Project Blue Book, but this is a question for defense specialists rather than research scientists."

## The Omnipresent Memorandum

The project report included a review of the history of UFO sightings, some of which was written as a result of one of Bob Low's contracts. Dr. Condon himself, however, wrote of the history of these sightings from 1947 to 1968—from the highly-publicized sighting of Kenneth Arnold, from which the term "flying saucer" arose, to the end of the Colorado Study.

Dr. Condon reviewed the various sighting reports, focusing particularly on the series of Air Force projects set up to deal with UFO reports, and various advisory panels used by the Air Force to guide their activities in this area. He discussed how the Colorado Project came into being, as the implementation of recommendations made in the report of the O'Brien Committee—a panel composed of both physical and social scientists organized by the Air Force to review Project Blue Book.

Regarding the by then infamous memorandum written by Robert Low during contract negotiations between Colorado University and the Air Force Office of Scientific Research, Dr. Condon pointed out that it did not represent official policy of the University. It was, he correctly said, at most, a preliminary "thinking out loud" about the proposed project by an individual having no authority to make formal decisions for the administration, the department of physics, or any other university body. (Low was, at the time of writing his memo, assistant dean of the graduate school.)

Continuing on the Low memorandum, Dr. Condon wrote, "Indeed, one of the proposals Low makes in it runs exactly contrary to the procedure actually followed by the project. Low proposed 'to stress investigation, not of physical phenomena, but rather of the people who do the observing—the psychology and sociology of persons and groups who report seeing UFOs.' It should be evident to anyone perusing this final report that the emphasis was placed where, in my judgment, it belonged: On the investigation of physical phenomena, rather than psychological or sociological matters. It should be equally obvious that, had the University elected to adopt Low's suggestion, it would have hardly chosen a physicist to direct such an investigation."

Dr. Condon went a step further in this regard. He stated that he would have declined to undertake a study focusing along psychological and sociological lines, considering himself unqualified to direct such an investigation.

Dr. Condon also pointed out that, not only were the views in the Low memorandum at variance with his own—but also that he was not aware of the existence of the memorandum until eighteen months after it was written. In Dr. Condon's words, "Since I knew nothing of the ideas Low had expressed, they had no influence on my direction of the project."

# Chapter 14

# The Alternative Report

The "Alternative Report" of the Colorado Study which, at the time of the suggested mutiny, Norm had cautiously inquired if I would participate in writing, was produced and published by Dr. David Saunders after he was discharged from the project staff. It was written in collaboration with newspaper reporter R. Roger Harkins, who, while working for the Boulder, Colorado, *Daily Camera*, had maintained deep interest in the Colorado project. The book was rushed into print for public release ahead of the project's final report, so that it might further discredit the Condon Report. Its intent was to present an alternate interpretation of the findings of the Colorado study—an interpretation which concluded that the presence of extraterrestrial intelligence was indicated by our examination of UFO reports. It carried the title "UFOs? Yes! Where the Condon Committee Went Wrong."

The introduction to the Saunders-Harkins book was written by John Fuller, author of the *Look* article which had called the Condon study a "fiasco." Mr. Fuller concluded his introduction of the new book with, "Unhindered by administrative dogma, and free from Air Force pressures, it is bound to be far more interesting than the official report of the Condon Committee, whose philosophy was expressed in Mr. Low's memo concerning 'the trick' to make the project 'appear' as an objective scientific study."

Since Fuller had been in Boulder talking with both Saunders and Harkins before he wrote either the *Look* article or this introduction, he presumably was quite aware that Dr. Condon had not known the Low memo existed. He presumably also knew, as revealed in the Saunders-Harkins book which he was introducing, that Dean Archer, one of the two university administrators to whom the Low memorandum was addressed, also had not known of the memo. According to Harkins, Dean Archer had a secretary get a copy of the Low memorandum, upon Harkin's request to see it, from the files of the graduate school where Low served as assistant dean when the memo was written. After reading the memo then for the first time, finding it incredible, and telling Harkins that he had never received a copy, Dean Archer, apparently distressed that he had not received a copy, allowed Harkins not only to see the memo but to have a copy of it.

Since Mr. Fuller must have known that the Low memorandum, reprehensible as it was, had no actual effect on Dr. Condon or the project, his claim that the Low memorandum expressed the philosophy of the Condon Committee seems to be a very specious propaganda "trick."

Dr. Saunders's alternate interpretation of the results of studies we made as part of the Colorado project, from which he concluded that extraterrestrial visitation actually was indicated, was based primarily on three arguments or cases. They were, first,

229

"orthoteny," second, the Mariana photographs, and third, Ubatuba magnesium.

The orthoteny argument that the locations of reports of UFO sightings during a given time period occurred on a straight-line gridwork—suggesting systematic surveillance of Earth by alien beings—seemed to me utter nonsense. As I had pointed out to Dr. Levine (see Chapter 11), all UFO investigators knew that at least ninety percent of UFO reports were misidentifications of planets, balloons, airplane lights, and other natural phenomena or man-made objects, or hoaxes. The locations of those ninety-plus percent, whether or not on straight lines, could not possibly indicate alien presence, and their inclusion in any alignment effort would so obscure any actual alignment of "real" UFO sightings, if such existed, that the actual alignment would never be apparent. I never discussed orthoteny with Dr. Condon, but I believe he also considered the argument to have no probative value whatsoever—although he was tolerant of Saunders's efforts to make something of it.

The two specific cases which Dr. Saunders considered to be convincing evidence of extraterrestrial visitation were ones which I personally had investigated (see Chapters 8 and 12).

I was never able to prove that the Air Force had confiscated some of the most telling frames of the Mariana movie of two lights moving together over Great Falls, Montana. A letter from the Air Force admitting that it had not returned all his film, which Mr. Mariana casually told me "must have got lost during the move to Portland" seemed to me one of the things which would *not* have gotten lost while moving—particularly since Mr. Mariana had taken legal action against a writer who had called his UFO claims fraudulent. It seemed to me that if such a letter had existed, copies certainly would have been made and used as evidence in court. Mr. Mariana still had a collection of news clippings about his UFO film and the 1956 documentary movie on UFOs which featured it. That collection had not been lost in the move.

The film itself withstood Dr. Hartmann's scrutiny, and, rejecting the official explanation of the lights as reflection of sunlight off two Air Force planes coming in for a landing at the Great Falls air base, Hartmann reported them as "unknowns" in the Condon Report.

In discussing the case in the Condon Report, as an example of the difficulties of field investigation of old UFO cases, I pointed out discrepancies which had come to light during my investigation. I did not report, however, the comment I considered most significant, which Mr. Mariana's ex-secretary made to me during a telephone interview. She had been the only other witness to the filming of the UFOs by Mr. Mariana. The fact that she recalled seeing only one object, when the movie clearly showed two, I did not consider particularly significant, as I did her very hesitant comment when I pressed for information or beliefs regarding clipping of the film by the Air Force. The very hesitant comment was, "What you have to remember in all this is. . . ahh . . . that Nick Mariana is a 'promoter'." That comment was adequate to close our conversation. I would not like to have to defend Dr. Saunders's conviction that the Mariana film is strong evidence that we have extraterrestrial visitors.

I was particularly surprised to see Ubatuba magnesium listed in Saunders's alternative report as one of the "facts" from which he concluded that extraterrestrial intelligence stands as the "least implausible" explanation of "real UFOs" (Saunders, p. 237). The analyses I had done on the magnesium samples (see Chapter 8) showed this material not to be unique and probably never part of a manufactured vehicle, as already noted.

The story of the origin of the Ubatuba samples as fragments of a disintegrated flying disc itself was one of the most highly suspect of the UFO reports we encountered.

Conditions which make the story highly suspect already have been given, but perhaps even more damning to the Ubatuba case is the fact that the "fragments" were nearly pure magnesium metal. In spite of its light weight, pure magnesium is among the least likely materials of construction for space vehicles. Magnesium burns so readily in air that, in the granular state, it has been used in incendiary bombs. Massive pieces must pass the melting point of 650 degrees Centigrade before they ignite. In mankind's early space programs, one of the most difficult problems was developing a material of construction for nose cones which could withstand the high temperatures due to friction as the space vehicle reentered the Earth's atmosphere. Most materials burn up, as would magnesium if not protected by some more resistant material.

Pure magnesium also has very low structural strength, and must be alloyed with such other elements as aluminum or zinc before it is a suitable material of construction. Such alloys have been widely used when light weight is desired and, because of their use in the Agena and other space programs, there may now be more magnesium than any other metal floating around in space near Earth. But it would not be pure magnesium. Magnesium has many merits, but pure magnesium simply is not an appropriate material of construction for space vehicles that are expected to enter oxygen-containing atmospheres.

In summary, Saunders and Harkins have every right to believe in extraterrestrial visitation if they wish. Such belief, however, rests on desire, not on reason applied to evidence provided by the cases Saunders listed. To claim that the Colorado Study developed any probative evidence to support a belief in extraterrestrial visitation is, perhaps unfortunately, simply but emphatically untrue. Dr. Condon gave his investigators a free hand to try to reveal such evidence, and Saunders, Levine, and several others of us made a serious effort to do so, as indicated in Chapters 1 through 10 above. The "alternative report" is not defensible as a scientific work.

Chapter 15

# The Impact of the Condon Report

## The Air Force Got What It Needed

As the Colorado Study got underway, the Air Force was receiving 3,000 letters a month from school children asking for information on UFOs. Major Hector Quintanilla, Director of Project Blue Book, told the Colorado group, "Last month we had twenty-five Presidential and seventeen Congressional inquiries regarding UFOs." The workload associated with Air Force involvement with UFOs was indeed impressive.

By Air Force Regulation, an officer at each Air Force facility had been designated to serve as the area "UFO Officer." He was to receive and investigate all local reports of unidentified flying objects, and send a report of each case and his findings to the Blue Book office at Wright-Patterson Air Base. After the Colorado Project was commissioned, Air Force Regulation 80-17A stipulated that a copy of each report to Blue Book also be sent to the Colorado Project.

The Colorado Project staff was still trying to settle on a methodology for carrying out the UFO study when the Air Force Advisory Panel held a special briefing for that staff in Boulder on 12 January 1967. Dr. Condon discussed the progress and future plans of the project and asked for Panel members' opinions on where the emphasis should be placed with respect to policy questions the study had to deal with. Although I had not yet joined the project staff at that time, I do have a transcript of that briefing, at which Lieutenant Colonel Robert Hippler, who was with the Air Force's Science Division, Directorate of Science and Technology, and was serving as the Project's contact at the Pentagon, commented, "You see, first of all, we (the Air Force) have not charged you, and you have not promised, to prove or disprove anything." Later, after Dr. J. Thomas Ratchford, who had represented the AFOSR in negotiating the project contract, said, "I think the only thing that we are really asking you to do is to take a look at the problem, first of all, and on the basis of what you determine recommend what the Air Force should do in the future." Col. Hippler then remarked, "I don't think we want any recommendation from you unless you feel strongly about it."

The Air Force may not have realized that what it really needed was a means of getting freed from the UFO responsibility altogether. But that was what it did need, and the recommendations of Dr. Condon in the Colorado Project Report gave it the means to do just that.

On 17 December 1969, the Secretary of the Air Force announced the termination of Project Blue Book. He stated that the decision to discontinue UFO investigations was based on an evaluation of a report prepared by the University of Colorado entitled, "Scientific Study of Unidentified Flying Objects"; on a review of the University of Colorado's report by the National

Academy of Sciences; on past UFO studies; and on Air Force experience investigating UFO reports during the past two decades.

Orders establishing a UFO officer at each air base were rescinded, and UFO sightings henceforth were to be reported to local law-enforcement agencies and/or amateur UFO investigating groups. Those UFO reports that had been classified "restricted" or "secret" were declassified, and all reports pertaining to the 12,618 UFO sightings reported to the Air Force from 1947 to 1969 were transferred to the Air Force Archives.

The Air Force had cause to breathe a sigh of relief. It had been relieved of a large load of unproductive work unrelated to its mission of national defense. Its public relations problem had been solved, as the public could no longer make convincing accusations that it was covering up the truth about flying saucers. Congressional investigations could look elsewhere, as could the thousands of children whose teachers encouraged them (mistakenly, in the view of Dr. Condon) to look into the UFO phenomenon as "science."

Students of history can find an excellent review of U.S. Air Force involvement in UFO investigations, written by Dr. Condon himself, including, in the appendix, copies of relevant panel reports and Air Force directives, all in the Colorado Project report—if they can find a library which has a copy of that report! (See "Erasing the Condon Report," below.)

## The Scientific Community Got What It Expected

Before the Colorado Project contract was signed, it was agreed that the project's report of its work and conclusions would be reviewed by a panel representing the National Academy of Science before it was released to the public.

An eleven-member panel, chaired by Gerald M. Clemence

of Yale University, was appointed by the Academy in late October and early November 1968. It began its review immediately after the project report became available on November 15. The panel was charged to provide an independent assessment of the scope, methodology, and findings of the University of Colorado study as reflected in the report.

In order to feel comfortable with its conclusions, panel members chose to examine not only the report, but also papers by technically trained persons who debunked extraterrestrial visitation and by those who professed belief that UFO reports indicated the presence of extraterrestrial vehicles. Three papers by Dr. James McDonald were included in the latter category.

As to scope—did the report, in the opinion of the panel, cover those topics that a scientific study of the UFO phenomena should have embraced? The panel concluded that the scope of the study was adequate to its purpose.

On methodology—did the report, in the opinion of the panel, reveal an acceptable scientific methodology and approach to the subject? The panel reported, "We think the methodology and approach were well chosen, in accordance with accepted standards of scientific investigation."

Since field investigations of UFO reports were one of my personal primary functions on the project, I was pleased to read that the panel considered the narration and interpretation of cases investigated in the field to be reasonable and adequate.

Regarding the findings of the project—were the conclusions and interpretations warranted by the evidence and analyses as presented in the report and were they reasonable?—the panel concurred with the report's findings and evaluations, and also with its recommendations of termination of Project Blue Book, non-involvement of Federal agencies in future UFO reports, and treatment of proposals by qualified scientists for funding and support of future UFO research on an equal basis with other research proposals.

In its conclusion, the panel stated, "We are unanimous in the opinion that this has been a very creditable effort to apply objectively the relevant techniques of science to the solution of the UFO problem."

The National Academy Panel apparently found Bob Low's office memorandum too insignificant to mention, for it made no reference to it.

Further indication of the general scientific community's acceptance of and agreement with the Colorado Study could be found in comments such as appeared in the 17 January 1969, edition of *Science* magazine, the official publication of the American Association for the Advance of Science. In *Science's* opinion, "The Colorado Study is unquestionably the most thorough and sophisticated investigation of the nebulous UFO phenomenon ever conducted." The *Science* writer also quoted Condon (page 262 of the report) stating that a conclusive demonstration that UFOs really are vehicles from another world would be the greatest single scientific discovery in the history of mankind. The report had found no evidence that such discovery was imminent, however, and that seemed to be what most of the scientific community expected.

## The Public Got More Than It Wanted

Public interest in UFOs has varied in intensity through the years, depending somewhat on influence of the press and other news media. That interest, however, involves a far greater segment of the public than a mere "fringe" group of people who believe religiously in flying saucers from outer space.

A 1966 Gallup Poll indicated that more than five million Americans claimed to have seen something they believe to be a "flying saucer." Other surveys showed that nearly half of the people surveyed who were under twenty-five years of age be-lieved that "flying saucers" are not only real, but that they come from outer space. While such belief decreased markedly in older age groups, to about one-third of those over fifty believing in their "reality" and about one-fifth in their origin from outer space, the figures indicate that belief in extraterrestrial visitation is held by many millions of Americans.

Extraterrestrial visitation, of course, was the "jackpot" ques-tion involved in the Colorado Study. It is there that public inter-est focused. Those who were interested in what the Condon Report said did not really care about scientific discussions of atmospheric conditions that cause mirages, whether the mirage is seen on radar or visually; of "auto kinesis," which causes sta-tionary lights to appear to the human observer to move and "dance about" when there are no visible reference objects near the light—even though almost everyone who observes such a stationary light will "see" such a motion; of light diffraction and scattering, which causes light sources to appear extended in di-mension, change color, and move about; of the crowd effect, of mass hysteria, and hysteric contagion; of processes of human perception and cognition; or of planets that can be seen in the daytime. But, in the Condon Report, the public got more than it wanted in more ways than scientific discussion.

It often was said that the American people wanted to know what really was being seen by those who reported UFO obser-vations. I don't believe this is what they actually wanted at all. The majority of those interested in the subject wanted confirma-tion of their beliefs, which often were based primarily on desire. They wanted the Condon Report to verify evidence that we are being visited by beings from another world.

Those of us working on the Colorado Study were quite aware that it is theoretically impossible to prove that all reported sightings, other than hoaxes, were misinterpretations of ordi-

239

nary things—that is, to *prove* that a flying saucer from outer space has *not* visited Earth. We were aware also that proof of extraterrestrial visitation, if it occurred, could be possible. However, we were not able to produce convincing evidence of the latter. Believers in extraterrestrial visitation wanted the Condon Report at least to leave the question open, to consider some sightings unexplainable as ordinary phenomena, and the mystery to remain alive and healthy. To the extent that the Condon Report did not do this, and therefore destroyed illusion, the public got more than it wanted. For human beings do not want to give up their illusions. Many, of course, will not do so, and will rationalize their illusions and simply reject non-conforming evidence (see Chapter 8).

Individuals and magazine publishers who had published articles and books about contacts with flying saucers from outer space fought desperately, as we already have seen, to discredit the Condon Report even before it was written. Author John Fuller surely did not want the public to believe a major report which implied that the Incident at Exeter, about which he had written in such a fascinating manner, probably never happened. *Look* magazine, which had achieved record sales by publishing Fuller's UFO articles, also did not want to be made to look ridiculous. It is not surprising that Fuller and *Look* tried desperately, and with considerable success, to discredit the Colorado Study before the Final Report could stand to defend itself.

*Look* had published not only the Fuller articles, but also a special edition entitled "Flying Saucers," which featured "authentic" pictures of UFOs. Dr. Condon commented on only two of those photos in his report. One, a pentagonal image which had appeared unexpectedly on a high school teacher's photograph of a milk can and sky, received Condon's comment because he found it hard to understand how the editors of a national illustrated magazine could be unfamiliar with this kind of

240

image, which is quite commonplace and arises from a malfunctioning of the iris of the camera. The other photo upon which he commented was of an allegedly "claw-shaped" marking on the dry sand of a beach where a strange "machine in the sky" had been reported. Some of the dark colored moist sand making up the "claw mark" had been shipped to Wright-Patterson AFB and analyzed. The liquid was found to be urine. Dr. Condon, with his ever-present sense of propriety, commented that some person or animal had "performed an act of micturition there." The type of pattern pictured, of course, is quite familiar to any boy who has taken a piss in snow.

The Fuller article in the 14 May 1968 issue of *Look*, calling the Colorado Study a "flying saucer fiasco," a "half-million dollar cover-up on whether UFOs really exist," and "the half-million dollar 'trick' to make Americans believe the Condon committee was conducting an objective investigation," was based almost entirely on a somewhat twisted interpretation of the office memorandum written by Robert Low before the project started. The *Look* article, which was given maximum public attention by newspapers across the country, was quoted on the floor of Congress on April 30 by Representative J. Edward Roush of Indiana, who commented, "The story in *Look* magazine raises grave doubts as to the scientific profundity and objectivity of the project conducted at the University of Colorado. The publication of this article will cast in doubt the results of that project in the minds of the American public; in the minds of the scientific community."

The next day, Mr. Roush again picked up on the issue, "Since reading this article and considering the situation there at the university, I have written to the Secretary of the Air Force asking for his comments on this deplorable situation, and I have written the Comptroller General of the United States asking for an immediate investigation of the incidents involving the use of public moneys at the University of Colorado." Believers in extraterrestrial visitation could be found in almost any group of Americans, and Congress was no exception.

Those believers now had a weapon—an indiscreet office memorandum—and hungrily latched onto it to join the campaign to discredit the forthcoming Condon Report.

Influenced by intense lobbying efforts of Dr. James McDonald, the Committee on Science and Astronautics, U.S. House of Representatives, scheduled a "symposium on unidentified flying objects" as an official committee hearing on 29 July 1968. The "symposium" was chaired by Representative Roush, who invited prepared statements from six scientists and written papers from six others to be included in the hearing record. Among the "others" was Dr. Donald Menzel, then of the Smithsonian Astrophysical Observatory, who responded with a telegram to Mr. Roush. "Received your letter and will contribute paper as you suggest. Am amazed, however, that you could plan so unbalanced a symposium, weighted by persons known to favor Government support of a continuing, expensive, and pointless investigation of UFOs without inviting me, the leading exponent of opposing views and author of two major books on the subject."

The scientists invited to present their views to the congressional committee were J. Allen Hynek, James E. McDonald, Carl Sagan, Robert L. Hall, James A. Harder, and Robert M. L. Baker, Jr. In his opening remarks, Mr. Roush said, "We are here today to listen to their [the six scientists'] assessment of the nature of the problem: to any tentative conclusions or suggestions they might offer, so that our judgment and our actions might be based on reliable and expert information." Mr. Roush did not mention that one can get any advice he wants by careful selection of his "experts."

Perhaps more significant than the scientific presentations at this hearing were comments on the Colorado Study by congress-men. Any evaluation of an Air Force contract came under the jurisdiction of the House Committee on Armed Services instead of the Committee on Science and Astronautics, and discussion of the Colorado Project at this hearing would, therefore, raise a jurisdictional issue. It was agreed that the Colorado Study, which had received such devastating attacks by the information me-dia, would not be discussed. Congressman William Ryan of New York, however, could not restrain himself. After McDonald's presentation, he asked, "I wondered, Dr. McDonald, if you would care to evaluate the research project at the University of Colo-rado and comment on that?" Symposium Chairman Roush at-tempted to shut off this line of questioning, reminding Mr. Ryan of the agreement that this was not the place to discuss the Colo-rado Project. Mr. Ryan rephrased his questions, and persisted with, "You wrote a letter to the National Academy of Sciences concerning this [the Colorado] project. Have you had any reac-tion from the National Academy of Sciences?" McDonald's re-sponse: "Yes, I received a letter from Dr. Seitz, saying for the time being we must let the Colorado Project run its course. That was the gist of the answer." At this point Mr. Roush again inter-jected, "I would appreciate it if we dispensed with that. Let me say that the National Academy is undertaking an evaluation of the University of Colorado project, and this will be published." But Mr. Ryan would not be cut off. "I'm suggesting maybe this committee should make an investigation of the University of Colorado project." At that point, Rep. George Miller, chairman of the Committee on Science and Astronautics, stated, "That is something we don't have authority to do here."

This hearing seemed ill-timed, since the Colorado Project was just nearing completion, and no one knew yet what its re-port would say. Whether or not the hearing had any lasting im-pact, it was clear that the impact of the Low memorandum had been felt even in the halls of Congress.

The office memorandum written by Bob Low mainly concerned the attitudes of non-university scientists in the Boulder area regarding whether or not they thought the University of Colorado should accept an Air Force contract for a UFO study. It is amazing how the memo's one indiscreet paragraph could be used so effectively to destroy, in the mind of the general public, the credibility of the project itself, even though it was neither written by nor reflective of the opinion of the project's director.

Representative Roush's predilections were perhaps revealed in his selection of hearing participants. He later was elected to the Governing Board of NICAP.

NICAP, of course, had joined the drive to keep the public from accepting the results and recommendations of the Colorado Study. In a special box with the *Look* article by Fuller, Major Donald E. Keyhoe, USMC, Retired, Director of NICAP, wrote, "After 17 months, NICAP has broken with the University of Colorado UFO Project. We join *Look* and John G. Fuller in disclosing the facts as a public service. . . . NICAP will submit plans to the President and Congress for a new official investigation. . . . Meantime, to offset the Colorado failure, our investigations will be intensified. . . ."

A year after the Condon Report was released, the American Association for the Advancement of Science (AAAS) held another symposium on UFOs. It did not succeed in getting Dr. Condon to participate. In fact, Condon vigorously opposed the holding of such a symposium by the AAAS, which he had once served as President. However, Condon did not prevail, and the symposium proceeded as part of the AAAS annual meeting, with fifteen invited papers. The "pros" and the "cons" were represented in a balanced presentation. Participants included astronomers, physicists, sociologists, psychologists, psychiatrists, and a representative of the newspaper industry.

Groups like NICAP saw this symposium as a last-ditch chance to rekindle the public interest in UFOs that it felt slipping away. Both Dr. Hynek and Dr. McDonald gave papers, pleading for additional UFO studies. McDonald stated, "I am enough of a realist to sense that, unless this AAAS symposium succeeds in making the scientific community aware of the seriousness of the UFO problem, little response to any call for new investigation is likely to appear." It apparently was for that reason that the proponents of major government involvement in UFO investigations put their strongest efforts into this last-ditch stand.

However, the Colorado Study had, by then, received unanimous endorsement by the reviewing committee of the National Academy of Sciences. Attacks on it were not to be popular at this meeting of scientists, as they had been at the U.S. House of Representatives' "symposium." In fact, Dr. Menzel commented, "The scientific world should be highly grateful to Dr. Edward U. Condon of the University of Colorado, who undertook, in the public interest, an independent and unbiased study of UFOs.... Condon's book deserves our support as well as our gratitude. I heartily endorse the report and concur with its general findings."

While Dr. Menzel was more pleased with the Condon Report than most, it was obvious that, with few exceptions, the Condon Report had won the day in scientific circles. Those who wanted to believe in extraterrestrial visitation were then fighting in the wrong arena.

Looking back at the UFO wars, one sees interesting parallels with other wars, complete with intrigue, infiltration, spy activity, and secrecy. The Air Force had stipulated that the Colorado Study was to be done by scientists who had no prior commitment regarding the nature of UFOs. Dr. David Saunders claimed, in order to qualify to participate in the Study, that he had joined NICAP only as the easiest means of obtaining NICAP publications. His subsequent actions and irrational evaluation of data to favor the extraterrestrial hypothesis, however, indicated that his membership in NICAP was quite fitting to his predilections.

The NICAP organization fully cooperated with the Colorado study as long as their man, Saunders, was working at Woodbury Hall. When Saunders was fired, and it became obvious that NICAP would have no influence on the study results, Major Keyhoe gave up his hope that the study would show that the Air Force had indeed conspired to withhold the truth about UFOs from the American public. Hence, his dramatic withdrawal of NICAP support for the project.

Fuller stated, in his *Look* article, that McDonald first became aware of the Low memorandum at the 12 December 1967, Denver meeting of Hynek, McDonald, Saunders, Levine, and Armstrong. However, Saunders's *UFOs Yes* book reveals that McDonald had been informed of the memo earlier by Keyhoe. Saunders had secretly taken a copy of the memo to NICAP Director Keyhoe, cautioning him that it was to be known only by members of the NICAP Governing Board. Saunders had, according to his own book, been surprised to learn that McDonald knew of the memo, since McDonald was not a member of that board. Since Saunders took a copy of the memo with him to the Denver meeting, it seems logical to assume that he intended to give it secretly to McDonald, to be used in any way it could be used to undercut the credibility of Dr. Condon's future report. I think it was significant that the memo was given to McDonald after Hynek left the meeting.

Condon and Low's reaction to McDonald's use of the memorandum played beautifully, for their enemies, into the enemies' hands. Condon's immediate firing of Saunders and Levine, making a major issue of the memorandum, brought the office memorandum to public attention and gave it its destructive power.

Condon's "enemies" had won a skirmish in the UFO wars.

## Casualties of the UFO Wars

References of statements and activities of Dr. McDonald have appeared repeatedly in this book. Dr. James E. McDonald had a distinguished career. Not only was he a Senior Physicist at the Institute of Atmospheric Physics, and Professor in the Department of Meteorology at the University of Arizona, but he was also a member of the National Academy of Sciences's Panel on Weather and Climate Modification; a member of the ESSA-Navy Project Stormfury Advisory Panel; a member of the American Meteorological Society's Commission on Publications; and a member of the National Science Foundation's Advisory Panel for Weather Modification.

Dr. McDonald told the U.S. House of Representatives Committee on Science and Astronautics, at its Symposium on UFOs, that he had a moderate interest in UFO reports for twenty years, and interviewed 150-200 witnesses in the Tucson area before 1966. His interest intensified in 1966, and he spent that summer vacation period examining official UFO reports at Project Blue Book and unofficial reports in the files of NICAP and APRO. He became convinced that the better UFO reports dealt with extraterrestrial devices of some surveillance nature.

For the next two years, Dr. McDonald spent nearly all his time on UFO concerns. He vigorously studied reports, interviewed witnesses, and tried to convince other scientists, newspaper editors, congressmen, and anyone else in the United States and Canada who would listen, that UFOs constituted "the greatest scientific problem of our times." He tried to convince congressional committees that greatly expanded scientific and public attention to the UFO problem was urgently needed. He suggested, at a General Seminar of the United Aircraft Research

Laboratories, East Hartford, Connecticut, that adequate proof that the extraterrestrial hypothesis was the most probable explanation of the UFO evidence would require monitoring and observational programs supported by budgets that probably would "dwarf the present NASA budgets."

In a lengthy presentation before the 1967 annual meeting of the American Society of Newspaper Editors, Dr. McDonald pleaded for the editors' support in bringing about Congressional hearings that could escalate the scientific study of the UFO problem to the top-level status he believed it deserved. He pointed out, "You members of the American Society of Newspaper Editors are in an ideal position to generate the pressures necessary to force Congressional investigation that will awaken scientists here and abroad to the real state of the UFO problem."

In April, 1967, Dr. McDonald received a report, written by an Anglican missionary in the Papuan Territory of New Guinea, of a series of UFO sightings that had taken place there. That report apparently intensified his interest in the international nature of UFO experiences. He pursued that interest while on a trip to Australia the following summer, and reported interviewing seventy-five or eighty UFO witnesses in Australia, New Zealand, and Tasmania. After the Australia trip, he came to Boulder to share with the Colorado Project the information he had gathered. He found UFO experiences elsewhere to be quite similar to those in the United States, and he believed many of them to be significant.

Dr. McDonald kept close watch on the Colorado Project, and criticized it frequently. After the Condon Report was published, he fought desperately, as we already have noted, to keep its recommendations from being accepted by the scientific community and the public. The common scientific rejection of his views, and the failure of his last-ditch effort, at the AAAS symposium mentioned above, to get the UFO problem elevated to a status where it would receive major effort and support, must have been devastating to him.

After completing my parts of the Condon Report, I spent a month or so in Colombia, South America, and on the Amazon River in Columbia, Brazil and Peru. Then I began my duties as a Visiting Professor at the University of Hawaii in Honolulu. After returning to the mainland, I stopped for a visit with Dr. Condon in Boulder. He told me the tragic news that Jim McDonald had gone out onto the desert, put a rifle to his head, and pulled the trigger. He was found there, still alive, and had survived, but would henceforth be blind.

Dr. Condon was obviously moved and saddened by this happening. Neither of us knew what other problems had left Jim so mentally anguished. We realized, however, that the rejection of his views on UFOs by his fellow scientists, after he had worked for about three years so energetically and brilliantly on this issue, must have had a major impact on his outlook.

Months later, I visited Dr. Condon again. Again, he had unpleasant news. Jim McDonald had gone back onto the desert and repeated his action. This time, it was fatal. Our sympathies were for Jim's wife and six children.

I believe it also was Dr. Condon who told me that Bob Low, who had accepted a position as Vice President for Administration at Portland State College, died soon thereafter in the crash of a private plane.

I don't suppose J. Allen Hynek's career should be considered a casualty of the UFO wars. He wrote a book on his UFO experiences and served as a consultant on the movie *Strange Encounters of the Third Kind*—in fact, he appeared briefly in that movie. He formed a UFO research organization to receive, investigate, and log UFO reports. Presumably the organization operated on private contributions, as Hynek was unsuccessful in getting federal or agency funding. He served the organiza-

249

tion as an elder statesman and advisor after he turned over its leadership to others. He reportedly became disappointed with the new leaders' performance, and wrote them, acrimoniously, that they had better "get their act together." Six months before his death in 1986, he was still contacting sympathetic scientists, such as Franklin Roach, seeking their support for proposals for funding of UFO studies. (Dr. Roach, who had participated in the Colorado Study, knew Dr. Hynek when they were in graduate school together at Yerkes Observatory.) The funding was not forthcoming. I suspect Dr. Hynek approached the wrong clients with the wrong arguments.

In 1995 a substantial sum of money was made available to the three major UFO organizations in the United States to enhance UFO research. Officers of the J. Allen Hynek Center for UFO Studies thereupon organized a workshop for invited scientists, including the author of this book, to discuss optimum utilization of such funds. Actually, Dr. Hynek simply didn't live long enough to see some of his dreams become reality.

As for Dr. Condon, the UFO wars made their contribution to the saddening of his later years. He lost no prestige as an outstanding scientist in the minds of his colleagues. However, it cannot make a devoted scientist happy to experience mutiny and denigration of his work, or to have a journalist who has a national public audience call the project he directed a "flagrant example of the misuse of the taxpayers' money and what has to be considered a dereliction of scientific duty."

When the project was over, Dr. Condon considered the editorial in *The Nation* to have been the most prescient of the many editorial comments made when the project was announced. *The Nation* had declared, "If Dr. Condon and his associates come up with anything less than the little green men from Mars, they will be crucified."

Dr. Condon also commented in the project report, "I had

some awareness of the passionate controversy that swirled around the subject, contributing added difficulty to the task of making a dispassionate study. This hazard proved to be much greater than was appreciated at the outset. Had I known of the extent of the emotional commitment of the UFO believers and the extremes of conduct to which their faith can lead them, I certainly would never have undertaken the study."

Dr. Condon died in 1974, five years after his UFO report was published.

Assuredly, the large organizations of UFO believers, NICAP and APRO, must be listed as casualties of the UFO wars. When the Colorado Project commenced, NICAP claimed to have 12,000 members—some of them scientists, engineers, and other technically-trained people. APRO claimed to have about 8,000 members. The wounds these organizations received were not fatal, and they continued to exist. After the Condon Report and its recommendations received acceptance by the scientific community, however, the two large organizations of UFO enthusiasts lost popularity and quietly faded toward oblivion.

The human need for a mythology acceptable to technically-oriented societies, however, did not fade with the large organizations which promoted belief in vehicles from outer space. The tremendous popularity of the movie *E. T.* and the *Star Trek* series speaks to that need, as does the continued existence of numerous small groups of UFO believers who support their beliefs and each other with meetings, newsletters, and testimonials. Speakers continue to attract large audiences, particularly in college settings, as they tell about Air Force or CIA conspiracies and frozen little green men kept at Wright-Patterson Air Force Base.

The number of flying saucer clubs that existed internationally at the time of the Colorado Project was suggested in the tenth anniversary issue of a newsletter *Saucers, Space, and Science*, written by Gene Duplantier of Ontario, Canada. The newsletter listed names and addresses of seventy clubs and newsletters in locations scattered about the United States; twenty-four in Great Britain; thirteen in Canada (including the Ottawa New Sciences Club with its publication *Topside*, discussed at length in Chapter 8); six in Australia; six in various countries of South America; and from one to four each in Belgium, Denmark, Finland, France, Germany, Holland, Iceland, Italy, Japan, New Zealand, Spain, Sweden, and Switzerland. Whether or not clubs of enthusiasts were then active in the Communist world is speculative. It was known, however, that UFO sightings frequently were reported there.

A number of the listed clubs may have been casualties of the UFO wars of the late 1960s. Some simply did not survive the passage of time. Some have survived and thrived, and they have been joined by new clubs that have appeared through the years in local areas, as the human psychic need continues to assert itself.

To a large segment of the general public, as well as to club members, the symbolic flying saucer represents acceptance of the belief that intelligent beings exist elsewhere in the universe. It is a significant, and probably now permanent, part of human culture.

## Erasing the Condon Report

At the time the Condon Report was completed, E. P. Dutton and Company had purchased publication rights for hardback distribution, and Bantam Books had paperback rights. Bantam was so sure there would be great public demand for the report that they rushed the re-setting of type and had the report ready for printing in something like seventy-two hours after its release. Their "first printing" of some huge number of copies (my recollection of the figure as 200,000 may be grossly erroneous) hit the market in rush fashion—and the market accepted it like a lead balloon. I often wondered if Bantam employees enjoyed a big bonfire to dispose of the unsold copies of their "first printing."

In 1989, I decided to try to learn how many copies of the Condon Report had been sold or otherwise distributed to the public. I didn't really expect Bantam or Dutton to give out their sales figures, but I sent carefully-worded and hopeful requests for the information, anyway. I also sent such a request to the U.S. Department of Commerce, National Technical Information Service. In 1969, the Air Force had let it be known to the public that photoduplicated copies of the Condon Report were available in a three volume set from what was then known as the Clearinghouse for Federal Scientific and Technical Information, for a mere three dollars per volume.

Since this source of the report was a government agency, I thought perhaps I could get sales information from it. I was overly optimistic. The people receiving my written request were not able to break out of their computer routine, and all I got back was an order form and information that the current price for photoduplicated copies was $42.95 for Volume 1, and $49.95 each for Volumes 2 and 3.

With the help of U.S. Representative Ben Nighthorse Campbell's office, I learned that the government had, by 1989, photocopied, on request, a mere 330 copies of Volume 1, 307 of Volume 2, and 301 copies of Volume 3. In addition, it had sent out 166 microfiches of the report. For the whole nation (or world), this was negligible distribution! But then, the Bantam edition initially was available for $1.95, so why should people order photocopies from the government at nine bucks?

Maybe Bantam Books sold more copies of the report than I thought. After switching from one party to another on a phone connection, I finally got connected with a lady at Bantam who wanted to be helpful. The trouble was, her computer failed to

253

show any book entitled *Scientific Study of Unidentified Flying Objects* as ever having been published by Bantam. She did say that other books published earlier than 1969 were still on her list, and ones now out of publication carried a notation to that effect. But there was no listing under "Scientific." I suggested that perhaps the book had been such a bomb that Bantam wanted to forget they had ever gotten involved with it, hence obliteration from the records. I probably will never know how many copies of the Bantam paperback were sold.

Of course, I got no reply from Dutton either. I assume quite a number of libraries purchased Dutton's hardback version of the report. It might be difficult to find a library which has a copy today, however. At the AAAS symposium in 1969, referring to the Bantam paperback, Dr. Menzel commented, "I am concerned to learn that this [Condon] report is disappearing from libraries around the country at a rate far greater than one would expect for a book that costs only $2.00. I wonder whether this might not be an attempt at suppression by various individuals who regard it harmful to the cause of UFOlogy."

Out of curiosity, in 1989, I checked the two libraries in Durango, Colorado. The public library had a copy of Saunders's book *UFOs Yes: Where the Condon Committee Went Wrong*, but had no record of ever having had the Condon Report. The Fort Lewis College library listed the Condon Report in its stack holdings. When I checked there, however, the copy was gone. It had been checked out, not returned, and was then listed as "lost." Perhaps Dr. Menzel's suspicions were correct. Computer listings for libraries in Denver and neighboring towns showed both the Condon Report and the Saunders book at the University of Colorado libraries, but only the Saunders book at three other universities in the area. Of seven of the public libraries in the Denver-Boulder region, three showed no listing of the Condon Report.

Conspiracy or not, it seems obvious that there has been very little reading of the Condon Report by the American public.

The American public also has not been informed of the Condon Study by TV or other media. Periodically through the years, TV audiences have been treated with "documentaries" on UFOs. The ones offered in 1985 and 1988 seemed typical. In 1985, the "documentary" pretended to present all aspects of the subject, yet it did not even mention the Condon Study. The Seligman Productions live TV program presented on 15 October 1988, entitled "UFO Cover-Up" lasted two hours. It mentioned that Project Blue Book was terminated in 1969, but it made no mention of why—nor of the Condon Study. Pretending the study had never happened, this production left viewers with two major questions: 1.) Is our government hiding the truth from us? and 2.) Should there be a Congressional investigation of the UFO phenomenon? I found it hard to believe the producers of this film were all so young that they were innocently ignorant of important past events which they had ignored in their film.

Time-Life Books published a series of Mysteries of the Unknown, beginning in 1985. One of these volumes was *The UFO Phenomenon*. The advertising flyer said, "UFO sightings are ignored or dismissed by the CIA and the NSA. Yet, U.S. government officials have denied release of documents requested under the Freedom of Information Act on the grounds that public knowledge of UFO details would threaten national security!" Of course, any serious discussion of the Condon Study would lead the reader to feel that this flyer statement, as well as much of the contents of the book, was utter nonsense.

By 1990, very few Americans, particularly those who were too young, at the time of the Condon study, to follow the news, or who were born after the 1968 study, had any idea that an official Scientific Study of Unidentified Flying Objects had ever been made. The popular Larry King Live TV show, in a 1994 multi-hour special presentation titled "The UFO Cover-Up?" also made no mention whatsoever of the Condon study. It did include Barry Goldwater, long-time U. S. Senator and once candidate for the office of President of the United States, indicating that he hoped he should live long enough to see the Air Force reveal the truth about UFOs. In *Omni* magazine's 1995 series focusing on how to search for and discover UFOs, the writer does list the Condon Report as an indispensable reference book for a serious UFO investigator. However, he pays little heed to the contents of that report.

In 1994, the Air Force again had to go through an investigation and explanation of the claimed UFO crash at Roswell, New Mexico, back in 1947—in spite of the by then long-standing Air Force policy to leave UFO investigations to civilian authorities. The Air Force apparently felt it had to do this, again, after U.S. Representative Steven Schiff of New Mexico asked the General Accounting Office to press the Pentagon to declassify documents relating to the Roswell event.

The Air Force found no classified documents to declassify, but, in an effort to put to rest persistent rumors that the government has conspired to hide the truth, spent several months reviewing archives and old news stories, and tracking down people involved, when possible. The 1994 conclusion, contained in a twenty-five-page report, plus thirty-three attachments, was that the debris found at Roswell probably came from a once top-secret balloon designed to monitor the atmosphere for evidence of Soviet nuclear tests. This conclusion, of course, was immediately rejected by UFO believers, who wrote it off as a continuation of the Air Force conspiracy to keep the truth from the public. The futility of trying to prove there is no conspiracy was again demonstrated. The Incident at Roswell lives on in tabloid newspapers, made-for-TV movies, and two UFO museums operated since 1992 in Roswell, New Mexico.

One might wonder if the campaign to publicly discredit the

Colorado study had been so successful that it relegated the study to oblivion. The discrediting campaign was certainly a factor. However, the book and film producers probably ignored the Condon Study and its results simply because the story was more interesting without them—perhaps less factual, but more interesting.

Representatives of the news media frequently state that their purpose is to "inform the public." Their bottom line, however, is not to "inform the public"—it is to "sell the paper," "sell the show," or, for the author, "sell the story." Walter Sullivan, science editor of *The New York Times*, who was the press representative at the 1969 AAAS symposium on UFOs, stated there:

> Reporters earn their bread and butter with good stories, and don't get full credit if they 'qualify to death' such a yarn. They are trained to check the source of an interesting report, then write it up 'colorfully'. But, they don't do a full research on it, and they hope that no one 'shoots it down' before the readers can appreciate it. We journalists should not be too proud of this shallow treatment, knowing that deeper investigation will often lose the story.

The way newspapers misinform the public was obvious to me while I worked on the Colorado Project. Colorful and sensational reports of UFO encounters typically were spread across the local newspapers' front pages. A day or two later, however, when it was shown that, for instance, the law enforcement officers who had chased a flying saucer in a dozen counties in Georgia had actually been chasing the planet Venus, the revealed facts of the case were reported in a small column buried in the back part of the paper. That was the case also when the flattened bullets that had dropped back off a flying saucer after a lumberyard guard in Los Angeles fired his pistol at it were revealed to have been flattened by encounter with a steel trash barrel which the very bored guard had used for target practice. These facts did not make an interesting story. Since the average reader didn't get to page twenty-two in the later newspaper, he was left with the belief that there had been a real UFO encounter in his neighborhood.

The thesis of Mr. Sullivan's paper at the AAAS symposium was that we have all been conditioned by the press, radio, and TV—by the general tone of our society—to a hierarchy of beliefs that include, for most of the population at least, the image of UFOs. Mr. Sullivan felt that public opinion was swinging away from UFOs, but it would be a disservice to science if everyone were conditioned to ignore strange sights in the sky.

Mr. Sullivan stated, "I disagree with Dr. Condon, who vehemently opposed this symposium, because I feel that UFOs represent a human phenomenon that is far more important than any of us realize. Our attitudes and perceptions are conditioned to a degree far beyond our capabilities of direct observation."

Sullivan had written the introduction in the Condon Report. His awareness of the newspaperman's contribution to the conditioning process, and the image of UFOs that the public was conditioned to believe in, may have told him why the media have chosen, in later years, not to recognize the creation or existence of the Condon Report.

A comment Dr. Condon buried in the project report displayed an attitude not unlike that indicated by Robert Low in his infamous memorandum. It seemed quite inconsistent with Dr. Condon's tolerance of views held by his investigative staff and with his recommendations in the project report. The comment was, "It is regarded by scientists today as essentially certain that ILE (Intelligent Life Elsewhere) exists, but with essentially no possibility of contact between the communities on planets associated with different stars. We, therefore, conclude that there is no relation between ILE at other solar systems and the UFO phenomenon as observed on Earth." This statement did not preclude a relation between UFOs and ILE within our own solar system, and at that time our space probes had not yet completely eliminated Mars as a possible home of ILE. Dr. Condon's dogmatic comment, however, is one which could as well have been made before the Colorado Study as afterwards. It had no dependence on the results of an investigation.

Economist John Kenneth Galbraith once wrote that the American public did not understand the importance in our society of the "no-business meeting," that is, a meeting whose purpose was not to conduct business, but to give the impression that business was being conducted. Bob Low's indiscreet paragraph in his office memorandum suggested the Colorado Study would be a "no-business" investigation. Dogmatic views like that of Condon, quoted above, would fit a situation in which a "no-business" non-investigation would be appropriate. The contents of this book, however, as well as the full contents of the Condon Report, show that the American public got a real "business" investigation in the Colorado Project, regardless of the implications of Low's office memorandum, regardless of the possible appropriateness of a non-investigation, and regardless of the campaign of magazines and newspapers to convince the public otherwise.

# Outlook

# Interstellar Travel And The Current State Of Human Knowledge

Periodically, there appears in a science magazine an argument which purportedly proves that a visitation on Earth of some being from outer space would be incompatible with the laws of physics. Therefore, of course, flying saucers cannot exist.

The authors of such articles often concede that life as we know it probably exists on perhaps as many as a million or more planets around the 200 thousand million stars of our Milky Way galaxy—to say nothing of the millions of similar galaxies in the observable universe. Other planets might contain life not as we know it but as we can imagine it, such as life based on ammonia instead of water, functioning at temperatures far below those at which we water beings would become solid objects. There might, of course, exist other forms of life of such a nature that our limited experience and intellects do not give us the ability to imagine.

It is the fantastic distance between stars that makes interstellar flight, according to present knowledge, seem incompatible with the laws of physics. Our concepts of space and time tell us that it would take years for anything traveling at the speed of light—perhaps many thousands of years—to get to or from Earth's nearest inhabited neighbor planet.

Relativity theory tells us that no material objects could travel as fast as the speed of light, and that the mass of moving objects increases as the velocity of motion increases, going to infinity if the speed of light were to be reached. The theory is upheld by experiment. Atomic particles accelerated in cyclotrons and synchrotons, for example, are observed to increase in mass as they achieve a significant fraction of the speed of light, in full agreement with expectations based on relativity. If the mass of an object increased to near infinity, it would take near infinite energy to push that mass to a still greater velocity, and the speed of light is therefore an unachievable maximum speed for a material object.

At the time of the Colorado UFO Project, Dr. Menzel, who was perhaps the most outspoken of scientists who felt that extraterrestrial visitation of Earth was not possible, wrote to the U.S. House Committee on Science and Astronautics:

"Please don't misunderstand me. I think it is very possible that intelligent life—perhaps more intelligent than we—may exist somewhere in the vast reaches of outer space. But it is the very vastness of this space that complicates the problem. The distances are almost inconceivable. The time required to reach the earth—even at speeds comparable with that of light—range in hundreds if not thousands of years for our near neighbors. And it takes light some billions of years to reach us from the most distant galaxies, times comparable with that for the entire life history of our solar system. The number of habitable planets in the universe is anybody's guess. Any figures you may have heard, including mine, are just guesses. I have guessed that our own Milky Way may contain as many as a million such planets. That sounds like a lot, but the chances are the nearest such inhabited planet would be so distant that if we send out a message to it today we should have to wait some 2,000 years for a reply."

Dr. Carl Sagan, who, at the time of the Committee on Science and Astronautics hearings in 1968, was already establishing programs to monitor radio waves coming to Earth from space and watching for signs of intelligent communication, and who since has become quite familiar to readers and TV audiences for his work in cosmology, was less dogmatic than was Dr. Menzel. While cautioning the House Committee that he was obviously speaking in the context of contemporary science when saying one cannot travel faster than light, he stated, "But that, of course, is a time-dependent statement. It may be that this isn't the ultimate truth." Dr. Sagan concluded, "It is not beyond any question of doubt that we can be visited."

But even Dr. Sagan's outlook brought little solace to UFOlogists. He also told the committee, "It would be rash to preclude, from our present vantage point, the possibility of its [interstellar space flight's] development by other civilizations. But if each of, say, a million advanced technical civilizations in our galaxy launched an interstellar spacecraft each year, and even if all of them could reach our solar system with equal facility, our system would, on the average, be visited only once every 100,000 years."

Such a conclusion stems from a reversion to the dogma of contemporary science. It also assumes random exploration and travel, in the absence of any universal intelligence or purpose.

I do not wish to denigrate contemporary science. Its achievements are fantastic, quite the match for miracles of other religions. And its miracles are reproducible and demonstrable. I find it almost unbelievable that a Voyager II spacecraft could send detailed pictures of the planet Neptune and its moons to a tiny receiver on Earth some three billion miles away. Or that a spherical dish a few feet in diameter behind my house could pick up radio transmissions from a stationary satellite about 24,000 miles high, when the satellite sends only a trivial few watts of power toward an area covering many American states, particularly when those transmissions are received in stereo from station WQXR in New York, two thousand miles away, for example, with such fidelity and clarity that closed eyes would let one think he is sitting in the middle of the performing orchestra. Or that so much information is contained in a single cell of the human body, or can be stored on and retrieved from a computer chip.

However, amazing as are the achievements of contemporary science, our knowledge of the universe may well seem backward and rudimentary to civilizations elsewhere. For anyone to claim that contemporary science knows the ultimate truth about the nature of the universe is the ultimate in arrogance. We really know very little about time and space. We study how the components of this universe function and how the processes of creation operate; yet, we know nothing about why.

Subatomic particles called mu-mesons are created naturally in Earth's upper atmosphere, several miles above ground, from the impact of energetic particles from space upon atmospheric molecules. Many of these mu-mesons reach sea level, traveling at speeds about 0.998 times the speed of light. When created in Earth laboratories, mu-mesons, which are unstable and disintegrate spontaneously, have an average life span of only two millionths of a second. Even moving at 0.998 the speed of light, an object would traverse only three-eighths of a mile in two millionths of a second. Yet, mu-mesons travel several miles to the earth's surface before disintegrating. They do this because, traveling so near the speed of light, the relative motion causes significant dilation of time. According to our clocks, the life of the mu-meson would be extended, because of its speed, to about sixteen times the life span of a slow-moving mu-meson, and it therefore can travel sixteen times farther, by our measurement of distance (not the mu-meson's), during its life span.

The fact that the meson does exist longer, in our Earth frame of reference, because of its high speed, is in accordance with expectations of relativistic mechanics. If human beings could travel near the speed of light, they similarly could reach distant stars during a portion of their normal life span. According to current science, however, such speeds are not even theoretically attainable by a vehicle for human transport. Man seems destined to age during space flight at essentially the same rate as his brothers on Earth.

Of course, we know nothing of the nature of life or intelligence elsewhere in the universe, assuming such exists. Individual life spans could be such that human lives would seem, by comparison, as fleeting as the mu-meson seems to human beings.

I can remember when conventional wisdom said man's airplanes could never fly faster than the speed of sound, for at that speed the plane would shudder and shatter into pieces. Just a few years later, those of us on the ground heard the loud cracks of "sonic booms" as plane after plane cracked the sound barrier and flew on at greater speeds. During the Condon Study, the then quite secret SR-71 of the U.S. Air Force, flying at 1,800 miles per hour—about three times the speed of sound—sometimes appeared on radar screens, or was seen visually, and was reported to us as a UFO because "airplanes could not fly that fast."

I also recall, as a student at Caltech, listening to a highly respected scientist-administrator there tell us why man's rockets would never be able to escape Earth's gravitational field, though they might go into orbit around the earth. It took just another blip on the time scale, and the simple innovation of staged rocketry, for him to be proven dead wrong.

Although our space probes now fly at tens of thousands of miles per hour, we are not even near the ballpark of the 670 million miles per hour speed of light. But our advanced technology and advanced scientific knowledge of the universe are in their 100-year infancy. What will another 50,000 years bring?

It took Columbus a couple of months to cross the Atlantic, yet today we could have breakfast in Palos and be in San Salvador before time for lunch. Columbus would never have dreamed that his destination might someday be reached by traveling through air rather than on water.

There have been suggestions of how the speed-distance barrier to interstellar travel might possibly be averted. The June, 1989, issue of *Discover* magazine, for instance, discussed the concept of "cosmic wormholes," which are sort of bottomless Black Holes, which, like Black Holes, have appeared as possible solutions to equations of Einstein's general relativity theory. Wormholes could conceivably serve as shortcuts from one region of space to another. They are favored by science fiction writers, including Carl Sagan, who wrote of interaction of aliens and Earthlings in his 1985 novel, *Contact*. The traversable wormhole concept is given some scientific recognition simply because of its invention by Caltech's Kip Thorne—who brought Black Holes into reasonable scientific acceptance—with one of his students, Michael Morris. Though Thorne and the rest of the scientific world look upon traversable wormholes as no more than fantasy at this point, their discussion does serve to show how little we actually know yet about the universe in which we live.

The state of man's current knowledge not only makes him unable to travel to other solar systems, but it also limits his ability to even imagine currently unknown features of the universe which eventually may make interaction with life elsewhere commonplace.

It is my personal belief that the intelligence responsible for existence of the universe would not permit interaction of human beings with extraterrestrial beings unless or until humanity overcomes its predilections toward violence. Fighting among individuals of a species has a major role, through survival of the fittest, in species elevation. In the case of human beings, however, that role vanished with invention of guns. Guns have been touted as "the great equalizer," giving the small person as much power as the giant, and serving to tame the brute. However, guns tend to degrade the species when they are used by the less fit to destroy the "fittest."

We have, during the latter part of the twentieth century, observed with gratitude the subsidence of the threat of major international warfare, which itself now could destroy humanity. That expression of group violence, however, has been replaced by individual violence on the streets and factional warfare within states or nations. Until mankind surmounts its addiction to violence, the species is perhaps not worthy of survival—and not worthy of interaction with extraterrestrial beings.

The creator of the universe has provided mankind a planet home of fantastic intricacy and beauty. When I view the Southwest Colorado mountains with trees and bushes in Fall color, or the patterns of a single feather of a bird, or the alignment of colorful "eyes" on individual feathers of a peacock's fanned tail, and as I hear the sounds of rippling brooks, of singing birds—and of man's musical symphonies—I cannot imagine a Heaven more beautiful than Earth.

There may not be room on Earth for sustained existence of the numbers of people mankind has procreated on this planet. If human intelligence proves incapable of managing the population problem, human beings will have been merely a malignant disease that Earth contracted for a time. The possibility of survival still exists, however. And, while space on Earth is limited, there is unlimited room in the collective mind of mankind for mystery, for awe, for reverence, for love, for wonder—and for UFOs.

# Index

121–28; photographs in
Pennsylvania, 28–37; patrolman with time loss, 98–104;
pilot photographs in Denver,
38–51; "Sheets, Mr.," 151–56;
sightings in New York state,
52–71; Ubatuba, Brazil,
magnesium fragments, 105–
13
Italy, 252

Jackson, Mississippi, 136
Japan, 252
Jefferson Hill, New York, 52, 70–
71
Jung, C. G., 129, 132

Keyhoe, Donald E., xi, 244, 246
Kreith, Frank and Marian, xvii

La Boca Ranch, 177–78
"Larry King Live," 255–56
Leary, Wallace, 121
LeBailly, E. B., xiii
Levine, Norman, 86, 109, 187,
190–91, 192–93, 194, 196, 200,
201 203, 230, 246
Life, x, xxiii, 16–18, 20, 22
Lincoln, Nebraska, 159
Look, 204, 205, 229 240, 241, 244,
246
Lorenzen, Coral, ix, 114; and
Jim, 105, 107–109, 113
Los Alamos, xvi
Los Angeles, California, 73,
257–58
Low, Robert, xvii–xviii, 169 187,
178–83, 188, 194, 195, 196–97,
199, 202–203, 205, 206–207,
216, 222; memo, 194–95, 196,
197, 200–201, 202, 204, 206,

225–27, 229, 238, 241, 243,
249, 258–59

McClure, Frank, 142–45
McCoid, James, 142–45
McDivitt, James (astronaut),
220, 221
McDonald, James, xiv, 148, 189,
190, 194, 200, 203; letter, 194–
95, 197, 202, 203, 212–13, 237,
242–43, 245, 247–49
McElroy, Jerry, xxiii
Mack, John E., 104
McMinnville, Oregon, 222
magnetic fields, 74–82
Malstrom Air Force Base,
Montana, 135, 171
Manning, Thurston E., 195, 196,
204
Mariana, Nick, 158, 161–62,
195–96, 230–31
Mars, 259
"Mason, Bobby," 32
"Mason, Mr.," 31–37
Maxwell Air Force Base, Ala-
bama, 148
Menzel, Donald H., xii, 242, 245,
254, 261–62
Milledgeville, Georgia, 42
Miller, George, 243
Millman, Peter M., 209–10
Mineral Production Laboratory,
(Brazil), 109
Minnaert, M., 49
Minturn, Robert, xxiii
Montgomery, Alabama, 148
Morris, Michael, 265
Mt. Vernon, Washington, 11
Moyer, David F., 75
Mysteries of the Unknown
(book series), 255